GENDER AND THE POLITICS OF HISTORY

GENDER AND CULTURE

Carolyn G. Heilbrun and Nancy K. Miller, EDITORS

GENDER AND CULTURE

A SERIES OF COLUMBIA UNIVERSITY PRESS

Edited by Carolyn G. Heilbrun and Nancy K. Miller

In Dora's Case: Freud, Hysteria, Feminism
Edited by Charles Bernheimer and Claire Kahane

Breaking the Chain: Women, Theory, and French Realist Fiction
Naomi Schor

Between Men: English Literature and Male Homosocial Desire
Eve Kosofsky Sedgwick

Romantic Imprisonment: Women and Other Glorified Outcasts
Nina Auerbach

The Poetics of Gender
Edited by Nancy K. Miller

Reading Woman: Essays in Feminist Criticism
Mary Jacobus

Honey-Mad Women: Emancipatory Strategies in Women's Writing
Patricia Yaeger

Subject to Change: Reading Feminist Writing
Nancy K. Miller

Thinking Through the Body
Jane Gallop

Dialogic and Difference: "An/Other Woman" in Virginia Woolf and Christa Wolf
Anne Herrmann

Inspiriting Influences: Tradition, Revision, and Afro-American Women's Novels
Michael Awkward

AND THE POLITICS OF HISTORY

JOAN WALLACH SCOTT

COLUMBIA UNIVERSITY PRESS
NEW YORK

COLUMBIA UNIVERSITY PRESS
NEW YORK OXFORD

LIBRARY OF CONGRESS
Library of Congress Cataloging-in-Publication Data

Scott, Joan Wallach.
Gender and the politics of history / Joan Wallach Scott.
p. cm.—(Gender and culture)
Bibliography: p.
Includes index.
ISBN 0-231-06554-X
ISBN 0-231-06555-8 (pbk.)
1. Women—History—19th century. 2. Women—History—20th century.
3. Sex role—History. 4. Working class women—History.
5. Women—Employment—France—History—19th century.
I. Title. II. Series.
HQ1154.S335 1988
305.4'09—dc19 88-9518
CIP

Book design by Jennifer Dossin

Printed in the United States of America

c 10 9 8 7 6 5 4 3

Hardback editions of Columbia University Press books are Smyth-sewn
and are printed on permanent and durable acid-free paper

FOR ELIZABETH

Contents

Acknowledgments

These essays owe their greatest debt to the Pembroke Center for Teaching and Research on Women at Brown University. Funding provided by Brown, the Ford Foundation, and the National Endowment for the Humanities supported an intense and exciting intellectual environment. The center would not have run smoothly without the skill, patience, and enthusiasm of Barbara Anton and Elizabeth Barboza; in fact it would not have run at all. I learned a great deal from both of them about what a cooperative enterprise really means and about the support women can provide for one another. I learned most of all from Elizabeth Weed, at once my colleague, mentor, and friend. She taught me how to think about theory and gender. She read and criticized each of these essays more than once and held out exacting standards that I have tried, not always successfully, to meet. Her influence on this book has been profound; for that reason it is dedicated to her.

Friends and colleagues have been unstinting with their time, advice, and criticism. I am especially indebted to Denise Riley whose work has had an important influence on my own. I am grateful, too, for close and attentive readings of the entire manuscript by Elisabetta Galeotti and Lynn Hunt.

Sarah Johns not only typed and retyped the manuscript but provided extraordinary and efficient organization for every aspect of my working life. This book owes a great deal to her energy, warmth, generosity, and intelligence. It owes a good deal, too, to the Institute for Advanced Study, my current "home," and to its unstinting support for scholarly activity.

For Donald Scott, gratitude is an inadequate expression. He has read and criticized these essays many times. He first pointed out that they warranted publication in a single volume and he both insisted on and encouraged the project. As an intellectual and emotional partner he has empowered all aspects of my life, proving that men can share in the feminist project and that equality is not only desirable but worth striving to achieve.

GENDER AND THE POLITICS OF HISTORY

Introduction

I think of these essays as my Pembroke Center essays for they were all inspired by discussions that took place during my years as director of Brown University's Pembroke Center for Teaching and Research on Women. There, a remarkable group of scholars engaged in the kind of direct and probing thinking that changes minds and opens new directions for research and writing. In the Pembroke Center seminar I was forced to take post-structuralist theory seriously and wrestle with its implications for a social historian. The process was at once rewarding and difficult. It addressed many of the most pressing philosophical questions I had confronted as a feminist trying to write women's history, but, at the same time, it brought me to a critique more fundamental than I had anticipated of the presuppositions of my discipline. Because I learned about post-structuralism largely from literary scholars, I also met problems inevitable for those who wander into new fields. These were problems of language and translation, of the adaptability of reigning disciplinary paradigms, and of the significance—if any—of supposed oppositions between the methods and projects of history and literature. I experienced these problems not only as abstract issues but acutely as questions of professional and political identity.

Since the essays served as a way of exploring these problems, they may seem partial, inconclusive, or disparate. The topics and the substantive materials they treat do vary, but they are linked, nonetheless, by the themes of gender and history and by an attempt to articulate the nature of the connection between those two terms. Taken as a whole, moreover, the essays are organized to build an argument cumulatively. For that reason they ought to be read not randomly as independent articles, but sequentially as chapters in a book. Although many of the chapters appeared originally as articles, most have been substantially rewritten to develop the common themes of gender and history.

Gender, in these essays, means knowledge about sexual difference. I use knowledge, following Michel Foucault, to mean the understanding produced by cultures and societies of human relationships, in this case of those between men and women.[1] Such knowledge is not absolute or true, but always relative. It is produced in complex ways within large epistemic frames that themselves have an (at least quasi-) autonomous history. Its uses and meanings become contested politically and are the means by which relationships of power—of domination and subordination—are constructed. Knowledge refers not only to ideas but to institutions and structures, everyday practices as well as specialized rituals, all of which constitute social relationships. Knowledge is a way of ordering the world; as such it is not prior to social organization, it is inseparable from social organization.

It follows then that gender is the social organization of sexual difference. But this does not mean that gender reflects or implements fixed and natural physical differences between women and men; rather gender is the knowledge that establishes meanings for bodily differences. These meanings vary across cultures, social groups, and time since nothing about the body, including women's reproductive organs, determines univocally how social divisions will be shaped. We cannot see sexual difference except as a function of our knowledge about the body and that knowledge is not "pure," cannot be isolated from its implication in a broad range of discursive contexts. Sexual difference is not, then, the originary cause from which social organization ultimately can be derived. It is instead a variable social organization that itself must be explained.

History figures in this approach not exclusively as the record of changes in the social organization of the sexes but also crucially as a participant in the production of knowledge about sexual difference. I assume that history's representations of the past help construct gender for the present. Analyzing how that happens requires attention to the assumptions, practices, and rhetoric of the discipline, to things either so taken for granted or so outside customary practice that they are not usually a focus for historians' attention. These include the notions that history can faithfully document lived reality, that archives are repositories of facts, and that categories like man and woman are transparent. They extend as well to examinations of the rhetorical practices of historians, the construction of historical texts, and the politics—that is, the power relationships—constituted by the discipline. In these essays history is as much the object of analytic attention as it is a method of analysis. Taken in both ways together, it provides a means for understanding and contributing to the process by which gender knowledge is produced.

If the themes of gender and history unite this book, so does a preoccupation with theory. Although historians are not trained (in the United States at least) to be reflective or rigorous about their theory, I found it imperative to pursue theoretical questions in order to do feminist history. This resulted, I think, from my sense of frustration at the relatively limited impact women's history was having on historical studies generally and my consequent need to understand why that was the case. My motive was and is one I share with other feminists and it is avowedly political: to point out and change inequalities between women and men. It is a motive, moreover, that feminists share with those concerned to change the representation of other groups left out of history because of race, ethnicity, and class as well as gender. Though simple to state, those operations are difficult to implement, especially if one lacks an analysis of how gender hierarchies are constructed, legitimated, challenged, and maintained.

The difficulties are apparent in some of the dilemmas encountered by women's history as it tried to work within the existing parameters of its discipline. By uncovering new information about women, historians assumed they would right the balance of long years of neglect. But what amounted to an almost naive endorsement of positivism soon led to a critique of it. New facts might document the existence of women in the past, but they did not necessarily change the importance (or lack of it) attributed to women's activities. Indeed, the separate treatment of women could serve to confirm their marginal and particularized relationship to those (male) subjects already established as dominant and universal.

Associated with the initial acceptance of history's positivism was an implicit belief in pluralism, in the possibility of expanding existing categories and topics to include women. But writing about women as, say, workers or members of the working class did not effectively change established definitions of those categories, nor did it shed light on why those writing labor history had ignored evidence about women for so long. Apart from allusions to male bias, there was nothing to account for the absence of attention to women in the past and, if male bias was the cause, there was nothing (but faith in the progress of democracy) to guarantee that it would not continue to stand in the way of pluralism's promise of equality. What seemed to be called for was an analysis of discrimination that extended to the categories themselves, categories such as class, worker, citizen—even man and woman.

The need to examine these categories in a new way was also provoked by the difficulty of analyzing gender inequality within the framework of social history. Here, whether explicitly theorized (as Marxism, behaviorism, or modernization) or simply taken as an accurate description of how things happen, the notion that categories of identity reflect objective experience seemed to lead to explanations that served more often to confirm than to challenge prevailing views about women. By assuming that women have inherent characteristics and objective identities consistently and predictably different from men's, and that these generate definably female needs and interests, historians imply that sexual difference is a natural rather than a social phenomenon. The search for an analysis of discrimination gets caught by a circular logic in which "experience" explains gender difference and gender difference explains the asymmetries of male and female "experience." Typically the visions of what constitutes male and female experience appeal to or incorporate existing normative definitions. Women's history written from this position, and the politics that follow from it, end up endorsing the ideas of unalterable sexual difference that are used to justify discrimination.

A more radical feminist politics (and a more radical feminist history) seems to me to require a more radical epistemology. Precisely because it addresses questions of epistemology, relativizes the status of all knowledge, links knowledge and power, and theorizes these in terms of the operations of difference, I think post-structuralism (or at least some of the approaches generally associated with Michel Foucault and Jacques Derrida) can offer feminism a powerful analytic perspective. I am not suggesting the dogmatic application of any particular philosopher's teachings and I am aware of feminist critiques of them. Still I want to indicate the places where and the ways in which, for me, the openings they provide to new intellectual directions have proved not only promising but fruitful.

Perhaps the most dramatic shift in my own thinking came through asking questions about *how* hierarchies such as those of gender are constructed or legitimized. The emphasis on "how" suggests a study of processes, not of origins, of multiple rather than single causes, of rhetoric or discourse rather than ideology or consciousness. It does not abandon attention to structures and institutions, but it does insist that we need to understand what these organizations mean in order to understand how they work.

Post-structuralists, of course, did not initiate concern with meaning, but they offer a distinctive way of studying it in their emphasis on its variability, its volatility, and the political nature of its construction. If the meanings of concepts are taken to be unstable, open to contest and redefinition, then they require vigilant repetition, reassertion, and implementation by those who have endorsed one or another definition. Instead of attributing a transparent and shared meaning to cultural concepts, post-structuralists insist that meanings are not fixed in a culture's lexicon but are rather dynamic, always potentially in flux.[2] Their study therefore calls for attention to the conflictual processes that establish meanings, to the ways in which such concepts as gender acquire the appearance of fixity, to the challenges posed for normative social definitions, and to the ways these challenges are met—in other words, to the play of force involved in any society's construction and implementation of meanings: to politics.

The mention of politics inevitably raises the question of causality: In whose interest is it to control or contest meanings? What is the nature of that interest, what is its origin? There are two ways to answer those questions. One, in terms of an objectively determined, absolute, and universal interest (economics or sexual domination, for example); the other in terms of a discursively produced, relative, and contextual concept of interest. The second is not the reverse of the first, rather it refuses the opposition between objective determination and its subjective effects. In both cases we grant the effects of "interest" in creating social groups (classes or genders, for example). But in the first case, there is a separation assumed between material conditions and the human thoughts and actions they are said to generate. In the second case, no such separation is possible since "interest" does not inhere in actors or their structural positions but is discursively produced. The objects of study are then epistemological phenomena, which include economics, industrialization, relations of production, factories, families, classes, genders, collective action, and political ideas, as well as one's own interpretive categories.

This second approach complicates the unilinear account of experience, identity, and politics that accompanies the first approach. Experience is not seen as the objective circumstances that condition identity; identity is not an objectively determined sense of self defined by needs and interests; politics is not the collective coming to consciousness of similarly situated individual subjects. Rather politics is the process by which plays of power and knowledge constitute identity and experience. Identities and experiences are variable phenomena in this view, discursively organized in particular contexts or configurations. It then follows that (as film theorist Teresa de Lauretis puts it) "consciousness is never fixed, never attained once and for all because discursive boundaries change with historical conditions."[3] It follows, as well, that political differences among women cannot be explained as false consciousness. This outlook renders feminist politics more self-conscious and self-critical and links it inextricably to analyses of gender as the production of knowledge about sexual difference. For political identity, like social institutions and cultural symbols, is a form of knowledge production. Rather than there being a separation between feminist politics and academic studies of gender, the two are part of the same political project: a collective attempt to confront and change existing distributions of power.

For the feminist historian this is an especially appealing theoretical perspective. It makes critical analyses of past and present a continuing operation; the historian can interpret the world while trying to change it. It also insists on the need to examine gender concretely and in context and to consider it a historical phenomenon, produced, reproduced, and transformed in different situations and over time. This is at once a familiar posture for a historian and a profoundly new way of thinking about history. For it calls into question the reliability of terms that have been taken as self-evident by historicizing them. The story is no longer about the things that have happened to women and men and how they have reacted to them; instead it is about how the subjective and collective meanings of women and men as categories of identity have been constructed. If identities change over time and are relative to different contexts, then we cannot use simple models of socialization that see gender as the more or less stable product of early childhood education in the family and the school. We must also eschew the compartmentalizing tendency of so much of social history that relegates sex and gender to the institution of the family, associates class with the workplace and the community, and locates war and constitutional issues exclusively in the domain of the "high politics" of governments and states. Since all institutions employ some divisions of labor, since the structures of many institutions are premised on sexual divisions of labor (even if such divisions exclude one sex or the other), since references to the body often legitimize the forms institutions take, gender is, in fact, an aspect of social organization generally. It can be found in many places, for the meanings of sexual difference are invoked and contested as part of many kinds of struggles for power. Social and cultural knowledge about sexual difference is therefore produced in the course of most of the events and processes studied as history.

To find gender in history, however, it is not enough to do the literal, thematic reading typical of the discipline; a different kind of exegesis is required. Here the work of literary critics associated with post-structuralism has been extremely helpful for me. They point to the importance of textuality, to the ways arguments are structured and presented as well as to what is literally said. And they draw attention to the need carefully to tease out what Barbara Johnson calls "the warring forces of signification within the text itself."[4] This approach rests on the assumption that meaning is conveyed through implicit or explicit contrast, through internal differentiation.

Positive definitions rest always, in this view, on the negation or repression of something represented as antithetical to it. And categorical oppositions repress the internal ambiguities of either category. Any unitary concept rests on—contains—repressed or negated material and so is unstable, not unified. As Johnson puts it, "Difference is not engendered in the space between identities; it is what makes all totalization of the identity of a self or the meaning of a text impossible."[5] Fixed oppositions conceal the heterogeneity of either category, the extent to which terms presented as oppositional are interdependent—that is, derive their meaning from internally established contrast rather than from some inherent or pure antithesis. Furthermore, the interdependence is usually hierarchical, with one term dominant, prior, and visible, the opposite subordinate, secondary, and often absent or invisible. Yet precisely through this arrangement, the second term is present and central because required for the definition of the first. Although some oppositional pairs seem to recur predictably in certain cultures, their specific meanings are conveyed through new combinations of contrasts and oppositions. Contests about meaning involve the introduction of new oppositions, the reversal of hierarchies, the attempt to expose repressed terms, to challenge the natural status of seemingly dichotomous pairs, and to expose their interdependence and their internal instability. This kind of analysis, theorized by Jacques Derrida as "deconstruction," makes it possible to study systematically (though never definitively or totally) the conflictual processes that produce meanings. For the historian this adds an important new dimension to the exegetical project.[6]

It also undermines the historian's ability to claim neutral mastery or to present any particular story as if it were complete, universal, and objectively determined. Instead, if one grants that meanings are constructed through exclusions, one must acknowledge and take responsibility for the exclusions involved in one's own project. Such a reflexive, self-critical approach makes apparent the particularistic status of any historical knowledge and the historian's active role as a producer of knowledge. It undermines claims for authority based on totalizing explanations, essentialized categories of analysis (be they human nature, race, class, sex, or "the oppressed"), or synthetic narratives that assume an inherent unity for the past.

Although a great deal has been written about the problems of using methods associated primarily with texts (and therefore with literature) to study history, I think much of the debate is beside the point. Oppositions between text and context, fiction and truth, art and life structure the self-representations of the disciplines of literature and history. Each discipline defines its expertise through a contrast with the other's objects of inquiry and methods of interpretation. Each discipline also resolves the ambiguities of its own project by using the other as a foil. In the process, each articulates the rules and conventions that identify them as discrete fields of knowledge, necessarily emphasizing certain methods and materials. For some literary scholars single texts, the problem of reading, the act of writing, and the identity of the author have become in recent years so central as to preclude other kinds of social or political questions. For many social historians, archives are sacred places where one culls from documents "facts" about the past. Works of fiction, when they enter the historians' domain, are most often scrutinized for thematic materials that will further document the social processes or political events that are the primary focus of investigation.[7]

These differences can create obstacles to interdisciplinary work for those who define themselves entirely within disciplinary parameters, but they are less troublesome from the theoretical perspective I have been discussing. That perspective takes the production of cultural knowledge as its object and is concerned with analyzing how various forms of knowledge are produced. History and literature are such forms of knowledge, whether we take them as disciplines or as bodies of cultural information. As such, both are susceptible to the same kind of analysis, one that is directed to concepts, meanings, linguistic codes, and the organization of representation. This analytic approach takes seriously the boundaries of disciplines and the different genres they represent but makes these a matter for investigation, rather than a set of preconditions for scholarly work. An approach such as this tempers a certain kind of overly enthusiastic disciplinary borrowing, one example of which is the tendency among some historians influenced by literary critics to make written texts themselves the only viable subject for history; another example is the enthusiasm of some literary scholars for history as an external source of information that will explain what's going on in their texts. When, instead, we take the disciplines as analysts and producers of cultural knowledge, we find that what is at stake is not simply a literary technique for reading but an epistemological theory that offers a method for analyzing the processes by which meanings are made, by which we make meanings.

This theory is, moreover, profoundly political in its implications for it puts conflict at the center of its analysis, assuming that hierarchy and power are inherent in the linguistic processes being analyzed. Although deconstruction has been labeled "nihilistic" and "destructive" by its critics, these epithets seem to me to be substitutes for serious evaluations of its possibilities. It may be that some deconstructive critics pursue an endless exposure of contradiction and are thereby unable to endorse or comfortably advocate a political program of their own. But there are also evident examples of a politics empowered by this approach, politics that are not only critical of existing social hierarchies but able to point out the premises of their operations; politics that are self-consciously critical of their own justifications and exclusions, and so refuse an absolutist or totalizing stance. There are, for example, legal theorists and feminist theorists who formulate and act on ethical positions even while acknowledging complexity and contradiction.[8] Their advantage is an ability to address institutional and intellectual questions in the same way, to refuse such oppositions as those between materialism and idealism, subjects studied and disciplinary studies of them, by approaching all of these as aspects of the production of knowledge and power—conceived not as a unitary process but as multiple and conflicting processes.

This epistemological perspective permits the kind of critical assessment of their discipline that feminist historians need in order to pursue their goal of making women historical subjects. For history, too, creates its meanings through differentiation and in this way organizes knowledge about the world. The form that knowledge has taken—the remarkable absence or subordination of women in the narratives of the "rise of civilization," their particularity in relation to Universal Man, their confinement to studies of the domestic and private—indicates a politics that sets and enforces priorities, represses some subjects in the name of the greater importance of others, naturalizes certain categories, and disqualifies others. It is not a conspiratorial politics, nor is it narrowly self-interested; rather it protects an established corporate tradition. Nonetheless, the discipline of history, through its practices, produces (rather than gathers or reflects) knowledge about the past generally and, inevitably, about sexual difference as well. In that way, history operates as a particular kind of cultural institution endorsing and announcing constructions of gender.

A relativized concept of gender as historically specific knowledge about sexual difference allows feminists to forge a double-edged analytic tool that offers a way to generate new knowledge about women and sexual difference *and* to inspire critical challenges to the politics of history, or for that matter, any other discipline. Feminist history then becomes not just an attempt to correct or supplement an incomplete record of the past but a way of critically understanding how history operates as a site of the production of gender knowledge.

The essays in this volume are attempts, tentative efforts, to perform the kinds of analyses I have been describing, to exemplify a feminist approach to gender, politics, and history. I have tried to deal critically with history as discipline, written text, and record of events in the past, to suggest how we might produce new knowledge through critical reflection on the processes by which knowledge is and has been produced. My specific concern as a feminist is with knowledge about sexual difference, with gender. As a historian I am particularly interested in historicizing gender by pointing to the variable and contradictory meanings attributed to sexual difference, to the political processes by which those meanings are developed and contested, to the instability and malleability of the categories "women" and "men," and to the ways those categories are articulated in terms of one another, although not consistently or in the same way every time.

Even as I want to insist that questions about gender will illuminate not only the history of relations between the sexes but also all or most history whatever its specific topic, I am aware of the necessarily partial results such an approach will produce. I make no claim to total vision, nor to having found *the* category that will finally explain all inequality, all oppression, all history. My claim is more modest: that gender offers both a good way of thinking about history, about the ways in which hierarchies of difference—inclusions and exclusions—have been constituted, and of theorizing (feminist) politics. Such an admission of partiality, it seems to me, does not acknowledge defeat in the search for universal explanation; rather it suggests that universal explanation is not, never has been possible. Indeed, it turns critical attention to the politics (that is, the power dynamics) of "totality," whether advanced as (mono)causal analysis or master narrative, whether invoked by historians or political activists.

There has been some worry expressed in historical and political circles that this kind of critical stance makes both history and politics as we know them impossible. That may be true, but it also grants to established practices a permanent existence that they have never had. It is precisely by exposing the illusion of the permanence or enduring truth of any particular knowledge of sexual difference that feminism necessarily historicizes history and politics and opens the way for change. If gender is to be rethought, if new knowledge about sexual difference is to be produced (knowledge that calls into question even the primacy of the male/female opposition), then we must also be willing to rethink the history of politics and the politics of history. This book is an inevitably partial attempt to do some of that rethinking.

I

TOWARD A FEMINIST HISTORY

I

Women's History

What one wants, I thought—and why does not some brilliant student at Newnham or Girton supply it?—is a mass of information; at what age did she marry; how many children had she as a rule; what was her house like; had she a room to herself; did she do the cooking; would she be likely to have a servant? All these facts lie somewhere, presumably, in parish registers and account books; the life of the average Elizabethan woman must be scattered about somewhere, could one collect it and make a book of it. It would be ambitious beyond my daring, I thought, looking about the shelves for books that were not there, to suggest to the students of those famous colleges that they should rewrite history, though I own that it often seems a little queer as it is, unreal, lop-sided; but why should they not add a supplement to history? calling it, of course, by some inconspicious name so that women might figure there without impropriety?

VIRGINIA WOOLF, *A Room of One's Own*

During the last decade, Virginia Woolf's call for a history of women—written more than fifty years ago—has been answered.[1] Inspired directly or indirectly by the political agenda of the women's movement, historians have not only documented the lives of average women in various historical periods but they have charted as well changes in the economic, educational, and political positions of women of various classes in city and country and in nation-states. Bookshelves are being filled with biographies of forgotten women, chronicles of feminist movements, and the collected letters of female authors; the book titles treat subjects as disparate as suf-

The original version of this essay appeared in *Past and Present: A Journal of Historical Studies* (1983) 101:141–57, under the title "Women in History: The Modern Period." The world copyright is held by The Past and Present Society, 175 Banbury Rd., Oxford, England. For their suggestions on the first version, I wish to thank Ellen Furlough and Sherri Broder. Although I have substantially revised the original article, the bibliographic references in the notes have not been fully updated.

frage and birth control. Journals have appeared that are devoted exclusively to women's studies and to the even more specialized area of women's history.[2] And, at least in the United States, there are major conferences devoted entirely to the presentation of scholarly papers on the history of women.[3] All of this adds up to what is justifiably termed "the new knowledge about women."

The production of this knowledge is marked by remarkable diversity in topic, method, and interpretation, so much so that it is impossible to reduce the field to a single interpretive or theoretical stance. Not only is a vast array of topics studied, but in addition, on the one hand, many case studies, and, on the other hand, large interpretive overviews, which neither address one another nor a similar set of questions. Moreover, women's history does not have a long-standing and definable historiographic tradition within which interpretations can be debated and revised. Instead, the subject of women has been either grafted on to other traditions or studied in isolation from them. While some histories of women's work, for example, address contemporary feminist questions about the relationship between wage-earning and status, others frame their studies within the context of debates among Marxists and between Marxists and modernization theorists about the impact of industrial capitalism.[4] Reproduction covers a vast terrain in which fertility and contraception are variously studied. Sometimes they are treated within the confines of historical demography as aspects of the "demographic transition." Alternatively they are viewed within the context of discussions about conflicting political analyses by Malthusian political economists and socialist labor leaders, or within the very different framework of evaluations of the impact of nineteenth-century "ideology of domesticity" on the power of women in their families. Yet another approach stresses feminist debates about sexuality and the history of women's demands for the right to control their own bodies. Additionally, some Marxist-feminists have redefined reproduction as the functional equivalent of production in an effort to incorporate women into the corpus of Marxist theory.[5] In the area of politics, investigations have sought to demonstrate simply that women were to be found "in public," or to illustrate the historical incompatibility between feminist claims, on the one hand, and the structure and ideology of organized trade unions and political parties, on the other hand (the "failure" of socialism, for example, to accommodate feminism). Another quite different approach to politics examines the interior organization of women's political movements as a way of documenting the existence of a distinctively female culture.[6]

More than in many other areas of historical inquiry, women's history is characterized by extraordinary tensions: between practical politics and academic scholarship; between received disciplinary standards and interdisciplinary influences; between history's atheoretical stance and feminism's need for theory. Feminist historians feel these tensions in many ways, perhaps most acutely as they try to identify the presumed audiences for their work. The disparate nature of these audiences can lead to uneven and confusing arguments in individual books and essays and it makes impossible the usual kind of synthetic essay on the state of the field.[7]

What is possible, instead, is an attempt to tease out from this vast accumulation of writings some insight into the problems historians face as they produce new knowledge about women. For whatever the topical range and variety, there is a common dimension to the enterprise of these scholars of different schools. It is to make women a focus of inquiry, a subject of the story, an agent of the narrative —whether that narrative is a chronicle of political events (the French Revolution, the Swing riots, World War I or II) and political movements (Chartism, utopian socialism, feminism, women's suffrage), or a more analytically cast account of the workings or unfoldings of large-scale processes of social change (industrialization, capitalism, modernization, urbanization, the building of nation-states). The titles of some of the books that launched the women's history movement in the early 1970s explicitly conveyed their authors' intentions: those who had been "Hidden from History" were "Becoming Visible."[8] Although recent book titles announce many new themes, the mission of their authors remains to construct women as historical subjects. That effort goes far beyond the naïve search for the heroic ancestors of the contemporary women's movement to a reevaluation of established standards of historical significance. It culminates in the set of questions raised so tellingly by Woolf: can a focus on women "add a supplement to history" without also "rewriting history"? Beyond that, what does the feminist rewriting of history entail?

These questions have established the framework for debate and discussion among historians of women during the past fifteen years. Although there are clear lines of difference discernible, they are better understood as matters of strategy than as fundamental divides. Each has particular strengths and limits, each addresses the difficulty of writing women into history in a somewhat different way. The cumulative effect of these strategies has been the creation of a new field of knowledge marked not only by tensions and contradictions but also by an increasingly complex understanding of what the project of "rewriting history" entails.

Not only has that understanding emerged from debates internal to the field of women's history; it has also been shaped in relation to the discipline of history itself. As feminists have documented the lives of women in the past, provided information that challenged received interpretations of particular periods or events, and analyzed the specific conditions of women's subordination, they have encountered the powerful resistance of history—as a disciplined body of knowledge and as a professional institution. Meeting this resistance has been an occasion variously for anger, retreat, and the formulation of new strategies. It has also provoked analyses of the deeply gendered nature of history itself. The entire process has generated a search for terms of criticism, conceptual reorientations, and theory that are the preconditions for feminist rewritings of history.

Much of the search has revolved around the issue of woman as a subject, that is as an active agent of history. How could women achieve the status of subjects in a field that subsumed or ignored them? Would making women visible suffice to rectify past neglect? How could women be added to a history presented as a universal human story exemplified by the lives of men? Since the specificity or particularity of women already made them unfit representatives of humankind, how could attention to women undercut, rather than reinforce, that notion? The history of women's history during the last decade and a half illustrates the difficulty of finding easy answers to these questions.

In this essay I will examine that history as a way of exploring the philosophical and political problems encountered by the producers of the new knowledge about women. I will draw most heavily on North American scholarship that focuses on the nineteenth and twentieth centuries because I am most familiar with it, and because in the United States there has been the fullest elaboration of theoretical debates about women's history.[9]

One approach—the first chronologically—to the problem of constituting women as historical subjects was to gather information about them and write (what some feminists dubbed) "her-story." As the play on the word "history" implied, the point was to give value to an experience that had been ignored (hence devalued) and to insist on female agency in the making of history. Men were but one group of actors; whether their experiences were similar or different, women had to be taken explicitly into account by historians.

"Her-story" has had many different uses. Some historians gather evidence about women to demonstrate their essential likeness as historical subjects to men. Whether they uncover women participating in major political events or write about women's political action on their own behalf, these historians attempt to fit a new subject—women—into received historical categories, interpreting their actions in terms recognizable to political and social historians. One example of this approach looks at a women's political movement from the perspective of its rank-and-file members rather than its leaders. In the best traditions of the social histories of labor (which were inspired by the work of E. P. Thompson), Jill Liddington and Jill Norris offer a sensitive and illuminating account of working-class women's participation in the English suffrage campaign. Their material, drawn largely from Manchester records and from oral histories they collected, documents the involvement of working-class women in the struggle to win the vote (previous histories described it as almost entirely a middle-class movement) and links demands by these women for suffrage to their work and family lives and to the activities of trade union and Labor Party organizers. The predominance and wisdom of the Pankhurst wing of the movement is called into question for its elitism and its insistence on female separatism (a position rejected by the majority of suffragettes).[10] A book on the history of the French women's suffrage movement by Steven Hause offers another illustration. The author interprets the weakness and small size of the movement (in comparison with its English and American counterparts) as the product of the ideologies and institutions of French Catholicism, the legacy of Roman law, the conservatism of French society, and the peculiar political history of French republicanism, especially the Radical Party during the Third Republic.[11]

Another strategy associated with "her-story" takes evidence about women and uses it to challenge received interpretations of progress and regress. In this regard an impressive mass of evidence has been compiled to show that the Renaissance was not a renaissance for women,[12] that technology did not lead to women's liberation either in the workplace or at home,[13] that the "Age of Democratic Revolutions" excluded women from political participation,[14] that the "affective nuclear family" constrained women's emotional and personal development,[15] and that the rise of medical science deprived women of autonomy and a sense of feminine community.[16]

A different sort of investigation, still within the "her-story" position, departs from the framework of conventional history and offers a new narrative, different periodization, and different causes. It seeks to illuminate the structures of ordinary women's lives as well as those of notable women, and to discover the nature of the feminist or female consciousness that motivated their behavior. Patriarchy and class are usually assumed to be the contexts within which nineteenth- and twentieth-century women defined their experience, and moments of cross-class collaboration among women directly addressed to women's oppression are stressed. The central aspect of this approach is the exclusive focus on female agency, on the causal role played by women in their history, and on the qualities of women's experience that sharply distinguish it from men's experience. Evidence consists of women's expressions, ideas, and actions. Explanation and interpretation are framed within the terms of the female sphere: by examinations of personal experience, familial and domestic structures, collective (female) reinterpretations of social definitions of women's role, and networks of female friendship that provided emotional as well as physical sustenance.

The exploration of women's culture has led to the brilliant insights of Carroll Smith-Rosenberg about the "female world of love and ritual" in nineteenth-century America,[17] to an insistence on the positive aspects of the domestic ideology of the same period,[18] to a dialectical reading of the relationship between middle-class women's political action and the ideas of womanhood that confined them to domestic realms,[19] and to an analysis of the "reproductive ideology" that constructed the world of the bourgeoises of northern France in the mid-nineteenth century.[20] It has also led Carl Degler to argue that American women themselves created the ideology of their separate sphere in order to enhance their autonomy and status. In his rendering of the story, women created a world neither within nor in opposition to oppressive structures or ideas that others imposed, but to further a set of group interests, defined and articulated from within the group itself.[21]

The "her-story" approach has had important effects on historical scholarship. By piling up the evidence about women in the past it refutes the claims of those who insist that women had no history, no significant place in stories of the past. It goes further, by altering some of the standards of historical significance, asserting that "personal, subjective experience" matters as much as "public and political activities," indeed that the former influence the latter.[22] And it demonstrates that sex and gender need to be conceptualized in historical terms, at least if some of the motives for women's actions are to be understood. It establishes not only the legitimacy of narratives about women but the general importance of gender difference in the conceptualization and organization of social life. At the same time, however, it runs several risks. First, it sometimes conflates two separate operations: the valuation of women's experience (considering it worthy of study) and the positive assessment of everything women said or did.[23] Second, it tends to isolate women as a special and separate topic of history, whether different questions are asked, different categories of analysis offered, or only different documents examined. For those interested there is now a growing and important history of women to supplement and enrich conventional histories, but it can too easily be consigned to the "separate sphere" that has long been associated exclusively with the female sex.

"Her-story" developed in tandem with social history; indeed, it often took its lead from the methods and conceptions developed by social historians. Social history offered important support for women's history in several ways. First, it provided methodologies in quantification, in the use of details from everyday life, and in interdisciplinary borrowings from sociology, demography, and ethnography. Second, it conceptualized as historical phenomena family relationships, fertility, and sexuality. Third, social history challenged the narrative line of political history ("white men make history") by taking as its subject large-scale social processes as they were realized in many dimensions of human experience. This led to the fourth influence, the legitimation of a focus on groups customarily excluded from political history. Social history's story is ultimately about processes or systems (such as capitalism or modernization, depending on the theoretical stance of the historian), but it is told through the lives of particular groups of people who are the ostensible, though not always the actual, subjects of the narrative. Since human relationships of all kinds constitute society, one can study a variety of groups and topics to assess the impact of processes of change and it is relatively easy to extend the list from workers, peasants, slaves, elites, and diverse occupational or social groups to include women. Thus, for example, studies of women's work were undertaken, much as studies of workers had been, to assess capitalism's impact or to understand its operations.

These studies have led to a proliferation of that "mass of information" Virginia Woolf asked for. They have documented the extraordinary range of jobs women held and drawn patterns of female labor force participation according to age, marital status, and household income—belying the notion that one could generalize categorically about women and work. The studies have shown that women formed labor unions and went on strike, albeit at different rates from men; they have examined wage-scales and charted changes in employment opportunities, suggesting the greater importance of demand than supply in structuring female job markets.[24]

There is as well a rich interpretive debate. Some historians insist that wage-earning enhanced women's status; others that women were exploited as a cheap labor supply and that, as a result, men perceived women as a threat to the value of their own labor. While some historians point out that family divisions of labor attributed economic value to a wife's domestic role, others have argued that family conflict centered on control of wages. Those who maintain that sex-segregation undermined women's job control and hence their ability to organize and strike are challenged by those who suggest that when women command sufficient resources they engage in collective action identical to men. All of this indicates a need not only to look at women but to analyze their situation in relation to men, to introduce into general studies of labor history questions about family organization and sex-segregated labor markets.[25]

At the same time that it has enabled documentation of topics like the history of women's work, social history has also raised problems for feminist historians. On the one hand, social history made room for the study of women by particularizing and pluralizing the subjects of historical narratives—no single universal figure could possibly represent the diversity of humankind. On the other hand, it reduced human agency to a function of economic forces and made gender one of its many by-products. Women are just one of the groups mobilizing resources, being modernized or exploited, contending for power, or being excluded from a polity. Feminist questions about the distinctiveness of women and the centrality of social relations between the sexes tend to be displaced by or subsumed within economist and behaviorist models.

Both "her-story" and social history establish women as historical subjects; indeed, they are often overlapping or intersecting approaches in the work of historians of women. They differ, however, in their ultimate implications because each is associated with a somewhat different analytic perspective. Social history assumes that gender difference can be explained within its existing frame of (economic) explanation; gender is not an issue requiring study in itself. As a result, social history's treatment of women tends to be too integrationist. "Her-story," in contrast, assumes that gender explains the different histories of women and men, but it does not theorize about how gender operates historically. For that reason, its stories seem to be uniquely about women and can be read in too separatist a manner.

Attempts to conceptualize gender are, of course, also part of the history of women's history, and they have run through the discussions and debates from the beginning. The late Joan Kelly set as the goal for women's history the making of sex "as fundamental to our analysis of the social order as other classifications such as class and race."[26] For Natalie Zemon Davis the aim was "to understand the significance of the sexes, of gender groups in the historical past."[27] This could be accomplished by examining social definitions of gender as they were expressed by men and women, constructed in and affected by economic and political institutions, expressive of a range of relationships that included not only sex but also class and power. The results, it was argued, would throw new light not only on women's experience but on social and political practice as well.

For historians, studying gender has been largely a matter of method so far. It consists of comparing women's situation implicitly or explicitly to men's by focusing on law, prescriptive literature, iconographic representation, institutional structure, and political participation. Temma Kaplan's *Anarchists of Andalusia,* for example, examined the different appeals of that political movement to men and women and the different but complementary ways in which male and female peasants and workers were organized to revolutionary struggle. Her parallel treatment of men and women within anarchism shows how aspects of gender relationships in Andalusian society were used to articulate this particular political movement's attack on capitalism and the state.[28] Tim Mason developed important insights about the "reconciliatory function of the family" in Nazi Germany as a result of an inquiry into the position of women and policies toward women. The factual material he gathered about women, who he says were largely "non-actors" in the politics of the period, "provided an exceptionally fruitful new vantage point from which the behaviour of the actors could be—indeed, had to be—reinterpreted."[29] Taking Foucault's suggestion (in the *History of Sexuality*) that sexuality was not repressed, but at the center of modern discourses, Judith Walkowitz delved into Josephine Butler's campaign against the Contagious Diseases Acts in late Victorian England. She placed her account of this successful woman's movement, aimed at combating the double standard of sexual morality, in the context of economic, social, religious, and political divisions in English society.[30] The study establishes the centrality for members of parliament as well as for leading professional figures, male and female, of debates about sexual conduct. These debates were carried on "in public," and resulted in institutional and legal change. Sexual conduct was, therefore, an explicit political issue for at least several decades. The articulation of the meanings of sexual differences was also crucial at certain moments in the French Revolution, when citizenship and political participation were being defined. Darlene Levy and Harriet Applewhite have studied the proclamations that outlawed women's clubs in 1793 in the name of protecting femininity and domesticity. And Lynn Hunt has called attention to the way the Jacobins used masculinity to represent the sovereign people.[31]

These studies share a common preoccupation with politics and more specifically with governments as the realm in which power relationships are formally negotiated. As such, they indicate the importance of connecting the study of gender with the study of politics. Since political structures and political ideas shape and set the boundaries of public discourse and of all aspects of life, even those excluded from participation in politics are defined by them. "Non-actors," to use Mason's term, are acting according to rules established in political realms; the private sphere is a public creation; those absent from official accounts partook nonetheless in the making of history; those who are silent speak eloquently about the meanings of power and the uses of political authority.

This emphasis brings women's history directly to political historians, those most committed to writing narratives with male subjects at their center. It also begins to develop a way of thinking historically about gender, for it draws attention to the ways in which changes happen in laws, policies, and symbolic representations. Furthermore, it implies a social rather than a biological or characterological explanation for the different behaviors and the unequal conditions of women and men. At the same time, however, it seems to undercut the feminist project by neglecting female agency and by implicitly diminishing the historical importance of personal and social life—family, sexuality, sociability—the very areas in which women have been visible participants.

The contradictions encountered by these various approaches to women's history have not prevented the production of new knowledge. That is evident in the multiplication of women's history jobs and courses and in the thriving journals and book market on which publishers have so readily capitalized. The contradictions have been productive in other ways as well. They have generated a search for resolution, an effort to formulate theories, and have set off reflection on the process of writing history itself. When put into dialogue with one another, these different approaches can move the entire discussion forward. But they can only do so, it seems to me, if the key terms of analysis are examined and redefined. These terms are three: woman as subject, gender, and politics.

Although there is a growing literature (informed especially by psychoanalysis) on the question of the "subject" that ought to be brought to bear on any discussion of women in history, I want to take up only a small point here. That has to do with the issue—made so apparent by the experience of "her-story"—of the particularity of women in relation to the universality of men. The abstract rights-bearing individual who came into being as the focus of liberal political debate in the seventeenth and eighteenth centuries somehow became embodied in male form and it is his-story that historians have largely told. Feminists' scholarship has repeatedly come up against the difficulty of including women in this universal representation since, as their work reveals, it is a contrast with feminine particularity that secures the universality of the masculine representation.

It seems clear that to conceive of women as historical actors, equal in status to men, requires a notion of the particularity and specificity of all human subjects. Historians cannot use a single, universal representative for the diverse populations of any society or culture without granting differential importance to one group over another.[32] Particularity, however, raises questions about collective identities and about whether all groups can ever share the same experience. How do individuals become members of social groups? How are group identities defined and formed? What influences people to act as members of groups? Are processes of group identification common or variable? How do those marked by multiple differences (black women, or women workers, middle-class lesbians, or black lesbian workers) determine the salience of one or another of these identities? Can these differences, which together constitute the meanings of individual and collective identities, be conceived of historically? How could we realize in the writing of history Teresa de Lauretis's suggestion that differences among women are better understood as "differences within women?"[33]

If the group or category "women" is to be investigated, then gender—the mutiple and contradictory meanings attributed to sexual difference—is an important analytic tool.[34] The term "gender" suggests that relations between the sexes are a primary aspect of social organization (rather than following from, say, economic or demographic pressures); that the terms of male and female identities are in large part culturally determined (not produced by individuals or collectivities entirely on their own); and that differences between the sexes constitute and are constituted by hierarchical social structures.

The turn to political history by those interested in writing about gender has introduced notions of contest, conflict, and power into the process of the cultural determination of the terms of sexual difference. But by studying power as it is exercised by and in relation to formal governmental authorities, historians unnecessarily eliminate whole realms of experience from consideration. This would not happen if a broader notion of "politics" were employed, one that took all unequal relationships as somehow "political" because involving unequal distributions of power, and asked how they were established, refused, or maintained. Here Foucault's discussion of power relations in Volume I of *The History of Sexuality* seems worth quoting at length:

> The question that we must address, then, is not: Given a specific state structure, how and why is it that power needs to establish a knowledge of sex? Neither is the question: What over-all domination was served by the concern, evidenced since the eighteenth century, to produce true discourses on sex? Nor is it: What law presided over both the regularity of sexual behavior and the conformity of what was said about it? It is rather: In a specific type of discourse on sex, in a specific form of extortion of truth, appearing historically and in specific places (around the child's body, apropos of women's sex, in connection with practices restricting births and so on), what were the most immediate, the most local power relations at work? How did they make possible these kinds of discourses, and conversely, how were these discourses used to support power relations? . . . In general terms: rather than referring all the infinitesimal violences that are exerted on sex, all the anxious gazes that are directed at it, and all the hiding places whose discovery is made into an impossible task, to the unique form of a great Power, we must immerse the expanding production of discourses on sex in the field of multiple and mobile power relations.[35]

This approach would end such seeming dichotomies as state and family, public and private, work and sexuality. And it would pose questions about the interconnections among realms of life and social organization now treated quite separately from one another. With this notion of politics, one could offer a critique of history that characterized it not simply as an incomplete record of the past but as a participant in the production of knowledge that legitimized the exclusion or subordination of women.

Gender and "politics" are thus antithetical neither to one another nor to recovery of the female subject. Broadly defined they dissolve distinctions between public and private and avoid arguments about the separate and distinctive qualities of women's character and experience. They challenge the accuracy of fixed binary distinctions between men and women in the past and present, and expose the very political nature of a history written in those terms. Simply to assert, however, that gender is a political issue is not enough. The realization of the radical potential of women's history comes in the writing of histories that focus on women's experiences *and* analyze the ways in which politics construct gender and gender constructs politics. Feminist history then becomes not the recounting of great deeds performed by women but the exposure of the often silent and hidden operations of gender that are nonetheless present and defining forces in the organization of most societies. With this approach women's history critically confronts the politics of existing histories and inevitably begins the rewriting of history.

2

Gender: A Useful Category of Historical Analysis

> *Gender. n. a grammatical term only. To talk of persons or creatures of the masculine or feminine gender, meaning of the male or female sex, is either a jocularity (permissible or not according to context) or a blunder.*
>
> FOWLER'S *Dictionary of Modern English Usage*

Those who would codify the meanings of words fight a losing battle, for words, like the ideas and things they are meant to signify, have a history. Neither Oxford dons nor the Académie Française has been entirely able to stem the tide, to capture and fix meanings free of the play of human invention and imagination. Mary Wortley Montagu added bite to her witty denunciation "of the fair sex" ("my only consolation for being of that gender has been the assurance of never being married to any one among them") by deliberately misusing the grammatical reference.[1] Through the ages, people have made figurative allusions by employing grammatical terms to evoke traits of character or sexuality. For example, the usage offered by the *Dictionnaire de la langue française* in 1876 was: "On ne sait de quel genre il est, s'il est mâle ou femelle, se dit d'un homme très-caché, dont on ne connait pas les sentiments."[2] And Gladstone made this distinction in 1878: "Athene has nothing of sex except the gender, nothing of the woman except the form."[3] Most recently—too recently to find its way into dictionaries or the *Encyclopedia of the Social Sciences*—feminists have in a more literal and serious vein begun to use "gender" as a way of referring to the social organization of the relationship between the sexes. The connection to grammar is both explicit and full of unexamined possibilities. Explicit because

This essay was first prepared for delivery at the meetings of the American Historical Association in December 1985. It was subsequently published in its current form in the *American Historical Review,* Vol. 91, No. 5 (December 1986). Discussions with Denise Riley, Janice Doane, Yasmine Ergas, Anne Norton, and Harriet Whitehead helped formulate my ideas on the various subjects touched in the course of this paper. The final version profited from comments by Ira Katznelson, Charles Tilly, Louise Tilly, Elisabetta Galeotti, Rayna Rapp, Christine Stansell, and Joan Vincent. I am also grateful for the unusually careful editing done at the *AHR* by Allyn Roberts and David Ransell.

the grammatical usage involves formal rules that follow from the masculine or feminine designation; full of unexamined possibilities because in many Indo-European languages there is a third category —unsexed or neuter. In grammar, gender is understood to be a way of classifying phenomena, a socially agreed upon system of distinctions rather than an objective description of inherent traits. In addition, classifications suggest a relationship among categories that makes distinctions or separate groupings possible.

In its most recent usage, "gender" seems to have first appeared among American feminists who wanted to insist on the fundamentally social quality of distinctions based on sex. The word denoted a rejection of the biological determinism implicit in the use of such terms as "sex" or "sexual difference." "Gender" also stressed the relational aspect of normative definitions of femininity. Those who worried that women's studies scholarship focused too narrowly and separately on women used the term "gender" to introduce a relational notion into our analytic vocabulary. According to this view, women and men were defined in terms of one another, and no understanding of either could be achieved by entirely separate study. Thus Natalie Davis suggested in 1975, "It seems to me that we should be interested in the history of both women and men, that we should not be working only on the subjected sex any more than a historian of class can focus entirely on peasants. Our goal is to understand the significance of the *sexes,* of gender groups in the historical past. Our goal is to discover the range in sex roles and in sexual symbolism in different societies and periods, to find out what meaning they had and how they functioned to maintain the social order or to promote its change."[4]

In addition, and perhaps most important, "gender" was a term offered by those who claimed that women's scholarship would fundamentally transform disciplinary paradigms. Feminist scholars pointed out early on that the study of women would not only add new subject matter but would also force a critical reexamination of the premises and standards of existing scholarly work. "We are learning," wrote three feminist historians, "that the writing of women into history necessarily involves redefining and enlarging traditional notions of historical significance, to encompass personal, subjective experience as well as public and political activities. It is not too much to suggest that however hesitant the actual beginnings, such a methodology implies not only a new history of women, but also a new history."[5] The way in which this new history would both include and account for women's experience rested on the extent to which gender could be developed as a category of analysis. Here the analogies to class and race were explicit; indeed, the most politically inclusive of scholars of women's studies regularly invoked all three categories as crucial to the writing of a new history.[6] An interest in class, race, and gender signaled, first, a scholar's commitment to a history that included stories of the oppressed and an analysis of the meaning and nature of their oppression and, second, scholarly understanding that inequalities of power are organized along at least three axes.

The litany of class, race, and gender suggests a parity for each term, but, in fact, that is not at all the case. While "class" most often rests on Marx's elaborate (and since elaborated) theory of economic determination and historical change, "race" and "gender" carry no such associations. No unanimity exists among those who employ concepts of class. Some scholars employ Weberian notions, others use class as a temporary heuristic device. Still, when we invoke class, we are working with or against a set of definitions that, in the case of Marxism, involve an idea of economic causality and a vision of the path along which history has moved dialectically. There is no such clarity or coherence for either race or gender. In the case of gender, the usage has involved a range of theoretical positions as well as simple descriptive references to the relationships between the sexes.

Feminist historians, trained as most historians are to be more comfortable with description than theory, have nonetheless increasingly looked for usable theoretical formulations. They have done so for at least two reasons. First, the proliferation of case studies in women's history seems to call for some synthesizing perspective that can explain continuities and discontinuities and account for persisting inequalities as well as radically different social experiences. Second, the discrepancy between the high quality of recent work in women's history and its continuing marginal status in the field as a whole (as measured by textbooks, syllabi, and monographic work) points up the limits of descriptive approaches that do not address dominant disciplinary concepts, or at least that do not address these concepts in terms that can shake their power and perhaps transform them. It has not been enough for historians of women to prove either that women had a history or that women participated in the major political upheavals of Western civilization. In the case of women's history, the response of most nonfeminist historians has been acknowledgment and then separation or dismissal ("women had a history separate from men's, therefore let feminists do women's history which need not concern us"; or "women's history is about sex and the family and should be done separately from political and economic history"). In the case of women's participation, the response has been minimal interest at best ("my understanding of the French Revolution is not changed by knowing that women participated in it"). The challenge posed by these responses is, in the end, a theoretical one. It requires analysis not only of the relationship between male and female experience in the past but also of the connection between past history and current historical practice. How does gender work in human social relationships? How does gender give meaning to the organization and perception of historical knowledge? The answers depend on gender as an analytic category.

[I]

For the most part, the attempts of historians to theorize about gender have remained within traditional social scientific frameworks, using long-standing formulations that provide universal causal explanations. These theories have been limited at best because they tend to contain reductive or overly simple generalizations that undercut not only history's disciplinary sense of the complexity of social causation but also feminist commitments to analyses that will lead to change. A review of these theories will expose their limits and make it possible to propose an alternative approach.

The approaches used by most historians fall into two distinct categories. The first is essentially descriptive; that is, it refers to the existence of phenomena or realities without interpreting, explaining, or attributing causality. The second usage is causal; it theorizes about the nature of phenomena or realities, seeking an understanding of how and why these take the form they do.

In its simplest recent usage, "gender" is a synonym for "women." Any number of books and articles whose subject is women's history have, in the past few years, substituted "gender" for "women" in their titles. In some cases, this usage, though vaguely referring to certain analytic concepts, is actually about the political acceptability of the field. In these instances, the use of "gender" is meant to denote the scholarly seriousness of a work, for "gender" has a more neutral and objective sound than does "women." "Gender" seems to fit within the scientific terminology of social science and thus dissociates itself from the (supposedly strident) politics of feminism. In this usage, "gender" does not carry with it a necessary statement about inequality or power nor does it name the aggrieved (and hitherto invisible) party. Whereas the term "women's history" proclaims its politics by asserting (contrary to customary practice) that women are valid historical subjects, "gender" includes, but does not name women, and so seems to pose no critical threat. This use of "gender" is one facet of what might be called the quest of feminist scholarship for academic legitimacy in the 1980s.

But only one facet. "Gender" as a substitute for "women" is also used to suggest that information about women is necessarily information about men, that one implies the study of the other. This usage insists that the world of women is part of the world of men, created in and by it. This usage rejects the interpretive utility of the idea of separate spheres, maintaining that to study women in isolation perpetuates the fiction that one sphere, the experience of one sex, has little or nothing to do with the other. In addition, gender is also used to designate social relations between the sexes. Its use explicitly rejects biological explanations, such as those that find a common denominator for diverse forms of female subordination in the facts that women have the capacity to give birth and men have greater muscular strength. Instead, gender becomes a way of denoting "cultural constructions"—the entirely social creation of ideas about appropriate roles for women and men. It is a way of referring to the exclusively social origins of the subjective identities of men and women. Gender is, in this definition, a social category imposed on a sexed body.[7] Gender seems to have become a particularly useful word as studies of sex and sexuality have proliferated, for it offers a way of differentiating sexual practice from the social roles assigned to women and men. Although scholars acknowledge the connection between sex and (what the sociologists of the family called) "sex roles," these scholars do not assume a simple or direct linkage. The use of gender emphasizes an entire system of relationships that may include sex, but is not directly determined by sex nor directly determining of sexuality.

These descriptive usages of gender have been employed by historians most often to map out a new terrain. As social historians turned to new objects of study, gender was relevant for such topics as women, children, families, and gender ideologies. This usage of gender, in other words, refers only to those areas—both structural and ideological—involving relations between the sexes. Because, on the face of it, war, diplomacy, and high politics have not been explicitly about those relationships, gender seems not to apply and so continues to be irrelevant to the thinking of historians concerned with issues of politics and power. The effect is to endorse a certain functionalist view ultimately rooted in biology and to perpetuate the idea of separate spheres (sex or politics, family or nation, women or men) in the writing of history. Although gender in this usage asserts that relationships between the sexes are social, it says nothing about why these relationships are constructed as they are, how they work, or how they change. In its descriptive usage, then, gender is a concept associated with the study of things related to women. Gender is a new topic, a new department of historical investigation, but it does not have the analytic power to address (and change) existing historical paradigms.

Some historians were, of course, aware of this problem, hence the efforts to employ theories that might explain the concept of gender and account for historical change. Indeed, the challenge was to reconcile theory, which was framed in general or universal terms, and history, which was committed to the study of contextual specificity and fundamental change. The result has been extremely eclectic: partial borrowings that vitiate the analytic power of a particular theory or worse, employ its precepts without awareness of their implications; or accounts of change that, because they embed universal theories, only illustrate unchanging themes; or wonderfully imaginative studies in which theory is nonetheless so hidden that these studies cannot serve as models for other investigations. Because the theories on which historians have drawn are often not spelled out in all their implications, it seems worthwhile to spend some time doing that. Only through such an exercise can we evaluate the usefulness of these theories and begin to articulate a more powerful theoretical approach.

Feminist historians have employed a variety of approaches to the analysis of gender, but the approaches come down to a choice among three theoretical positions.[8] The first, an entirely feminist effort, attempts to explain the origins of patriarchy. The second locates itself within a Marxian tradition and seeks there an accommodation with feminist critiques. The third, fundamentally divided between French post-structuralist and Anglo-American object-relations theorists, draws on these different schools of psychoanalysis to explain the production and reproduction of the subject's gendered identity.

Theorists of patriarchy have directed their attention to the subordination of women and found their explanation for it in the male "need" to dominate the female. In Mary O'Brien's ingenious adaptation of Hegel, she defined male domination as the effect of men's desire to transcend their alienation from the means of the reproduction of the species. The principle of generational continuity restores the primacy of paternity and obscures the real labor and the social reality of women's work in childbirth. The source of women's liberation lies in "an adequate understanding of the process of reproduction," an appreciation of the contradiction between the nature of women's reproductive labor and (male) ideological mystifications of it.[9] For Shulamith Firestone, reproduction was also the "bitter trap" for women. In her more materialist analysis, however, liberation would come with transformations in reproductive technology, which might in some not too distant future eliminate the need for women's bodies as the agents of species reproduction.[10]

If reproduction was the key to patriarchy for some, sexuality itself was the answer for others. Catherine MacKinnon's bold formulations were at once her own and characteristic of a certain approach: "Sexuality is to feminism what work is to marxism: that which is most one's own, yet most taken away." "Sexual objectification is the primary process of the subjection of women. It unites act with word, construction with expression, perception with enforcement, myth with reality. Man fucks woman; subject verb object."[11] Continuing her analogy to Marx, MacKinnon offered, in the place of dialectical materialism, consciousness-raising as feminism's method of analysis. By expressing the shared experience of objectification, she argued, women come to understand their common identity and so are moved to political action. Although sexual relations are defined in MacKinnon's analysis as social, there is nothing except the inherent inequality of the sexual relation itself to explain why the system of power operates as it does. The source of unequal relations between the sexes is, in the end, unequal relations between the sexes. Although the inequality of which sexuality is the source is said to be embodied in a "whole system of social relationships," how this system works is not explained.[12]

Theorists of patriarchy have addressed the inequality of males and females in important ways, but, for historians, their theories pose problems. First, while they offer an analysis internal to the gender system itself, they also assert the primacy of that system in all social organization. But theories of patriarchy do not show what gender inequality has to do with other inequalities. Second, whether domination comes in the form of the male appropriation of the female's reproductive labor or in the sexual objectification of women by men, the analysis rests on physical difference. Any physical difference takes on a universal and unchanging aspect, even if theorists of patriarchy take into account the existence of changing forms and systems of gender inequality.[13] A theory that rests on the single variable of physical difference poses problems for historians: it assumes a consistent or inherent meaning for the human body—outside social or cultural construction—and thus the ahistoricity of gender itself. History becomes, in a sense, epiphenomenal, providing endless variations on the unchanging theme of a fixed gender inequality.

Marxist feminists have a more historical approach, guided as they are by a theory of history. But, whatever the variations and adaptations have been, the self-imposed requirement that there be a "material" explanation for gender has limited or at least slowed the development of new lines of analysis. Whether a so-called dual-systems solution is profered (one that posits the separate but interacting realms of capitalism and patriarchy) or an analysis based more firmly in orthodox Marxist discussions of modes of production is developed, the explanation for the origins of and changes in gender systems is found outside the sexual division of labor. Families, households, and sexuality are all, finally, products of changing modes of production. That is how Engels concluded his explorations of the *Origins of the Family;*[14] that is where economist Heidi Hartmann's analysis ultimately rests. Hartmann insists on the importance of taking into account patriarchy and capitalism as separate but interacting systems. Yet, as her argument unfolds, economic causality takes precedence, and patriarchy always develops and changes as a function of relations of production.[15]

Early discussions among Marxist feminists circled around the same set of problems: a rejection of the essentialism of those who would argue that the "exigencies of biological reproduction" determine the sexual division of labor under capitalism; the futility of inserting "modes of reproduction" into discussions of modes of production (it remains an oppositional category and does not assume equal status with modes of production); the recognition that economic systems do not directly determine gender relationships, indeed, that the subordination of women pre-dates capitalism and continues under socialism; the search nonetheless for a materialist explanation that excludes natural physical differences.[16] An important attempt to break out of this circle of problems came from Joan Kelly in her essay "The Doubled Vision of Feminist Theory," where she argued that economic and gender systems interact to produce social and historical experiences; that neither system was casual, but both "operate simultaneously to reproduce the socioeconomic and male-dominant structures of . . . [a] particular social order." Kelly's suggestion that gender systems have an independent existence provided a crucial conceptual opening, but her commitment to remain within a Marxist framework led her to emphasize the causal role of economic factors even in the determination of the gender system. "The relation of the sexes operates in accordance with, and through, socioeconomic structures, as well as sex/gender ones."[17] Kelly introduced the idea of a "sexually based social reality," but she tended to emphasize the social rather than the sexual nature of that reality, and, most often, "social," in her usage, was conceived in terms of economic relations of production.

The most far-reaching exploration of sexuality by American Marxist feminists is in *Powers of Desire,* a volume of essays published in 1983.[18] Influenced by increasing attention to sexuality among political activists and scholars, by French philosopher Michel Foucault's insistence that sexuality is produced in historical contexts, and by the conviction that the current "sexual revolution" requires serious analysis, the authors make "sexual politics" the focus of their inquiry. In so doing, they open the question of causality and offer a variety of solutions to it; indeed, the real excitement of this volume is its lack of analytic unanimity, its sense of analytic tension. If individual authors tend to stress the causality of social (by which is often meant "economic") contexts, they nonetheless include suggestions about the importance of studying "the psychic structuring of gender identity." If "gender ideology" is sometimes said to "reflect" economic and social structures, there is also a crucial recognition of the need to understand the complex "link between society and enduring psychic structure."[19] On the one hand, the editors endorse Jessica Benjamin's point that politics must include attention to "the erotic, fantastic components of human life," but, on the other hand, no essays besides Benjamin's deal fully or seriously with the theoretical issues she raises.[20] Instead, a tacit assumption runs through the volume that Marxism can be expanded to include discussions of ideology, culture, and psychology and that this expansion will happen through the kind of concrete examination of evidence undertaken in most of the articles. The advantage of such an approach lies in its avoidance of sharp differences of position, the disadvantage in its leaving in place an already fully articulated theory that leads back from relations of the sexes to relations of production.

A comparison of American Marxist-feminist efforts, exploratory and relatively wide-ranging, to those of their English counterparts, tied more closely to the politics of a strong and viable Marxist tradition, reveals that the English have had greater difficulty in challenging the constraints of strictly determinist explanations. This difficulty can be seen most dramatically in the debates in the *New Left Review* between Michèle Barrett and her critics, who charge her with abandoning a materialist analysis of the sexual division of labor under capitalism.[21] It can be seen as well in the replacement of an initial feminist attempt to reconcile psychoanalysis and Marxism with a choice of one or another of these theoretical positions by scholars who earlier insisted that some fusion of the two was possible.[22] The difficulty for both English and American feminists working within Marxism is apparent in the work I have mentioned here. The problem they face is the opposite of the one posed by patriarchal theory. For within Marxism, the concept of gender has long been treated as the by-product of changing economic structures; gender has had no independent analytic status of its own.

A review of psychoanalytic theory requires a specification of schools, since the various approaches have tended to be classified by the national origins of the founders and the majority of the practitioners. There is the Anglo-American school, working within the terms of theories of object-relations. In the United States, Nancy Chodorow is the name most readily associated with this approach. In addition, the work of Carol Gilligan has had a far-reaching impact on American scholarship, including history. Gilligan's work draws on Chodorow's, although it is concerned less with the construction of the subject than with moral development and behavior. In contrast to the Anglo-American school, the French school is based on structuralist and post-structuralist readings of Freud in terms of theories of language (for feminists, the key figure is Jacques Lacan).

Both schools are concerned with the processes by which the subject's identity is created; both focus on the early stages of child development for clues to the formation of gender identity. Object-relations theorists stress the influence of actual experience (the child sees, hears, relates to those who care for it, particularly, of course, to its parents), while the post-structuralists emphasize the centrality of language in communicating, interpreting, and representing gender. (By "language," post-structuralists do not mean words but systems of meaning—symbolic orders—that precede the actual mastery of speech, reading, and writing.) Another difference between the two schools of thought focuses on the unconscious, which for Chodorow is ultimately subject to conscious understanding and for Lacan is not. For Lacanians, the unconscious is a critical factor in the construction of the subject; it is the location, moreover, of sexual division and, for that reason, of continuing instability for the gendered subject.

In recent years, feminist historians have been drawn to these theories either because they serve to endorse specific findings with general observations or because they seem to offer an important theoretical formulation about gender. Increasingly, those historians working with a concept of "women's culture" cite Chodorow's or Gilligan's work as both proof of and explanation for their interpretations; those wrestling with feminist theory look to Lacan. In the end, neither of these theories seems to me entirely workable for historians; a closer look at each may help explain why.

My reservation about object-relations theory concerns its literalism, its reliance on relatively small structures of interaction to produce gender identity and to generate change. Both the family division of labor and the actual assignment of tasks to each parent play a crucial role in Chodorow's theory. The outcome of prevailing Western systems is a clear division between male and female: "The basic feminine sense of self is connected to the world, the basic masculine sense of self is separate."[23] According to Chodorow, if fathers were more involved in parenting and present more often in domestic situations, the outcome of the oedipal drama might be different.[24]

This interpretation limits the concept of gender to family and household experience and, for the historian, leaves no way to connect the concept (or the individual) to other social systems of economy, politics, or power. Of course, it is implicit that social arrangements requiring fathers to work and mothers to perform most child-rearing tasks structure family organization. Where such arrangements come from and why they are articulated in terms of a sexual division of labor is not clear. Neither is the issue of inequality, as opposed to that of asymmetry, addressed. How can we account within this theory for persistent associations of masculinity with power, for the higher value placed on manhood than on womanhood, for the way children seem to learn these associations and evaluations even when they live outside nuclear households or in households where parenting is equally divided between husband and wife? I do not think we can without some attention to signifying systems, that is, to the ways societies represent gender, use it to articulate the rules of social relationships, or construct the meaning of experience. Without meaning, there is no experience; without processes of signification, there is no meaning.

Language is the center of Lacanian theory; it is the key to the child's induction into the symbolic order. Through language, gendered identity is constructed. According to Lacan, the phallus is the central signifier of sexual difference. But the meaning of the phallus must be read metaphorically. For the child, the oedipal drama sets forth the terms of cultural interaction, since the threat of castration embodies the power, the rules of (the Father's) law. The child's relationship to the law depends on sexual difference, on its imaginative (or fantastic) identification with masculinity or femininity. The imposition, in other words, of the rules of social interaction is inherently and specifically gendered, for the female necessarily has a different relationship to the phallus than the male does. But gender identification, although it always appears coherent and fixed, is, in fact, highly unstable. As meaning systems, subjective identities are processes of differentiation and distinction, requiring the suppression of ambiguities and opposite elements in order to ensure (create the illusion of) coherence and common understanding. The principle of masculinity rests on the necessary repression of feminine aspects—of the subject's potential for bisexuality—and introduces conflict into the opposition of masculine and feminine. Repressed desires are present in the unconscious and are constantly a threat to the stability of gender identification, denying its unity, subverting its need for security. In addition, conscious ideas of masculine or feminine are not fixed, since they vary according to contextual usage. Conflict always exists, then, between the subject's need for the appearance of wholeness and the imprecision of terminology, its relative meaning, its dependence on repression.[25] This kind of interpretation makes the categories of "man" and "woman" problematic by suggesting that masculine and feminine are not inherent characteristics but subjective (or fictional) constructs. This interpretation also implies that the subject is in a constant process of construction, and it offers a systematic way of interpreting conscious and unconscious desire by pointing to language as the appropriate place for analysis. As such, I find it instructive.

I am troubled, nonetheless, by the exclusive fixation on questions of the individual subject and by the tendency to reify subjectively originating antagonism between males and females as the central fact of gender. In addition, although there is openness in the concept of how "the subject" is constructed, the theory tends to universalize the categories and relationship of male and female. The outcome for historians is a reductive reading of evidence from the past. Even though this theory takes social relationships into account by linking castration to prohibition and law, it does not permit the introduction of a notion of historical specificity and variability. The phallus is the only signifier; the process of constructing the gendered subject is, in the end, predictable because always the same. If, as film theorist Teresa de Lauretis suggests, we need to think in terms of the construction of subjectivity in social and historical contexts, there is no way to specify those contexts within the terms offered by Lacan. Indeed, even in de Lauretis's attempt, social reality (that is, "material, economic and interpersonal [relations] which are in fact social, and in a larger perspective historical") seems to lie outside, apart from the subject.[26] A way to conceive of "social reality" in terms of gender is lacking.

The problem of sexual antagonism in this theory has two aspects. First, it projects a certain timeless quality, even when it is historicized as well as it has been by Sally Alexander. Alexander's reading of Lacan led her to conclude that "antagonism between the sexes is an unavoidable aspect of the acquisition of sexual identity. . . . If antagonism is always latent, it is possible that history offers no final resolution, only the constant reshaping, reorganizing of the symbolization of difference, and the sexual division of labor."[27] It may be my hopeless utopianism that gives me pause before this formulation, or it may be that I have not yet shed the episteme of what Foucault called the Classical Age. Whatever the explanation, Alexander's formulation contributes to the fixing of the binary opposition of male and female as the only possible relationship and as a permanent aspect of the human condition. It perpetuates rather than questions what Denise Riley refers to as "the dreadful air of constancy of sexual polarity." She writes: "The historically constructed nature of the opposition [between male and female] produces as one of its effects just that air of an invariant and monotonous men/women opposition."[28]

It is precisely that opposition, in all its tedium and monotony, that (to return to the Anglo-American side) Carol Gilligan's work has promoted. Gilligan explains the divergent paths of moral development followed by boys and girls in terms of differences of "experience" (lived reality). It is not surprising that historians of women have picked up her ideas and used them to explain the "different voices" their work has enabled them to hear. The problems with these borrowings are manifold, and they are logically connected.[29] The first is a slippage that often happens in the attribution of causality: the argument moves from a statement such as "women's experience leads them to make moral choices contingent on contexts and relationships" to "women think and choose this way because they are women." Implied in this line of reasoning is the ahistorical, if not essentialist, notion of woman. Gilligan and others have extrapolated her description, based on a small sample of late twentieth-century American schoolchildren, into a statement about all women. This extrapolation is evident especially, but not exclusively, in the discussions by some historians of "women's culture" that take evidence from early saints to modern militant labor activists and reduce it to proof of Gilligan's hypothesis about a universal female preference for relatedness.[30] This use of Gilligan's ideas provides sharp contrast to the more complicated and historicized conceptions of "women's culture" evident in the *Feminist Studies* 1980 symposium.[31] Indeed, a comparison of that set of articles with Gilligan's formulations reveals the extent to which her notion is ahistorical, defining woman/man as a universal, self-reproducing binary opposition—fixed always in the same way. By insisting on fixed differences (in Gilligan's case, by simplifying data with more mixed results about sex and moral reasoning to underscore sexual difference), feminists contribute to the kind of thinking they want to oppose. Although they insist on the revaluation of the category "female" (Gilligan suggests that women's moral choices may be more humane than men's), they do not examine the binary opposition itself.

We need a refusal of the fixed and permanent quality of the binary opposition, a genuine historicization and deconstruction of the terms of sexual difference. We must become more self-conscious about distinguishing between our analytic vocabulary and the material we want to analyze. We must find ways (however imperfect) continually to subject our categories to criticism, our analyses to self-criticism. If we employ Jacques Derrida's definition of deconstruction, this criticism means analyzing in context the way any binary opposition operates, reversing and displacing its hierarchical construction, rather than accepting it as real or self-evident or in the nature of things.[32] In a sense, of course, feminists have been doing this for years. The history of feminist thought is a history of the refusal of the hierarchical construction of the relationship between male and female in its specific contexts and an attempt to reverse or displace its operations. Feminist historians are now in a position to theorize their practice and to develop gender as an analytic category.

[II]

Concern with gender as an analytic category has emerged only in the late twentieth century. It is absent from the major bodies of social theory articulated from the eighteenth to the early twentieth century. To be sure, some of those theories built their logic on analogies to the opposition of male and female, others acknowledged a "woman question," still others addressed the formation of subjective sexual identity, but gender as a way of talking about systems of social or sexual relations did not appear. This neglect may in part explain the difficulty that contemporary feminists have had incorporating the term "gender" into existing bodies of theory and convincing adherents of one or another theoretical school that gender belongs in their vocabulary. The term "gender" is part of the attempt by contemporary feminists to stake claim to a certain definitional ground, to insist on the inadequacy of existing bodies of theory for explaining persistent inequalities between women and men. It seems to me significant that the use of the word "gender" has emerged at a moment of great epistemological turmoil that takes the form, in some cases, of a shift from scientific to literary paradigms among social scientists (from an emphasis on cause to one on meaning, blurring genres of inquiry, in anthropologist Clifford Geertz's phrase)[33] and, in other cases, the form of debates about theory between those who assert the transparency of facts and those who insist that all reality is construed or constructed, between those who defend and those who question the idea that "man" is the rational master of his own destiny. In the space opened by this debate and on the side of the critique of science developed by the humanities, and of empiricism and humanism by post-structuralists, feminists have begun to find not only a theoretical voice of their own but scholarly and political allies as well. It is within this space that we must articulate gender as an analytic category.

What should be done by historians who, after all, have seen their discipline dismissed by some recent theorists as a relic of humanist thought? I do not think we should quit the archives or abandon the study of the past, but we do have to change some of the ways we've gone about working, some of the questions we have asked. We need to scrutinize our methods of analysis, clarify our operative assumptions, and explain how we think change occurs. Instead of a search for single origins, we have to conceive of processes so interconnected that they cannot be disentangled. Of course, we identify problems to study, and these constitute beginnings or points of entry into complex processes. But it is the processes we must continually keep in mind. We must ask more often how things happened in order to find out why they happened; in anthropologist Michelle Rosaldo's formulation, we must pursue not universal, general causality but meaningful explanation: "It now appears to me that women's place in human social life is not in any direct sense a product of the things she does, but of the meaning her activities acquire through concrete social interaction."[34] To pursue meaning, we need to deal with the individual subject as well as social organization and to articulate the nature of their interrelationships, for both are crucial to understanding how gender works, how change occurs. Finally, we need to replace the notion that social power is unified, coherent, and centralized with something like Michel Foucault's concept of power as dispersed constellations of unequal relationships, discursively constituted in social "fields of force."[35] Within these processes and structures, there is room for a concept of human agency as the attempt (at least partially rational) to construct an identity, a life, a set of relationships, a society within certain limits and with language—conceptual language that at once sets boundaries and contains the possibility for negation, resistance, reinterpretation, the play of metaphoric invention and imagination.

My definition of gender has two parts and several subsets. They are interrelated but must be analytically distinct. The core of the definition rests on an integral connection between two propositions: gender is a constitutive element of social relationships based on perceived differences between the sexes, and gender is a primary way of signifying relationships of power. Changes in the organization of social relationships always correspond to changes in representations of power, but the direction of change is not necessarily one way. As a constitutive element of social relationships based on perceived differences between the sexes, gender involves four interrelated elements: first, culturally available symbols that evoke multiple (and often contradictory) representations—Eve and Mary as symbols of woman, for example, in the Western Christian tradition—but also, myths of light and dark, purification and pollution, innocence and corruption. For historians, the interesting questions are, Which symbolic representations are invoked, how, and in what contexts? Second, normative concepts that set forth interpretations of the meanings of the symbols, that attempt to limit and contain their metaphoric possibilities. These concepts are expressed in religious, educational, scientific, legal, and political doctrines and typically take the form of a fixed binary opposition, categorically and unequivocally asserting the meaning of male and female, masculine and feminine. In fact, these normative statements depend on the refusal or repression of alternative possibilities, and sometimes overt contests about them take place (at what moments and under what circumstances ought to be a concern of historians). The position that emerges as dominant, however, is stated as the only possible one. Subsequent history is written as if these normative positions were the product of social consensus rather than of conflict. An example of this kind of history is the treatment of the Victorian ideology of domesticity as if it were created whole and only afterwards reacted to instead of being the constant subject of great differences of opinion. Another kind of example comes from contemporary fundamentalist religious groups that have forcibly linked their practice to a restoration of women's supposedly more authentic "traditional" role, when, in fact, there is little historical precedent for the unquestioned performance of such a role. The point of new historical investigation is to disrupt the notion of fixity, to discover the nature of the debate or repression that leads to the appearance of timeless permanence in binary gender representation. This kind of analysis must include a notion of politics and reference to social institutions and organizations—the third aspect of gender relationships.

Some scholars, notably anthropologists, have restricted the use of gender to the kinship system (focusing on household and family as the basis for social organization). We need a broader view that includes not only kinship but also (especially for complex modern societies) the labor market (a sex-segregated labor market is a part of the process of gender construction), education (all-male, single-sex, or coeducational institutions are part of the same process), and the polity (universal male suffrage is part of the process of gender construction). It makes little sense to force these institutions back to functional utility in the kinship system, or to argue that contemporary relationships between men and women are artifacts of older kinship systems based on the exchange of women.[36] Gender is constructed through kinship, but not exclusively; it is constructed as well in the economy and the polity, which, in our society at least, now operate largely independently of kinship.

The fourth aspect of gender is subjective identity. I agree with anthropologist Gayle Rubin's formulation that psychoanalysis offers an important theory about the reproduction of gender, a description of the "transformation of the biological sexuality of individuals as they are enculturated."[37] But the universal claim of psychoanalysis gives me pause. Even though Lacanian theory may be helpful for thinking about the construction of gendered identity, historians need to work in a more historical way. If gender identity is based only and universally on fear of castration, the point of historical inquiry is denied. Moreover, real men and women do not always or literally fulfill the terms either of their society's prescriptions or of our analytic categories. Historians need instead to examine the ways in which gendered identities are substantively constructed and relate their findings to a range of activities, social organizations, and historically specific cultural representations. The best efforts in this area so far have been, not surprisingly, biographies: Biddy Martin's interpretation of Lou Andreas Salomé, Kathryn Sklar's depiction of Catharine Beecher, Jacqueline Hall's life of Jessie Daniel Ames, and Mary Hill's discussion of Charlotte Perkins Gilman.[38] But collective treatments are also possible, as Mrinalina Sinha and Lou Ratté have shown in their respective studies of the terms of construction of gender identity for British colonial administrators in India and for British-educated Indians who emerged as anti-imperialist, nationalist leaders.[39]

The first part of my definition of gender consists, then, of all four of these elements, and no one of them operates without the others. Yet they do not operate simultaneously, with one simply reflecting the others. A question for historical research is, in fact, what the relationships among the four aspects are. The sketch I have offered of the process of constructing gender relationships could be used to discuss class, race, ethnicity, or, for that matter, any social process. My point was to clarify and specify how one needs to think about the effect of gender in social and institutional relationships, because this thinking is often not done precisely or systematically. The theorizing of gender, however, is developed in my second proposition: gender is a primary way of signifying relationships of power. It might be better to say, gender is a primary field within which or by means of which power is articulated. Gender is not the only field, but it seems to have been a persistent and recurrent way of enabling the signification of power in the West, in the Judeo-Christian as well as the Islamic tradition. As such, this part of the definition might seem to belong in the normative section of the argument, yet it does not, for concepts of power, though they may build on gender, are not always literally about gender itself. French sociologist Pierre Bourdieu has written about how the "di-vision du monde," based on references to "biological differences and notably those that refer to the division of the labor of procreation and reproduction," operates as "the best founded of collective illusions." Established as an objective set of references, concepts of gender structure perception and the concrete and symbolic organization of all social life.[40] To the extent that these references establish distributions of power (differential control over or access to material and symbolic resources), gender becomes implicated in the conception and construction of power itself. The French anthropologist Maurice Godelier has put it this way: "It is not sexuality which haunts society, but society which haunts the body's sexuality. Sex-related differences between bodies are continually summoned as testimony to social relations and phenomena that have nothing to do with sexuality. Not only as testimony to, but also testimony for—in other words, as legitimation."[41]

The legitimizing function of gender works in many ways. Bourdieu, for example, showed how, in certain cultures, agricultural exploitation was organized according to concepts of time and season that rested on specific definitions of the opposition between masculine and feminine. Gayatri Spivak has done a pointed analysis of the uses of gender and colonialism in certain texts of British and American women writers.[42] Natalie Davis has shown how concepts of masculine and feminine related to understandings and criticisms of the rules of social order in early modern France.[43] Historian Caroline Bynum has thrown new light on medieval spirituality through her attention to the relationships between concepts of masculine and feminine and religious behavior. Her work gives us important insight into the ways in which these concepts informed the politics of monastic institutions as well as of individual believers.[44] Art historians have opened a new territory by reading social implications from literal depictions of women and men.[45] These interpretations are based on the idea that conceptual languages employ differentiation to establish meaning and that sexual difference is a primary way of signifying differentiation.[46] Gender, then, provides a way to decode meaning and to understand the complex connections among various forms of human interaction. When historians look for the ways in which the concept of gender legitimizes and constructs social relationships, they develop insight into the reciprocal nature of gender and society and into the particular and contextually specific ways in which politics constructs gender and gender constructs politics.

Politics is only one of the areas in which gender can be used for historical analysis. I have chosen the following examples relating to politics and power in their most traditionally construed sense, that is, as they pertain to government and the nation-state, for two reasons. First, the territory is virtually uncharted, since gender has been seen as antithetical to the real business of politics. Second, political history—still the dominant mode of historical inquiry—has been the stronghold of resistance to the inclusion of material or even questions about women and gender.

Gender has been employed literally or analogically in political theory to justify or criticize the reign of monarchs and to express the relationship between ruler and ruled. One might have expected that the debates of contemporaries over the reigns of Elizabeth I in England and Catherine de Medici in France would dwell on the issue of women's suitability for political rule, but, in the period when kinship and kingship were integrally related, discussions about male kings were equally preoccupied with masculinity and femininity.[47] Analogies to the marital relationship provide structure for the arguments of Jean Bodin, Robert Filmer, and John Locke. Edmund Burke's attack on the French Revolution is built around a contrast between ugly, murderous *sansculotte* hags ("the furies of hell, in the abused shape of the vilest of women") and the soft femininity of Marie Antoinette, who escaped the crowd to "seek refuge at the feet of a king and husband" and whose beauty once inspired national pride. (It was in reference to the appropriate role for the feminine in the political order that Burke wrote, "To make us love our country, our country ought to be lovely.")[48] But the analogy is not always to marriage or even to heterosexuality. In medieval Islamic political theory, the symbols of political power alluded most often to sex between man and boy, suggesting not only forms of acceptable sexuality akin to those that Foucault's last work described in classical Greece but also the irrelevance of women to any notion of politics and public life.[49]

Lest this last comment suggest that political theory simply reflects social organization, it seems important to note that changes in gender relationships can be set off by views of the needs of state. A striking example is Louis de Bonald's argument in 1816 about why the divorce legislation of the French Revolution had to be repealed:

> Just as political democracy, "allows the people, the weak part of political society, to rise against the established power," so divorce, "veritable domestic democracy," allows the wife, "the weak part, to rebel against marital authority. . . . in order to keep the state out of the hands of the people, it is necessary to keep the family out of the hands of wives and children."[50]

Bonald begins with an analogy and then establishes a direct correspondence between divorce and democracy. Harking back to much earlier arguments about the well-ordered family as the foundation of the well-ordered state, the legislation that implemented this view redefined the limits of the marital relationship. Similarly, in our own time, conservative political ideologues would like to pass a series of laws about the organization and behavior of the family that would alter current practices. The connection between authoritarian regimes and the control of women has been noted but not thoroughly studied. Whether at a crucial moment for Jacobin hegemony in the French Revolution, at the point of Stalin's bid for controlling authority, the implementation of Nazi policy in Germany, or with the triumph in Iran of the Ayatollah Khomeini, emergent rulers have legitimized domination, strength, central authority, and ruling power as masculine (enemies, outsiders, subversives, weakness as feminine) and made that code literal in laws (forbidding women's political participation, outlawing abortion, prohibiting wage-earning by mothers, imposing female dress codes) that put women in their place.[51] These actions and their timing make little sense in themselves; in most instances, the state had nothing immediate or material to gain from the control of women. The actions can only be made sense of as part of an analysis of the construction and consolidation of power. An assertion of control or strength was given form as a policy about women. In these examples, sexual difference was conceived in terms of the domination or control of women. These examples provide some insight into the kinds of power relationships being constructed in modern history, but this particular type of relationship is not a universal political theme. In different ways, for example, the democratic regimes of the twentieth century have also constructed their political ideologies with gendered concepts and translated them into policy; the welfare state, for example, demonstrated its protective paternalism in laws directed at women and children.[52] Historically, some socialist and anarchist movements have refused metaphors of domination entirely, imaginatively presenting their critiques of particular regimes or social organizations in terms of transformations of gender identities. Utopian socialists in France and England in the 1830s and 1840s conceived their dreams for a harmonious future in terms of the complementary natures of individuals as exemplified in the union of man and woman, "the social individual."[53] European anarchists were long known not only for refusing the conventions of bourgeois marriage but for their visions of a world in which sexual difference did not imply hierarchy.

These examples are of explicit connections between gender and power, but they are only a part of my definition of gender as a primary way of signifying relationships of power. Attention to gender is often not explicit, but it is nonetheless a crucial part of the organization of equality or inequality. Hierarchical structures rely on generalized understandings of the so-called natural relationships between male and female. The concept of class in the nineteenth century relied on gender for its articulation. While middle-class reformers in France, for example, depicted workers in terms coded as feminine (subordinated, weak, sexually exploited like prostitutes), labor and socialist leaders replied by insisting on the masculine position of the working class (producers, strong, protectors of their women and children). The terms of this discourse were not explicitly about gender, but they were strengthened by references to it. The gendered "coding" of certain terms established and "naturalized" their meanings. In the process, historically specific, normative definitions of gender (which were taken as givens) were reproduced and embedded in the culture of the French working class.[54]

The subject of war, diplomacy, and high politics frequently comes up when traditional political historians question the utility of gender in their work. But here, too, we need to look beyond the actors and the literal import of their words. Power relations among nations and the status of colonial subjects have been made comprehensible (and thus legitimate) in terms of relations between male and female. The legitimizing of war—of expending young lives to protect the state—has variously taken the forms of explicit appeals to manhood (to the need to defend otherwise vulnerable women and children), of implicit reliance on belief in the duty of sons to serve their leaders or their (father the) king, and of associations between masculinity and national strength.[55] High politics itself is a gendered concept, for it establishes its crucial importance and public power, the reasons for and the fact of its highest authority, precisely in its exclusion of women from its work. Gender is one of the recurrent references by which political power has been conceived, legitimated, and criticized. It refers to but also establishes the meaning of the male/female opposition. To vindicate political power, the reference must seem sure and fixed, outside human construction, part of the natural or divine order. In that way, the binary opposition and the social process of gender relationships both become part of the meaning of power itself; to question or alter any aspect threatens the entire system.

If significations of gender and power construct one another, how do things change? The answer in a general sense is that change may be initiated in many places. Massive political upheavals that throw old orders into chaos and bring new ones into being may revise the terms (and so the organization) of gender in the search for new forms of legitimation. But they may not; old notions of gender have also served to validate new regimes.[56] Demographic crises, occasioned by food shortages, plagues, or wars, may have called into question normative visions of heterosexual marriage (as happened in some circles, in some countries in the 1920s), but they have also spawned pronatalist policies that insist on the exclusive importance of women's maternal and reproductive functions.[57] Shifting patterns of employment may lead to altered marital strategies and to different possibilities for the construction of subjectivity, but they can also be experienced as new arenas of activity for dutiful daughters and wives.[58] The emergence of new kinds of cultural symbols may make possible the reinterpreting or, indeed, rewriting of the oedipal story, but it can also serve to reinscribe that terrible drama in even more telling terms. Political processes will determine which outcome prevails—political in the sense that different actors and different meanings are contending with one another for control. The nature of that process, of the actors and their actions, can only be determined specifically, in the context of time and place. We can write the history of that process only if we recognize that "man" and "woman" are at once empty and overflowing categories. Empty because they have no ultimate, transcendent meaning. Overflowing because even when they appear to be fixed, they still contain within them alternative, denied, or suppressed definitions.

Political history has, in a sense, been enacted on the field of gender. It is a field that seems fixed yet whose meaning is contested and in flux. If we treat the opposition between male and female as problematic rather than known, as something contextually defined, repeatedly constructed, then we must constantly ask not only what is at stake in proclamations or debates that invoke gender to explain or justify their positions but also how implicit understandings of gender are being invoked and reinscribed. What is the relationship between laws about women and the power of the state? Why (and since when) have women been invisible as historical subjects, when we know they participated in the great and small events of human history? Has gender legitimized the emergence of professional careers?[59] Is (to quote the title of a recent article by French feminist Luce Irigaray) the subject of science sexed?[60] What is the relationship between state politics and the discovery of the crime of homosexuality?[61] How have social institutions incorporated gender into their assumptions and organizations? Have there ever been genuinely egalitarian concepts of gender in terms of which political systems were projected, if not built?

Investigation of these issues will yield a history that will provide new perspectives on old questions (about how, for example, political rule is imposed, or what the impact of war on society is), redefine the old questions in new terms (introducing considerations of family and sexuality, for example, in the study of economics or war), make women visible as active participants, and create analytic distance between the seemingly fixed language of the past and our own terminology. In addition, this new history will leave open possibilities for thinking about current feminist political strategies and the (utopian) future, for it suggests that gender must be redefined and restructured in conjunction with a vision of political and social equality that includes not only sex but class and race.

II

GENDER AND CLASS

— 3 —

On Language, Gender, and Working-Class History

This essay is an attempt to address a problem that seems to me increasingly evident and stubbornly resistant to easy solution. That problem is the one faced by feminist historians in their attempts to bring women as a subject and gender as an analytic category into the practice of labor history. If women as subjects have increased in visibility, the questions raised by women's history remain awkwardly connected to the central concerns of the field. And gender has not been seriously considered for what it could provide in the way of a major reconceptualization of labor history. Some feminist historians (myself included) have therefore viewed with cautious optimism their colleagues' increasing interest in theories of language. Those theories (contained in the writings of post-structuralists and cultural anthropologists), and better referred to as epistemological theories, offer a way of thinking about how people construct meaning, about how difference (and therefore sexual difference) operates in the construction of meaning, and about how the complexities of contextual usages open the way for changes in meaning.

These theories are potentially of great use for the conceptualization of gender and the reconceptualization of historical practice. And yet,

This essay is based on an article that was originally published in *International Labor and Working Class History* (1987) 31:1–13. It has been revised and expanded to address critiques, published also in that issue, by Brian Palmer, Anson Rabinbach, and Christine Stansell. It includes as well portions of my reply to these critiques, published in (1987) 32:39–45. It is printed here with permission from the University of Illinois Press, which holds the copyright. I am grateful to Palmer, Rabinbach, and Stansell for comments that pointed up problems in the original essay, all of which will not have been corrected here to their satisfaction. I am appreciative, as well, of suggestions from Denise Riley and Elliott Shore, which substantially improved the argument.

for the most part, they have not been used that way. Instead they have been superficially applied, giving feminist historians some cause for frustration, if not pessimism about the kinds of changes we can expect from labor history. The recent spate of articles by labor historians on "language" demonstrates my point, for they reduce this important concept to the study of "words."[1] Words taken at their face value as literal utterances become one more datum to collect and the notion of how meaning is constructed—as a complex way of interpreting and understanding the world—is lost. With the loss of an understanding of meaning, the importance and usefulness of thinking about labor history in terms of gender also disappears. We are left with separate studies of women and of words and those may add new material, but they will never alone transform the way we think about the history we write.

Among labor historians attention to "language" has become the order of the day. Words like "discourse" and "rhetoric" appear with increasing frequency in journals and books and analyses of ideology have acquired renewed prominence. Even as historians resist the searing critique of their practice offered by post-structuralist writers (and perhaps as part of the resistance), they appropriate the terminology used by their critics. Thus "language," "discourse," "symbolic," and "deconstruct" now pop up in ordinary historical conversation, stripped of the terrifying relativist consequences they have in the writings of Saussure, Foucault, Lacan, Althusser, Barthes, or Derrida. This transformation of meaning, so easily accomplished by the relocation of words into different discursive fields, ought to carry a lesson about the difficulties of establishing clear and fixed definitions and thus of analyzing the operations of linguistic systems, but it does not. Instead, "language" has become another item to be scrutinized, words a kind of datum to be collected. Studying "language" may permit familiar questions to be opened up; some historians have thereby questioned the status of categories of class or experience as transparent, real, unmediated phenomena. But the operations of meaning remain remarkably unproblematic in their usages and, as a result, "language" loses its theoretical interest and its analytic force.

I will return to this point, but first I want to introduce a second, related theme.

Among labor historians attention to "gender" has acquired a certain legitimacy, though it has nothing of the fashionable status of "language." Some labor historians, acting on a kind of popular-front mentality, now place gender (along with race) on the list of variables they acknowledge as important, but don't have time to study; class, after all, is still the issue that really counts. Others, rejecting gender as a useful category, do refer to women (or note their absence or exclusion) as a gesture of sympathy or solidarity, but with little interest or attention. Most, however, ignore gender entirely, insisting either that it is absent from their sources or that (unfortunately) women played only a minor role in the working-class politics that mattered. Women and children may come up in discussions of working-class family life, for here they are visible actors, filling discernibly different social roles; in this way gender is equated with and hence reduced to a set of self-evident social categories (the roles played by women or men) and has no critical effect on the way labor history is conceived. Thus, for example, while notions of "language" have allowed historians to call for a major epistemological shift, "gender" has had no such effect on their conceptions of politics or class.

For the most part, labor historians seem quite willing to let women write women's history and they are usually supportive and even encouraging to their female students and colleagues. The antifeminist reaction so violent in certain quarters of the historical profession (which vehemently and passionately denounces feminist historians as "zealots" and "ideologues," subverters of supposedly timeless canons and established truths) is less apparent among labor historians.[2] Still, the halfhearted attention to gender is dismaying. For the relegation of this potentially radical conception to a set of descriptive social roles vitiates the theoretical interest and the analytic force feminist history could have.

My purpose in this essay is to argue that there is a connection between the study of "language" and the study of gender, when both are carefully defined; that certain epistemological theories, by providing historians with a way to analyze how gender figures in the construction of social and political meaning, thereby provide us with a way to recast our understanding of the place of gender in history, of the operations of sexual difference in the "making" of the working class. By "language" I mean not simply words in their literal usage but the creation of meaning through differentiation. By gender I mean not simply social roles for women and men but the articulation in specific contexts of social understandings of sexual difference. If meaning is constructed in terms of difference (by distinguishing explicitly or implicitly what something is from what it is not), then sexual difference (which is culturally and historically variable, but which always seems fixed and indisputable because of its reference to natural, physical bodies) is an important way of specifying or establishing meaning. My argument, then, is that if we attend to the ways in which "language" constructs meaning we will also be in a position to find gender. Especially in Western Europe and North

America in the nineteenth and twentieth centuries—the places and periods with which I am most familiar and in which most labor historians work—the connections are unavoidable. The connections are unavoidable as well because it was precisely in this period that gender was articulated as a problematic issue.

How then have historians managed to avoid the connections for so long? A look at Gareth Stedman Jones's *Languages of Class*, especially his "Introduction" and the long essay called "Rethinking Chartism," may provide something of an answer.[3] I choose Stedman Jones not because his work is bad but because it is so good. It seems to me he provides one of the best and clearest discussions so far of some of the uses of "language" for labor historians and for that reason he has sparked an excited renewal of thinking in the field. Yet his incomplete apprehension of the theories he draws on limits his work methodologically and conceptually; it would be a pity if this were to become the "new" approach to labor history for it falls far short of the radical promise post-structuralist theory holds out for us and it would perpetuate the marginal status of feminist inquiry in the field of labor history.

[I]

The theoretical claim of "Rethinking Chartism" (one I agree with) is that the backgrounds, interests, and structural positions of members of the movement cannot explain its emergence or decline. We get nowhere, Stedman Jones tells us, pursuing lines of inquiry that assume social causation because there is no social reality outside or prior to language. Hence class is not a thing whose existence predetermines or is reflected in class consciousness; rather it is "constructed and inscribed within a complex rhetoric of metaphorical associations, causal inferences and imaginative constructions" (p. 102). Class and class consciousness are the same thing—they are political articulations that provide an analysis of, a coherent pattern to impose upon, the events and activities of daily life. Although the rhetoric of class appeals to the objective "experience" of workers, in fact such experience only exists through its conceptual organization; what counts as experience cannot be established by collecting empirical data but by analyzing the terms of definition offered in political discourse (by the state, employers, discrete political movements, etc.). The categories within which empirical data are placed, after all, are not objective entities but ways of perceiving or understanding, of assigning importance or significance to phenomena or events. The origins of class must be sought then not in objective material conditions, nor in the consciousness said to reflect those conditions, but in the language of political struggle. "[I]t was not consciousness (or ideology) that produced politics, but politics that produced consciousness" (p. 19).

This philosophical assumption led Stedman Jones to redefine the nature of Chartism itself—above all it was a political movement—and to propose a new way of studying it—as a "language" providing the interpretive definition for experience within which action could be organized. Practically, this meant looking at what people wrote and said, but without assuming that the external reality of class explained their words. Stedman Jones's essay is an attempt to illustrate his method. It is a careful reading of "terms and propositions" (p. 21) that uncovers the lineage (in radicalism) of Chartist thought and that reveals a real struggle to define the lines of affiliation and opposition for the movement. Without question it "restores politics to its proper importance" (p. 21), but only in the most literal way.

Stedman Jones's essay conflates two different definitions of politics: one labels as politics any contest for power within which identities such as class are created; the other characterizes as politics (or political) those goals of a collective movement aimed at formal participation in government or the state. The first definition is by far the more radical for it contains the nonreferential conception Stedman Jones endorses in his Introduction. It suggests that there is always a politics—in the sense of a power relationship—in the operations of discourse. The second is essentially descriptive, employing the approach of conventional intellectual history—establishing continuities of thought, pointing out underlying assumptions, and organizing into a coherent outlook the diverse ideas of various proponents. Stedman Jones means to use the first definition, but in his essay on Chartism he uses the second. He cannot put into practice the theory he espouses in his Introduction because of the methods he employs to analyze history. First, he reads "language" only literally, with no sense of how texts are constructed. Second, he slips back to the notion that "language" reflects a "reality" external to it, rather than being constitutive of that reality.

By treating meaning as "language" and reading only literally, Stedman Jones finds Chartism to be a political movement because it was interested in formal political representation as a solution to social problems. The key to Chartism, he says, was its use of radical "vocabulary," the importation of older words and ideas into an early nineteenth-century context. He spends much of the essay showing that the message of Chartism was similar to that of Owenism, trade unionism, and the "Ricardian socialism" of the period—all understood the state as the ultimate source of oppression. Chartism was a heterogeneous movement, including all the unenfranchised in its notion of class; the contents of the message, in other words, was political in a formal and literal sense. This procedure shows class to be a political concept not so much because it was formulated in a particular kind of (discursive) conflict but because it contained or referred to political ideas (the vestiges of English radicalism). These ideas, moreover, were the "effect of" or a "response to" "legislative measures of the Whig government" (p. 175). Political ideas, then, *reflected* changes in political practice and in the position of those who espoused them. Stedman Jones concludes that the rise and fall of Chartism, cannot be "related . . . to movements in the economy, divisions in the movement or an immature class consciousness" but rather to "the changing character and policies of the state—the principal enemy upon whose actions radicals had always found that their credibility depended" (p. 178).

Although the word "related" is admittedly ambiguous, the conclusion is less so. Historians of Chartism have misplaced causality, Jones implies, for state policies and not relations of production *determined* the composition and the goals of the movement. As a corrective to a reductive economic determinism, this is an important contribution, but it is not a major transformation of how we think about history. Stedman Jones uses theories of language, which have a far more radical potential, in an essentially conservative manner, to correct certain conclusions that historians have made, but not to make us rethink entire questions. His analysis is less informed by a notion of the "materiality of language itself" (p. 20) than it is by an idea that attention to the words people used (rather than how words acquire and construct meaning) provides a way to determine which reality mattered most in a particular historical context. His reinterpretation of Chartism argues for a closer fit between the "vocabulary" of the movement and our description of it; rather than reversing the direction of our causal thinking he merely shifts the causality from the economic to the political sphere. Stedman Jones does not entertain the possibility that economic grievances are about power and politics, that Chartists might have sought economic change by political means, that their visions of power intertwined economics and politics. He wants to argue that Chartist politics were not immanent in productive relations and that Chartism drew on many different socioeconomic groups in the population. Its political appeal, in other words, created the identity of individuals in the movement. But Stedman Jones's literalism leads him to deny the possibility that "class" was part of the political identity that was created. He rejects economic causality and class when, in fact, it would have been more useful for his argument to acknowledge "class" but locate its origins in political rhetoric. Stedman Jones stops short of opening up a reconceptualization of Chartist history because he treats "language" simply as a vehicle for communicating ideas rather than as a system of meaning or a process of signification.

For Stedman Jones to achieve the radical promise of the theory he espouses, he would have to attend to certain aspects he ignores. These are, first, the notion that "language" reveals entire systems of meaning or knowledge—not only ideas people have about particular issues but their representations and organizations of life and the world. To say, as Stedman Jones does, that Chartism was not a class movement because it sought participation in government is to miss the opportunity to see a larger politics at work, to see, that is, how an identity of class constructed (and contained) social practice, through which people established, interpreted, and acted on their place in relation to others. These relations to others—of subordination or dominance, equality or hierarchy—constituted social organization. The problem comes, in part, from using the word "language" itself, for it somehow reduces the idea of meaning to instrumental utterances—words people say to one another—rather than conveying the idea of meaning as the patterns and relationships that constitute understanding or a "cultural system." Stedman Jones's confusion also stems from his use of "class" as an objective category of social analysis, instead of as an identity historically and contextually created.

The second related aspect of this theory that Stedman Jones overlooks is the way meaning is constructed through differentiation. He assumes a kind of one-dimensional quality for "language"—that words have a shared and stable definition in all contexts (a "vocabulary") through which communication occurs. Yet the theorists by whom he is inspired (he cites Saussure) maintained that words acquired meaning by implicit or explicit contrasts established in specific contexts (or discourses). One cannot read Foucault (another presence—albeit implicit—in Stedman Jones's work) without understanding that meaning is multidimensional, established relationally, directed at more than one auditor, framed in an already existing (discursive) field, establishing new fields at the same time. Positive definitions depend on negatives, indeed imply their existence in order to rule them out. This kind of interdependence has ramifications well beyond literal definitions, for it involves other concepts, other relationships in any particular usage. (Thus, for example, seventeenth-century political theorists made analogies between marriage contracts and social contracts that affected how people understood both; and nineteenth-century socialists depicted capitalist exploitation of workers as prostitution, thereby intertwining economic and sexual spheres.) Meaning is developed relationally and differentially and so constitutes relationships. Thus, to apply this to Stedman Jones's subject, one would expect that the category of the working class rested not only on antitheses (capitalists, aristocrats) but on inclusions (wage-earners, the unrepresented) and exclusions (those who held no property in their labor, women and children). The universal category of class, like the universal category of worker, secured its universality through a series of oppositions. The goal of a reading of Chartism from this perspective, it seems to me, is not to reduce it neatly to a formal political struggle or a particular strategy offered by an organized group but to examine the process through which Chartist politics constructed class identity.

It is in analyzing the process of making meaning that gender becomes important. Concepts such as class are created through differentiation. Historically, gender has provided a way of articulating and naturalizing difference. If we look closely at the "languages of class" of the nineteenth century we find they are built with, in terms of, references to sexual difference. In these references, sexual difference is invoked as a "natural" phenomenon; as such it enjoys a privileged status, seemingly outside question or criticism. Those who do criticize it (and there were those who did) have a difficult time challenging its authority for they seem to be disputing nature instead of social construction. Gender becomes so implicated in concepts of class that there is no way to analyze one without the other. One cannot analyze politics separately from gender, sexuality, the family. These are not compartments of life but discursively related systems; "language" makes possible the study of their interrelationships. As Chartists set forth their program they offered the terms of political collective identity. This identity rested on a set of differentiations—inclusions and exclusions, comparisons and contrasts—that relied on sexual difference for their meaning. Had Stedman Jones attended to the way meaning was constructed he would have seen *how* the particular category of class developed by this group relied on gender. By failing to attend to how meanings rest on differentiation he missed both class and gender in their specific manifestation in Chartism.

[II]

How might Stedman Jones have "read" Chartism and better captured the process by which the working class was conceived? My answer can only be partial for I do not have the full texts of the documents he cites, nor (since I do not do research on Chartism) can I claim to command detailed knowledge of the field. Still, it seems worthwhile to suggest with the material he offers what a somewhat different conceptual approach to "languages of class" might have offered.

First, it is necessary to ask whether class, as a concept, appears in Chartist discourse. Stedman Jones's emphasis on the movement's rise and fall keeps him within the bounds of a more conventional explanation than he wants to employ and mutes the significance of his insights for an understanding of how class might be signified. Moreover, by insisting on the political thrust of the popular movement (and at one point stating that it was not displaced in the late 1830s by a "more class conscious mode of thought" [p. 153]), Stedman Jones underestimates the importance and complexity of the definition of class that was elaborated by Chartists. For they did develop a notion of "class." In the material he cites, there is clearly evident a conception of the particular position, the identity, of "working men" whether antagonistic to or in cooperation with masters, the middle classes, shopkeepers, or aristocrats. What is striking is how various orators grapple with the lines of distinction contrasting producers and idlers, laborers and profiteers, workers/middle classes/aristocrats, wage slaves and tyrants, honest democrats and usurious monopolists. The blame for inequality and injustice was placed, for the most part, on the government system, but there is no doubt that "class" was being signified—developed as a way of organizing collective identity through an appeal to shared economic, political, and social "experience." The interesting questions to ask, it seems to me, are how all these contrasts created a place in social and political discourse for a working class identity, and what that vision was.

Here the issue of discursive field(s) should enter the analysis. It might be more useful to place Chartism in a multidimensional field than to argue only for a linear continuity with radicalism. For political movements develop tactically and not logically, improvising appeals, incorporating and adapting various ideas to their particular cause. By conceiving of such movements as mélanges of interpretations and programs (instead of as coherently unified systems of thought) we come closer not only to how they operated but to the web of relationships within which they developed. Chartism spoke to issues about political rights and representation articulated in the debates leading to the Reform Bill of 1832; it inserted itself in the many and sometimes conflicting discussions of industrialization associated with Luddism, Owenism, cooperation and various union movements of the early nineteenth century (the movements E. P. Thompson writes about in *The Making of the English Working Class*). These, in turn, engaged with the teachings and critiques of political economy and social reform. Chartism spoke across these realms by evolving the notion of property in labor for disenfranchised and otherwise propertyless working men.

The Chartists located themselves squarely within the discourse on natural rights. (And Stedman Jones is surely right that the Reform Bill agitation had a great deal to do with the timing of the movement.) They did this by pointing out the affinity of their constituents—as propertied citizens—with those already enfranchised. Stedman Jones cites rhetoric that projected a future democratic world still consisting of employers and employees to demonstrate that Chartists were not fully "class conscious." This kind of reasoning misses the point, for it focuses on the literal content of words instead of on the way meaning was constructed. Stedman Jones tries to prove that Chartism did not reflect real economic conditions by showing that Chartists were not "class conscious" and he thereby dismisses the way in which class was indeed understood. The terms of his debate with English Marxists overtake his theoretical premises at this point as Stedman Jones tries to show that Chartists were not the forerunners of contemporary socialists. But he grants too much to his opponents, taking their notion of class as the only possible one and arguing that Chartism was not about class at all, instead of insisting that Chartism's "class" identity was fundamentally different from what later socialists would label "class." If one wants to argue that all categories of identity are politically constructed then it makes sense to relativize and historicize the categories. No theoretical ground is gained by reifying the category of class and using that frozen definition as if it were the only possible one.

Not only was the Chartist language setting out the terms of political coalition, but it worked to establish the similarity or comparability of different social groups. The point was to organize working men to demand entry into the political realm by insisting on a common denominator despite certain differences. That common denominator was property, albeit of different types. Chartists developed one aspect of Lockean theory that associated property with the enjoyment of individual political rights, by claiming that the fruit of one's labor or labor power was itself property.[4] As they did so they acknowledged another similarity to those already represented—the fact that all were men. The Chartist demand for universal manhood suffrage acknowledged (what was already in effect in franchise requirements) that only men concluded and entered the social contract; indeed, the identity Chartists claimed with those already represented was that all were male property holders.[5]

At the same time, Chartism used references to gender to position itself within debates of the popular movement and differentiated itself from certain of its threads, notably those that were expressive, associational, and religious. It did so by casting those utopian movements as "feminine," itself as "masculine." (That the Utopians played with gender quite differently is surely significant in this conflict; they projected a future harmonious world in terms of the complementarity of the sexes or of androgyny, positively valuing both feminine and masculine principles.)[6] This gendered differentiation served not only to clarify Chartism's goals but to underscore its argument about the eligibility of workingmen for the vote.

Those who contest the notion that the working class (and sometimes, in this rhetoric, "the people") was embodied in masculine form usually point to the fact that women participated in and supported the movement. This is undoubtedly true, but it does not contradict the argument. Rather, it confuses masculine/feminine with male/female; the former are a set of symbolic references, the latter physical persons, and though there is a relationship between them, they are not the same. Masculine/feminine serves to define abstract qualities and characteristics through an opposition perceived as natural: strong/weak, public/private, rational/expressive, material/spiritual are some examples of gender coding in Western culture since the Enlightenment. There is nothing in such usage to prevent individuals of either sex from accepting these definitions, nor from reinterpreting them to explain their own situations. That women supported a "masculine" movement was not a contradiction, it was rather an affirmation of Chartism's particular interpretation.[7]

The gendered representation of class that Chartism offered, however, *was* a factor in the ways women participated in that movement and in the ways general programs and policies addressed them. And it probably contributed in the long run to firming up a concept of class that endured long after Chartism's decline. For one, no matter how much later struggles stressed the need for a reorganization of the economy and a redistribution of wealth, the invocation of universal human rights was carried on within the masculine construction of property and rationalist politics. One result of this was to push alternative conceptions of class such as those offered by utopian socialists to the periphery. Another effect was to render sexual difference itself invisible. Class, after all, was offered as a universal category even though it depended on a masculine construction. As a result, it was almost inevitable that men represented the working class. Women then had two possible representations. They were either a specific example of the general experience of class and then it was unnecessary to single them out for separate treatment; for they were assumed to be included in any discussion of the working class as a whole. Or, women were a troubling exception, asserting particular needs and interests detrimental to class politics, objecting to husbands using household money for union dues, demanding different kinds of strategies in strikes, insisting on continuing religious affiliations in an age of secular socialism. Both representations are evident in the history of labor movements and in the writing of their histories and they help us locate reasons for the invisibility of women in the making of the working class.

The masculine representation of class also affected the labor movement's definition of workers' problems. Since women were not considered to have property in labor, it was difficult to find a solution other than removal of women from the workforce to the competitive crises created for certain male trades by the employment of women at very low wages. It was not lack of imagination or male chauvinism that prevented serious defense of the position of women workers, but a construction of class that equated productivity and masculinity. Even when attempts were made to extend unionizing efforts to women, these were awkward and difficult because women were not seen as appropriate political actors on behalf of the class. Instead, they were supposed to be represented by their men. The tension and anger between male and female workers in the 1830s that Sally Alexander has ascribed to a universal and enduring sexual hostility might better be understood as a debate about the very terms of this construction of class.[8] When we understand the gendered construction of the working class we gain new perspective on old problems—the problems of competition from women, of sexually differentiated wage scales, and of organizing women workers—problems central not only to women but to the working-class movement as a whole.

The "language" of class, as Chartists spoke it, placed women (and children) in auxiliary and dependent positions. If women mounted speakers' platforms, organized consumer boycotts, and founded special societies of their own, they did so under the Chartist aegis to demand male suffrage and thus assert property rights that came to them through their husbands' and fathers' labor. Eileen Yeo has characterized the Chartist women's position in these terms:

> In their public addresses Chartist women presented themselves mainly in a multi-faceted family role—as the primary tenders of the family, as contributors to the family wage and as auxiliaries who demanded the vote for their male kinfolk in a bid to help the family as a whole.[9]

This implied that women's welfare was included in men's, that consumer activities and childbearing were women's primary tasks, that however public and political these activities they carried a different status than did men's wage work. The masculine construction of class assumed a (gendered) family division of labor; that it reproduced what were thought by some to be natural arrangements makes it no less significant.

Sexual divisions of labor are, of course, neither natural nor fixed and the one that labeled men as the only propertied members of families was not endorsed by all groups in this period. Quite different arrangements were projected, for example, in the writings of some socialist and religious utopians. The 1830s was a moment of flux and experimentation; the lines of social affiliation were being redrawn and—as some of the wilder utopian schemes suggest—nothing was precluded as an imaginative possibility. The line Chartists chose, however, did limit the play of possibility for its own movement and, because of the extent of mobilization by Chartists, probably eclipsed the attraction of other more radical conceptions of class. The version of class that Chartists espoused affirmed a working-class family structure resembling middle-class ideals and susceptible to middle-class pressures: a family organization that no later radical theories of economics managed entirely to displace. From this perspective the working-class family was created within working-class political discourse, through the particular gendered conception of class evident in (though not invented by) the Chartist program. The experience of women in these families must thus be analyzed not as a separate problem but in terms of these interconnected concepts of gender and class.

[III]

Chartism, of course, did not "make" the working class in early nineteenth-century England. A full study of its discourse, however, could give insight not only into the particular politics of that movement but into the processes by which social relationships were conceived and constructed. To insist as Stedman Jones seems to do that our view of social relationships be confined to one-dimensional conflicts between such unquestioned or unproblematized categories as workers and employers, or the disenfranchised and the state, or to insist as some feminist historians do that the "real" story is about a struggle between women and men is so to compartmentalize our vision that we miss the fluidity and complexity of human interactions. A theory of meaning that assumes a multiplicity of references, a resonance beyond literal utterances, a play across topics and spheres makes it possible to grasp how connections and interactions work. When such a theory posits the multiple and contested aspects of all definitions, it also contains a theory of change since meanings are said to be open to reinterpretation, restatement, and negation. The questions, of course, are: how, by whom, and in what contexts do these reformulations take place? When, furthermore, we understand the ways in which contrasts and oppositions secure meanings, we can identify the various ways in which sexual difference was used to construct the working class.

Nineteenth-century "languages of class" were complicated, heterogeneous, and variable. They were, nonetheless, indisputably gendered, resting as they did on explicit appeals to nature and implicit evocations (not consciously intended) of sexual difference. We cannot understand how concepts of class acquired legitimacy and established political movements without examining concepts of gender. We cannot understand working-class sexual divisions of labor without interrogating concepts of class. There is no choice between a focus on class or on gender; each is necessarily incomplete without the other. There is no choice between analyses of gender and of women, unless we want to acknowledge the irrelevance of the history of women for the history of class. The link between gender and class is conceptual; it is a link every bit as material as the link between productive forces and relations of production. To study its history requires attention to "language" and a willingness to subject the very idea of the working class to historical scrutiny.

Attention to "language" should include an evaluation of the limits of that word for analyzing meaning systems. It seems always to be conflated, even when carefully defined, with "words," "vocabulary," and literal usage. Stedman Jones's difficulties, it seems to me, are contained in his reduction of the study of epistemology to the study of words. Perhaps discourse, following Foucault's definition, better characterizes the object of the kind of analysis I have proposed.

It may be visionary to hope that a more sophisticated theory of discourse will also open the way for a needed reconsideration of the politics of contemporary labor historians. Many of these historians, writing from a position that supports the democratic and socialist goals of past labor movements, uncritically accept masculine conceptions of class and rule out feminist demands for attention to women and gender as so many bourgeois distractions to the cause. In this they are unconsciously continuing the politics of an earlier age and they are, of course, the victims of their sources as well. For these sources build on some of the gendered notions that I have argued need exposure and analysis. Such analysis, moreover, is at once threatening and difficult. It is threatening because it requires a critical stance in relation not only to a movement one wants to uphold but often to one's own self-concept as a member of the "fraternal" order that will bring change to the world. Such an analysis is also difficult, for it requires the mastery of philosophically complex, often abstruse, theories and a willingness to shift the way one thinks about history. Despite the difficulties, however, I think there is a rich and challenging experience awaiting labor historians who are willing to take on these questions. Anyway, there really is no other alternative. By refusing to take gender seriously, labor historians only reproduce inequalities that their principles commit them to ending. It may be visionary to hope that we will ever find a way to end inequality, but I am both utopian *and* rationalist enough to think that, by pointing out the problem and suggesting a solution, we may come closer to our goal.

—— 4 ——

Women in *The Making of the English Working Class*

The Making of the English Working Class still stands as a classic text for labor historians, some twenty years after its publication. It at once prescribes and exemplifies a Marxist social history that conceives of class as a relationship (not a structure or category), of class consciousness as a cultural as much as an economic creation, of human agency as a crucial element in the making of history, and of politics as the central meaning of that history. The narrative E. P. Thompson constructs not only incites admiration for the dozens of heroes who move through his pages (rescuing them "from enormous condescension of posterity"),[1] but it also inserts its readers into what Fredric Jameson calls the "unity of a single great collective story . . . the collective struggle to wrest a realm of Freedom from a realm of Necessity."[2] If we are stirred by Thompson's comments about the outrages of child labor, we are also meant to share his endorsement of the politics of the artisans in the London Corresponding Society and of the Luddite "army of redressers" in the Midlands and industrial north. The artisans exemplify the possibility of an authentic humanist politics in the English working-class tradition; a tradition fundamentally rooted in the rank and file.[3]

The book makes little pretense of neutrality, despite Thompson's occasional claims to it (he is, he suggests, more objective than either

This essay was delivered first at the meetings of the American Historical Association in December 1983. It was then substantially rewritten and expanded for presentation at the Wesleyan Humanities Institute seminar in December 1986. I am grateful for the advice and criticism of Henry Abelove, Christina Crosby, Michael Denning, and Denise Riley that helped shape this final version.

the Hammonds, who confuse "history with ideology," or "some economic historians," who confuse "history with apologetics"); indeed, much of its excitement lies in its avowedly political purpose.[4] In 1963 it provided historians like myself with a model for writing socially relevant history. For us, *The Making of the English Working Class* embodied a scholarship that fit a New Left purpose: it exposed the workings of capitalist political economy and demonstrated (what Thompson had elsewhere described as) the virtues of "purposive historical commitment" and the possibilities for "the redemption of man through political action."[5] The timing of the book and its articulation of a socialist humanist position provided an intellectual alternative within Marxism to the frozen categories of Stalinist history. Thompson's emphasis on dynamic processes and on the culturally and historically specific experience of class formation opened the way for more contextualized readings of workers' collective action in the past and for a more flexible and imaginative contemporary politics. His insistence on the agency of ordinary people provided inspiration and confirmation for advocates of grass-roots organizing. In the United States, "history from below" was the academic correlate of the participatory democracy of Students of a Democratic Society (SDS). Activists who bridged the worlds of the university and the community made Thompson's text required reading in courses and study groups. In this way, *The Making of the English Working Class* achieved a kind of instant canonical status as the model for and expression of "the new labor history."

If Thompson's book provided a model for writing history, however, it was not meant to become a dogmatic text. Indeed, Thompson's insistence that he (like Marx) is not a Marxist—not committed to a fixed set of definitional categories that must be applied to historical events in the same way every time—has led some of his more literal-minded critics to deny him a place in the fellowship of the faithful. Yet the theoretical premises of the book sit comfortably within a quite orthodox Marxist tradition:

> . . . class happens when some men, as a result of common experiences (inherited or shared), feel and articulate the identity of their interests as between themselves, and as against other men whose interests are different from (and usually opposed to) theirs. The class experience is largely determined by the productive relations into which men are born—or enter involuntarily.[6]

The shared interest that constitutes class is somehow immanent in productive relations; it is the articulation of the experience that varies according to culture, time, and place.[7] The orthodoxy of Thompson's theoretical scheme now seems apparent, but when the book was written it introduced an important historicity into debates among Marxists in the late 1950s and early 1960s. Its concerns and emphases spoke to issues in that debate having to do with definitions of class, class consciousness, and class politics. *The Making of the English Working Class* was written to counter "economistic notations of Marxism" and to provide another way of thinking about the development of class consciousness than the one that posited the inevitable conversion of workers in factories to a proletarian class identification the terms of which could be assessed by some prior standard of political correctness. For Thompson, human subjects were active agents in the transformation of history. He explained that his purpose was

> to show the existing plebian consciousness refracted by new experiences in social being, which experiences were handled in cultural ways by the people, thus giving rise to a transformed consciousness. In this sense the questions being proposed and some of the theoretical equipment being brought to answer them arose out of that distinct ideological moment.[8]

In addition, the book sought to create a historical tradition of socialist humanism, to instill in the memory of Left politics a connection to an authentic, indigenous nineteenth-century worker radicalism.

> My own work for many years had been as a tutor in adult education, teaching evening classes of working people, trade unionists, white-collar people, teachers, and so on. The audience was there, and the audience of the Left also, of the labor movement and the New Left. I was thinking of that kind of reader when I wrote the book.[9]

Thompson's appeal to this audience was aimed against Leninist vanguardism, and against the notion that there would have been no popular revolts "if intellectuals had not dropped the seed of maladjustment in underprivileged soil."[10] Instead he sought to prove that workers were capable of formulating and acting on revolutionary ideas, that there was some basis in past history for a belief in participatory democratic politics.

Thompson's argument with his contemporaries had to do with the question of origins. Where had the idea of class come from? How had class consciousness taken shape? Class itself, as a set of conceptual terms for collective identity and political action, was not subjected to critical examination. For Thompson did not present himself as an analyst outside the historically situated discourse; instead he spoke from within it as an advocate. Positioning himself as the carrier of historical memory, Thompson brilliantly captured the terms of working-class discourse. He did so by using concepts of class that had been formulated by the nineteenth-century movement and used in the twentieth century. *The Making of the English Working Class* endorsed and reproduced a particular concept of class. As such, it can be read as a double historical document: it gathers rich evidence about how class became understood in the past and it incorporates those meanings in its own construction of working-class history. Analyzing the contents and the textual strategies of *The Making of the English Working Class* thus gives insight into the historical operations of a particular idea of the working class.

In this connection it is revealing to note the absence in the book (and in the preoccupations of the audience to whom it was addressed) of questions that have since become troubling for some labor historians; these are questions that were posed by the feminist movement of the late 1960s and early 1970s (well after the publication of Thompson's book) about the historical roles of women. When one rereads *The Making of the English Working Class* now, one is struck not by the absence of women in the narrative but by the awkward way in which they figure there. The book illuminates some of the reasons for the difficulty and frustration experienced by contemporary feminist socialists as they tried to convince themselves and their colleagues that there ought to be a place for women in the narrative of class formation and in the theory of politics that narrative contains. As such, Thompson's text, although it was not written within the new context created by feminist politics, must nonetheless be read as a precondition for the socialist-feminist discourse. It represents a crucial element in that discourse, for it articulates the assumptions of the tradition within which feminist socialists were located and which they had to confront as they formulated critical perspectives and wrote histories of their own.

[I]

"Class is defined by men as they live their own history, and in the end, this is its only definition."[11] Thus did Thompson refute the sociologists and politicians who reified a historically specific idea. The key to explaining the origins of the idea lay in an analysis of "the productive relations into which men are born—or enter involuntarily."[12] But the meaning of class could only be grasped by studying cultural and social processes "over a considerable historical period."[13] This suggested to Thompson the notion of a life history (in contrast to the identification of repeated appearances of an inert "thing") and so he likened his narrative to a kind of "biography of the English working class from its adolescence until its early manhood."[14] Although the book is hardly as coherent as most individual life histories, the analogy is nonetheless revealing. It suggests that Thompson conceives of the collective movement in the same unified terms he conceives of individual subjects. This kind of singular conceptualization has difficulty incorporating diversity or difference. So although "man" may stand for a neutral or universal human subject, the question of "woman" is hard to articulate or represent, for her difference implies disunity and challenges coherence.

In *The Making of the English Working Class,* the male designation of general concepts is literalized in the persons of the political actors who are described in strikingly detailed (and easily visualized) images. The book is crowded with scenes of men busily working, meeting, writing, talking, marching, breaking machines, going to prison, bravely standing up to police, magistrates, and prime ministers. This is preeminently a story about men, and class is, in its origin and its expression, constructed as a masculine identity, even when not all the actors are male. For, of course, there are women in *The Making of the English Working Class*. Women are identified by name, they are given a certain agency, and they are not all of one type. Indeed, the range is from Mary Wollstonecraft and Anna Wheeler, who spoke out for women's rights, through Richard Carlile's radical female followers, to religious visionaries like Joanna Southcott. Yet the organization of the story and the master codes that structure the narrative are gendered in such a way as to confirm rather than challenge the masculine representation of class. Despite their presence, women are marginal in the book; they serve to underline and point up the overwhelming association of class with the politics of male workers. A closer look at Thompson's women will provide some insight into how the concept and political meanings of class are established in the text.

The book begins with a dramatic scenario. The home of the radical shoemaker, Thomas Hardy, was ransacked in 1794 by officers of the King. The Hardys watched as their papers and clothing were strewn about; Mrs. Hardy "was pregnant and remained in bed." The officers then arrested Mr. Hardy for high treason and eventually sent him to Newgate prison. While he was there "Mrs. Hardy died in childbirth as a result of the shock sustained when her home was besieged by a 'Church and King' mob."[15] The immediacy of the description and its vivid impact evoke the entire story that will be told in the following pages: powerful forces invade the personal domain, the very life of the independent artisan. Hardy, the craftsman, resists in the name of the rights of the independent, freeborn Englishman. His wife and unborn child are the innocent victims of state repression. In subsequent pages, capitalism will wreak similar havoc, its dehumanizing operations ravaging families and disrupting the customary sexual divisions of labor. Men, rooted in historic traditions, will defend and claim their rights, while the distortions of women's traditional domestic experience will express the full measure of capitalist brutality.

This association of women and domesticity crops up even when the subject is women workers, even, that is, when women's experience is referred primarily to relations of production. Take, for example, Thompson's treatment of women textile workers, whose situation is discussed sympathetically and who are presented as the products of the new industrial system. "The mother who was also a wage-earner often felt herself to have the worst of both the domestic and the industrial worlds."[16] Their new status as wage-earners moved women to political action—to trade unions and Female Reform Societies. But, says Thompson, their unions tended to address immediate grievances and were thus less political than were the artisanal organizations that challenged the entire moral and political system. (Although this seems to have been the case for all industrial unions in the 1820s and 1830s, Thompson stresses the point in reference to the women's groups.) Furthermore, he says, the Female Reform Societies had no independent political status. "Paradoxically," says Thompson, the radicalism of these wage-earning women was an expression of nostalgia for a pre-industrial domestic economy. The women mourned the "loss in status and personal independence" of a "way of life centered on the home."[17] Instead of granting this as a valid political position (complementary to, indeed an aspect of, the artisan's longing for a return to his independent status), Thompson depicts it as "paradoxical" and links it to a subordinate status of women in the emerging radical movement. "Their role was confined to giving moral support to the men, making banners and caps of liberty which were presented with ceremony at reform demonstrations, passing resolutions and addresses, and swelling the numbers at meetings."[18] These women foreshadow "Carlile's womenfolk," described in later pages as those who "underwent trial and imprisonment more out of loyalty than conviction."[19] Since women's independence is cast in terms of a prior domesticity instead of work, their claims and political activities had less weight in the "making" of the class. In a sense, the domestic sphere operates as a double foil: it is the place where a presumably natural sexual division of labor prevails, as compared to the workplace, where relations of production are socially constructed; but it is also the place from which politics cannot emanate because it does not provide the experience of exploitation that contains within it the possibility of the collective identity of interest that is class consciousness. Domestic attachments, it seems, compromise the political consciousness even of women who work, in a way that does not happen (or is not seen as a problem) for men. Because of their domestic and reproductive functions, women are, by definition, only partial or imperfect political actors.

This perhaps implicitly explains a problem that is not directly addressed in *The Making of the English Working Class:* the absence of full or separate attention to the impact of industrial capitalism on women who did work. Except for textile workers, there is very little attention to working women in these pages. Women are referred to without comment as cheap labor used to substitute for men in the fields, workshops, and mills. The focus here is on capitalism's impact on male workers, not on the reasons for women's lower status and lower value in the labor market. Women artisans are also neglected, although, like their male counterparts, they had long traditions of independent economic activity that were disrupted by new capitalist practices. Women are not on Thompson's frequent listings of artisan trades (shoemakers, cabinetmakers, tailors, and the like), although sources he used such as Ivy Pinchbeck's *Women Workers and the Industrial Revolution* (and more recent studies that have gone over the same late eighteenth- and early nineteenth-century evidence) indicate milliners, seamstresses, lacemakers, tailoresses, and others forming a significant skilled labor force.[20] There are references in *The Making of the English Working Class* to female benefit societies and a long quotation describes a procession of the members of one such society in 1805. Thompson says that such societies were made up predominantly of artisans, but we are never told what trades the women belonged to. Indeed, while he stresses the formative influence such societies had on male artisans' political traditions, he discounts their influence on women. "In the last years of the eighteenth century female benefit societies and female Methodist classes may have given experience and self-confidence. . . . But it was in the textile districts that the changing economic status of women gave rise to the earliest widespread participation by working women in political and social agitation."[21] It may be that the absence of female artisans in movements of protest led Thompson to neglect them in his discussions of work. But this then raises a serious question about the immanence of class in relations of production. For the absence of artisan women from politics—if they were absent—confounds the theoretical premise that organizes the book. At the very least we need an analysis of the different relations of production experienced by male and female artisans to show why class was immanent in one set of relationships and not in the other. That such an analysis is not offered can be explained, I think, by the attribution to women of domestic associations that somehow discount them from full immersion in the economic relationships that give rise to the articulation of worker interest as class consciousness.

There is another explanation for the invisibility of women artisans, of course. That is that women artisans did participate in politics, but that Thompson felt there was no reason to signal the fact. This would follow from his assumption that the notion of class was a universal, comprehensive idea and from his principled commitment to a policy of equality between women and men. In a 1960 essay, "Outside the Whale," published in the New Left Books collection, *Out of Apathy*, Thompson lashed out against the forces that had led to quietism and resignation in the 1950s. "Custom, Law, the Monarchy, the Church, the State, the Family—all came flooding back. All were indices of the supreme good—stability."[22] Particularly significant was the fixing of human behavior in terms of functions and roles, the attribution of inevitable (because natural) sexual difference: "Sociologists, psychologists and husbands discovered that women are 'different'; and, under cover of talk about 'equality in difference,' the claim of women to full human equality with men was denied."[23] Thompson's (appropriate) refusal of functionalism carried with it a denial of *any* significant operation of difference; one could, after all, acknowledge that social processes involved the construction of gendered subjects without believing that the categories were natural and the meanings assigned to them fixed and inevitable. But his position seems to have been that singling out gender would introduce a presumption of natural difference that was discriminatory. A separate examination of artisanal women would have suggested a different (hence unequal) standard for their political behavior. Thompson's ideological commitment to equality ruled out special attention to sexual difference as a subject for discussion. At the same time, however, his egalitarianism was undermined by a textual strategy that depended on allusions to sexual difference to convey its meaning.

Thompson offered several varieties of female political behavior in *The Making of the English Class*. These were organized and evaluated according to a gendered scheme, a scheme that employed masculine and feminine symbols to identify the positive and negative poles of working-class politics. Indeed, if women are fleeting actors in the pages of the book, the feminine is a central figure in the representation of working-class politics. In the narrative of working-class political choices the masculine construction of the (universal) concept of class becomes clear and some of the confusions surrounding women's place in the story become more apparent.

Politics, the form of expression of class consciousness, is a cultural and historical product, according to Thompson, and it is politics that makes impossible any static definition of the meaning of class. The intersection of objective relations of production and available modes of political expression give distinctiveness to each appearance of class consciousness. "Consciousness of class arises in the same way in different times and places, but never in *just* the same way."[24] In Thompson's account, nineteenth-century working-class politics are traced to movements of eighteenth-century English rationalism and radicalism. The line is a direct one; the rights of freeborn Englishmen inform the claims of nineteenth-century workers. Somehow, this secular tradition is most appropriate to the "interests" of workers immersed in the emerging capitalist relations of production. There is an implication of immanence in this account, despite Thompson's call for history. He depicts rationalist, secular politics as the only possible form of class consciousness, thereby making its appearance natural or inevitable, instead of the product of struggle and debate. He achieves this effect not simply by endorsing particular movements but also by offering a negative contrast, depicting religious uses of sexual imagery as the antithesis of politics, the crazy strain in working-class discourse.

Orthodox Methodism represents the repressed side of this strain; its associations of sin and sexuality constituted a "perverted eroticism," which identified Satan with the phallus and Christ with feminine love. The unorthodox variant led by the poor working woman, Joanna Southcott, is characterized as frenzied and hysterical; unlike Methodism, it was almost exclusively a "cult of the poor." Marked by apocalyptic fervor, Southcott's preaching evoked a riot of lurid sexual imagery in which at times, Thompson says, "all tissue of sense disappears."[25] That Southcott had a following long after her death is undisputed; indeed, the least attractive aspects of Robert Owen's utopian messianism constituted a direct imitation of her: "Mr. Owen, the Philanthropist, threw the mantle of Joanna Southcott across his shoulders."[26] The evocation of a society in which there would be marital affection, sexual freedom, economic mutuality, and a balance between opposing forces—intellectual and physical power, city and country, agriculture and machinery, man and woman—marked

Owen's millenial vision. Its impracticality (there is no strategy other than coversion for effecting social change) leads Thompson, quoting Marx and Engels, to question its political efficacy.

Instead, Thompson distinguishes Owen's utopian claims from the *political* Radicalism of his Owenist artisanal followers expressed in cooperative societies, trade unions, and labor exchanges. Similarly, he distinguishes the religious contents of Southcottianism from the oath-swearing rituals that echoed into the Luddite movement. Indeed it is the *practices*—of community solidarity in Methodist churches, of lay preaching in independent sects, of cooperation of Owenism—that are transferred to working-class politics; according to Thompson, the contents of the religious teaching was not. "Southcottianism was scarcely a form of revolutionary Chiliasm; it did not inspire men to effective social action." Rather it was a psychic consequence of counter-revolution, "the Chiliasm of despair."[27]

Yet Eric Hobsbawm has argued exactly the reverse, that apocalyptic movements coincided with heightened revolutionary activity, indeed that religious and revolutionary movements often informed one another. Barbara Taylor has recently and brilliantly shown that the sexualized language of these visionary religious sects could be used to express profoundly radical critiques, and could lead women as well as men to participate in social action. The masculine imagery for Satan might translate into an attack on capitalism (depicted as aggressive, energetic, and manly in the middle-class rhetoric of the day). The feminine alternative projected a nonalienated, loving, cooperative social order. In another study, Deborah Valenze links traditions of "cottage religion" (presided over by female as well as male preachers, whose teachings offered a similar positive projection of feminine traits) to the household economy's resistance to the new industrial order. Sexualized imagery, with its insistence on affective and spiritual relationships in the household and the community, directly challenged the materialism and individualist values and practices of the new political economy. Taylor suggests, moreover, that the positive assessment of the feminine opened the way for the inclusion of women in Owenite movements. Clear connections were drawn in theory and practice among idealizations of the feminine, claims for women's rights, and plans for a new socialist order.[28]

The lines between political and religious critiques, between the language of politics and the language of sexuality, seem not to have been as clear as Thompson would have them. His insistence on drawing those lines singles out a particular strand of early nineteenth-century politics as the only example of working-class politics. This follows not only from his preference for rationalist politics but also from the implicit associations his theory makes between producers and effective political action. Although, as we have seen, he recognizes that all producers were not men, in fact in his scheme most are and, more important, production is represented as a masculine (if not exclusively male) activity. In this connection, a kind of symbolism attaches to certain characters in the narrative. Tom Paine is the quintessential political expression, the citizen of democratic revolutions. Paine appropriately provided, in his *Rights of Man,* a founding text of the working-class political movement. Joanna Southcott is the antithetical figure. Deluded, yet charismatic, she evoked in her utterances the lures of sexuality and religion; fantastic prophecy was her mode of expression, in her hysterical pregnancy one sees the sterility of her revolutionary appeal. Written into the narrative in this way, Paine and Southcott stand for the positive and negative possibilities for working-class politics; that they are man and woman simply underlines the power of the contrast between the masculine and feminine emphases of their respective appeals and of Thompson's emphatic endorsement of rationalist politics.

To be sure, all women in *The Making of the English Working Class* are not presented as frenzied prophetesses or domestic housewives. There are also women, like Mary Wollstonecraft, whose writings are linked to political traditions of radical individualism, and others, less well-known, who like her were fitting partners for Radical men. Susannah Wright, a Nottingham lace-mender, is described as "very different" from most of Richard Carlile's female volunteers. Prosecuted for selling one of Carlile's addresses, she defended herself in court, interrupted her appeal to suckle her infant, received thunderous applause from the spectators when she did so, and survived a stay in prison for her crime. While the press attacked her as the symbol of the shameless vulgarity of radicalism, Carlile wrote of her that she was a women "of very delicate health, and truly all spirit and not matter."[29] (The issue of how political threats are represented as sexual threats by the conservative press and how radicals are forced to defend their reputations on this score might provide an important perspective on the ways women are portrayed by working-class movements and on gender relationships in those movements. Thompson clearly finds the issue of press commentary worth noting, for he does so several times, but he does not pursue this line of analysis.)[30]

Another heroine is Susan Thistlewood, wife of the doomed Cato Street conspirator, Arthur Thistlewood. She was, Thompson tells us, "not a cypher" but a "spirited Jacobin in her own right, with a cold and intellectual manner and a readiness to take an active part in [her husband's] defense."[31] As in the description of Susannah Wright,

Thompson distinguishes Susan Thistlewood from most other women. She was "not a cypher" and the implication is that most other women were. Whether it is Thompson who thinks other women were cyphers or whether he assumes his readers believe that fact, the examples serve the same end. They show that exceptional women are capable of a type of political behavior most often practiced by men. Thompson's heroines serve to confirm the Paine/Southcott contrast by underscoring the fact that it *is* possible for women to understand and act according to the politics that exemplified English working-class consciousness in the 1820s and 1830s. When they eschew expressivity and act in rational ways, these unusual women can attain class consciousness.

[II]

Thompson placed *The Making of the English Working Class* in the context of the labor movement whose history he sought to write. The book's language and symbolic strategies constructed meanings in terms meant to be familiar to the constituents of that movement. Work, in the sense of productive activity, determined class consciousness, whose politics were rationalist; domesticity was outside production, and it compromised or subverted class consciousness often in alliance with (religious) movements whose mode was "expressive." The antitheses were clearly coded as masculine and feminine; class, in other words, was a gendered construction.

The expressive/rational contrast is a recurrent one in Thompson's political vocabulary. In a 1976 interview, for example, he compared the "expressive activity" of the "second New Left" to an earlier "more rational and open political activity":

> This New Left had elements within it that could be seen at once by a historian as the revolting bourgeoisie doing its own revolting thing—that is, the expressive and irrationalist, self-exalting gestures of style that do not belong to a serious and deeply rooted, rational revolutionary movement.[32]

Here the contrast is about class and politics, but it nonetheless resonates with the gendered meanings established in *The Making of the English Working Class* and at the same time adds a worker/bourgeois dimension. This gains additional significance when we remember that, in the 1890s, the dominant voices in the labor and socialist movements designated feminism as a bourgeois movement. The claim that women's interests constituted a definable political and social agenda was often dismissed as individualist, self-indulgent, and middle class, a distraction from the egalitarianism and the true needs of the working class as a whole. To the extent that, in the 1960s, feminism emerged in the context of the "second New Left," it could eventually (though not immediately) be perceived as antithetical to the (manly) political tradition with which Thompson identified.

All of this would be fairly straightforward to argue if Thompson held a simple rationalist position. In fact, however, much of his work lovingly embraces decidedly nonrationalist, romantic themes. One of his heroes, after all, is the Romantic socialist William Morris, about whom he wrote a major biography in 1955; another is William Blake, with whose "muggletonianism" he has declared himself in sympathy and with whose words he begins and ends *The Making of the English Working Class*. In that book Blake provides a crucial link between "the Romantics and the radical craftsmen" in their common resistance (in the years 1790–1830) to "the annunciation of Acquisitive Man": "After William Blake, no mind was at home in both cultures, nor had the genius to interpret the two traditions to each other."[33]

Blake embodied the possibility of poetry *and* politics, romantic yearning and rational resistance in a single movement. Similarly Morris offered a way to explore the limits of (romantic) utopian thinking, to distinguish between those utopias that can coexist with rational politics and those that are merely expressive. According to Thompson, utopias that permit critical assessment of the present in terms of some deep moral commitment and unleash imaginative longing for a particular kind of future are compatible with, indeed necessary for, practical politics. Hence his first interest in Morris had to do with Morris's ability to articulate what Thompson dubbed in 1955 a "Scientific Utopia." This involved an analysis of the motors of change, "mastery of historical process, understanding of the economic and social basis of Communism."[34] For Thompson the initial fascination of Morris was his appeal "to the moral consciousness as a vital agency of social change."[35]

In his 1976 postscript to the Morris biography, Thompson qualified some of his earlier attempts to write Morris fully into an orthodox Marxist tradition. But he maintained the distinction that concerns us here. While deemphasizing his initial insistence on science and stressing instead the importance of creative imaginative projections, Thompson still held to his original criteria for utopias: "To vindicate Utopianism does not . . . mean that *any* utopian work is as good as any other. . . . There are disciplined and undisciplined ways of 'dreaming,' but the discipline is of the imagination and not of science." The important point still was that Morris had offered an analysis of the direction of historical change, imbued his analysis with moral conviction, and indicated a preference for the best way to get there. His indications, moreover, were "placed within a firm controlling historical and political argument."[36]

Henry Abelove has offered an insightful way to read Thompson in the context of the post-1956 critique of Stalinism that sought a more open, democratic socialism. He points out that Thompson's stress on creativity and flexibility challenged the rigid "scientific" materialism of the British Communist party; his discovery of such imaginative play in earlier (British) socialist movements gave historical support to his endorsement of those values in the present. Poetry stood for deeply inspired action, informed by feelings that art could best express. The poet was crucial to revolutionary politics, for he could articulate the longings that, along with practical programs, inspired men to act.[37] It is important to note that the contrast being created here opposes the imaginative to the scientific, the poetic to an overly determined practicality. There is no suggestion that poetry is "spiritual" in opposition to materialism; rather it is included as a component of politics and material life.

At the same time Thompson's critique of democratic centralism required proof of the inherent rationality of working people. *The Making of the English Working Class* showed that they could be counted on to come up with a politics appropriate to the pursuit of their interest. The Luddites, after all, had maintained a certain grim, inventive humor as they carefully aimed their revenge at the appropriate targets: carriers of individualism and utilitarianism. Thompson's genius in the Luddite chapters was to identify the strategic thinking, the collectivist and mutualist motivation, the shared leadership (the participatory democracy) that informed what contemporary officials had (mistakenly) depicted as uncivilized, if not anarchic, behavior. Here the need to rule out "expressivity" was important as a way of correcting the evidence (most of it contained in law enforcement files) and as a way of insisting that secular, rational politics did not have to be imposed from above. Instead, left to their own invention workers were capable of great creativity. There was a wonderful kind of poetry evident to Thompson in the rational political movement developed "from below."

The role of poetry, according to Thompson, is to leaven politics with imagination, not to undermine it with undisciplined spirituality. In this careful definition, Abelove reminds us, Thompson's own sense of purpose is at stake. Thompson apparently wanted to be a poet; the title of *The Making of the English Working Class* plays on the old English term for poet, which was maker. "Making means poetry writing as well as building, achieving." In Abelove's words, "*The Making of the English Working Class* names both what Thompson has done and what the English working people have in struggle achieved for themselves."[38]

Thompson's work constantly examines the political role of the poet. In "Outside the Whale" he condemns W. H. Auden's defection from political struggle and insists that it is not the necessary path for anyone, least of all an artist.[39] For Thompson, there must be a middle ground between what Abelove calls disenchantment with perfectionist illusions and complete apostasy. That ground is the demanding, yet creative place of continuing aspiration, and it holds the most promise for political/poetic articulation.[40] The other alternatives are fruitless. Politics is mechanical and lifeless without poetry. Without politics, poetic aspiration is stillborn; it deteriorates into self-indulgent expressivity. The key to Morris, after all, was that his utopianism was "placed within a firm controlling historical and political argument." It was, in other words, the capture of romantic utopianism for socialist rationalism that made Morris appealing to Thompson.

In Thompson's representation of this relationship, the creative impulse was disciplined and directed to rational ends. Expressivity on its own was ruled out; but rational politics could be softened and enriched by the "vocabulary of desire," the directed play of socialist imagination. Indeed, without this kind of longing aspiration, rationalist politics would become sterile and incapable of stimulating human action for revolutionary social change. Although Thompson seemed to insist on a kind of organic complementarity (politics needs poetry and poetry needs politics), it is not a marriage he has in mind. Poetry is instead incorporated into politics to create a more perfect (masculine) activity. This merger is achieved conceptually by defining poetic politics in opposition to the subversive possibilities of (feminine) expressivity. The gendered contrast secures the masculinity of poetry by locating femininity in an excluded negative position. It is the integration of poetry into politics in this way that Thompson represents as the great political achievement of William Morris, William Blake, and himself.

Thompson's vision of politics is far more inclusive than the "economistic" notions against which he wrote. It makes imagination, art, moral passion, and intellect an inherent part of political struggle, vital for its well-being and success. The incorporation of these elements is achieved by a redefinition or enlargement of the definition of politics and by an extension of the notion of labor to include artistic creation (making intellectual productivity manly work), and by refining the gendered representation of politics and class. These retain their masculine coding; indeed, Thompson makes art acceptable by including it in the masculine, in opposition to a set of unacceptable, excluded terms—the domestic, the spiritual, the expressive, the religious, the undisciplined, and the irrational—all of which are coded as feminine. There might have been other ways to make this same appeal—by insisting, for example, on a notion of art that remained coded as feminine and was genuinely complementary to (masculine) politics—but Thompson's choice recognizes the powerful meanings already attached to class and politics in the tradition for which he writes, and he does not call these into question.

My point here is not to denounce Thompson's political vision in the name of some higher feminine expression but rather to uncover its reliance on gendered representations to convey its meaning. For it is in addressing these representations that we discover the subtle and central presence of gender in conceptions of working-class politics. Such an analysis ought to lead us not to condemn Thompson, for there is much in his conception of politics that is vital and relevant still. Rather, through the kind of analysis I have attempted, we can gain some sense of the enormity of the problem feminist socialists encountered. In trying to work within the boundaries set by canonical texts such as Thompson's, they faced a tradition that held to a universalized definition of class, the meaning of which was nonetheless constructed in gendered terms; a tradition committed to a literal egalitarianism that dismissed as reactionary any recognition of the stubborn complexity of sexual difference; a tradition that promised equality, but did not acknowledge its own uses of difference.

[III]

The power of this tradition has been difficult to challenge for it rests on the presumed social "reality" of the "working class." Historians like Thompson have depicted themselves as documenting that reality rather than as helping to construct it; in that way, they have precluded questions about the role of politics and of written history in the creation of concepts such as class. Yet the efforts of socialist feminist historians illustrate that we must, finally, raise such questions, interrogating both the meanings of fundamental categories and the politics of history itself. Such an interrogation recognizes the need not only to take sides in an ongoing class struggle but also, more radically, to understand the role of written history in the creation of individual and collective identities—identities of gender as well as of class.

The earliest efforts of feminists working in the Thompsonian tradition stopped short of radical reconceptualization of the terms of history itself. As a result, they were unable to produce the theoretical work that could explain and rectify the marginal place of women in the history of English working-class formation. The first of these attempts sought to include women in working-class history by collecting evidence about their participation in economic and political activities. These studies accepted class as an unproblematic sociological category and assumed that women had simply been ignored or neglected by earlier labor historians without asking how such neglect had occurred.[41] They assumed, as well, that a narrative parallel to the existing story of the working class would readily be incorporated into it, even with variations that included discussions of problems specific to women, such as childrearing and household responsibilities. In fact, however, this has not been the case. Instead, women either continue to be excluded from working-class history, or to be awkwardly included as special examples of the general (male) experience, or to be treated entirely separately. Women remain a particularized subject; their history has neither attained the canonical status of Thompson's, nor has it accounted in new ways for the making of the entire working class. Such an incorporation or revision will not be achieved until the troubling question raised by women's history is confronted: if women did work and engage in politics, how explain their invisibility, the lack of attention to them in theories of class formation and in the historical record?

Part of the answer lies in how the meanings of class itself were constructed; another part lies in how the history of class has been written. Thompson assumes there is one story of working-class formation; that is the point of his analogy to individual biography. Triumphant political visions become, in his account, the singular and necessary expressions of class consciousness, the only ones worth writing about in any detail. This kind of history is ultimately teleological because it assumes both a certain inevitability and a single, continuous link between present and past. Barbara Taylor has challenged the unitary view of working-class politics by introducing a discussion of competing traditions within the labor and socialist movements. Her work suggests a more complicated story, a struggle for hegemony among conflicting visions of a new society. Taylor argues that feminism was central to utopian socialism, to its most imaginative and radical designs, and she links the disappearance of feminist concerns and female voices to the displacement of utopianism by rationalist, "scientific socialism." Taylor's documentation of alternative attempts to define working-class politics aimed to legitimize contemporary feminist critiques by establishing their historical precedents.

> Socialist-feminists look back to the Owenites, then, not out of nostalgia for a transition long past but as a way of tracing the beginnings of a democratic-communist project which is still very much our own and with which we are still struggling to redefine the ends of modern Marxist movements. For, after, all, what count as Utopian answers depends on who is raising the questions.[42]

This approach signaled a far-reaching critique. For if evaluations of the meaning of political programs varied depending "on who is raising the questions," then not only Thompson's story but his theoretical premises needed revision. If class consciousness was inherent in certain relations of production, what could explain the fundamentally different expressions it had found? How could diversity and disagreement be introduced into the unified narrative Thompson had constructed?

Among socialist feminists several kinds of answers to these questions have been proposed, one based on psychoanalytic theory, another on a variation of Marxism, and a third on post-structuralist theories of discourse. The first two of these rewrite working-class history as a conflict not only between classes but between the sexes. They take class as an established fact and add another complicating strand—gender—to the story of working-class formation. The third, more fruitfully it seems to me, subjects the category of class to analytic scrutiny and rewrites its history from the perspective not of teleology but of (what Foucault, echoing Nietzsche, called) genealogy.[43]

Feminist historians have used psychoanalytic theory to address the question of diversity within the working class in terms of gender and to posit conflict between women and men as a fundamental fact of human experience and modern social organization, as fundamental as relations of production and conflicts of class. In addition, psychoanalysis insists on the importance of the unconscious as a factor in human behavior and so provides a powerful critique of the premises of rationalism and liberal egalitarianism. The historian Sally Alexander, for example, has opened a serious theoretical breach by introducing Lacanian notions into analyses of social behavior.[44] Too often, however, the premise of enduring sexual antagonism has been rendered literally, as the inevitability of conflict between real women and men. The complicated arguments of Freud and Lacan about the processes of construction of gender identification and the bisexuality of the individual subject are reduced to sociological discussions about objective differences of experience, interest, attitude, behavior, and political choice between women and men. "Men" and "women" are assumed to be fixed categories of identity, with historically variable (but inherently conflictual) needs. In fact, as Thompson's and Taylor's books show, clear-cut differences are not consistently evident. In the early nineteenth century women heroically engaged in rationalist politics, while men eagerly shared the delusions of the ranting Mrs. Southcott. If masculine/feminine is an enduring cultural opposition, men and women have not always been on opposite sides. How then account for the emergence of political movements with different programs addressed to the relations between the sexes; with different ways of expressing the meaning of class; with different representations of sexual difference encoded in their language?

An indirect answer to these questions addresses the connection between gender and class from the perspective of "dual systems" analysis. Patriarchy, in this approach, is a social system said to parallel and intersect with capitalism. Each system has its organization and relationships, its dynamic, its history, and its own distinctive ideology. Most often, the "origins" of patriarchy are located in family and kinship systems, including relations of household production and reproduction. Capitalist relations develop around the means of production and involve economic practices that are (in theory at least) "sex-blind" or impervious to gender.[45] The advent of capitalism, in this analysis, involved the application of patriarchal "gender ideology" to economic practices, the importation, as it were, of ideas from one realm (where they could be explained by material relationships) to another. Dual systems analysis avoids some of the more obvious pitfalls of psychoanalysis because the sometimes similar behavior of both women and men can be explained as a function of a mystifying "gender ideology," but it begs the questions of why that ideology so powerfully persists, how it relates to the articulation of class interest, and why different political strategies (involving the relations between gender and class) emerge within a sociologically similar group. It is a kind of mechanical solution framed within the logic of materialist analysis, which allows "gender ideology" to be introduced as an independent variable in analyses of capitalism while at the same time retaining the sociological imperative—the need ultimately to account for that ideology as the direct product of social/material organization.

Different as they are, dual systems and psychoanalytic theory have been used in the same sociologized way by feminist labor historians and so they have not addressed questions about politics such as those Barbara Taylor's work poses: What are the sources of different political programs articulated by workers? How explain the different ways in which class interest was expressed and defined? How account theoretically for the existence of different traditions, different "consciousness" among similar types of workers? Not by simple sociological correlations between social existence and political thought; not by holding to ideas about the immanence of consciousness in social experience; not by conceiving of class as a unified movement, rooted in a shared and singular perception of interest. Not, in other words, by remaining within the analytic frame of Thompson's history, but by problematizing all the connections it so readily assumes. How can that be done?

The direction has been at least indicated in some recent discussions of discourse and ideology by feminist historians. Thus Jane Lewis carefully documents the influence of "gender ideology" (whatever its origins) on workers' policies and she calls upon feminist historians to attend to "the way gender and class are constructed together," implying a conceptual reciprocity that defies the dual systems approach.[46] Alexander's deft summary of Lacan points to the crucial role language plays in the child's coming into consciousness; indeed, it suggests the need to rethink notions of consciousness as they have been used in recent labor history. For consciousness, this rethinking substitutes concepts of discourse and rhetoric, inserting into the connection between the objective reality of existence and the subject's perception of it the problems of representation and the contingency and variability of meaning.

Among British feminists, Denise Riley has perhaps historicized this approach most fully. In her book on feminism and the category of "women" she offers a discussion that might fruitfully be applied to the study of "women" in the "working class," or for that matter of any category whose origin has been located in nature or in objective social relations:

> To put it schematically: "women" is historically, discursively constructed, and always relatively to other categories which themselves change; "women" is a volatile collectivity in which female persons can be very differently positioned so that the apparent continuity of the subject of "women" isn't to be relied on; "women" is both synchronically and diachronically erratic as a collectivity, while for the individual "being a woman" is also inconstant, and can't provide an ontological foundation.[47]

If the same can be said for being a worker or a member of the working class, the question turns away from consciousness to the organization of representation, to the context and politics of any specified representational system. Identity becomes not a reflection of some essential reality but a matter of political allegiance. Feminist history approached this way changes Thompson's story. It refuses its teleology and retells it as a story of the creation of political identity through representations of sexual difference. Class and gender become inextricably linked in this telling—as representation, as identity, as social and political practice.

[IV]

In the preface to *The Making of the English Working Class,* Thompson elaborated a unitary definition of class: it was a historical relationship not a category or a thing; its meaning inhered in oppositional relationships and in the definitions men gave to those relationships. For Thompson the question was one of timing and context—when and under what circumstances was the common working-class identity discovered? The interests and the common experiences giving rise to such identity, he suggested, existed apart from class consciousness; they preceded it and structured the nature of men's perceptions. Class consciousness was the cultural expression of men's experience of productive relations and, although it might vary from place to place, it was an identifiable phenomenon. If we were to attend to discourse rather than consciousness in this account, we would open new interpretive possibilities. First, we would ask how categories of class were formulated through representation at specific historical moments, looking at once for the similarities that constituted the limits of linguistic possibilities as well as for different kinds of expression, different definitions, contests about definition: affirmations, negations, and repressions. We would attend to the processes by which one definition emerged as dominant, looking both for explicitly stated and implicitly structured political relationships. The result is not a unitary concept of class, not history as teleology, but a concept of class as a field that always contains multiple and contested meanings. Second, we would ask how appeals to sexual difference figured in the process: how did the exclusion or marginalization of that which was constructed as feminine, for example, work to ensure acceptance of masculine codings for particular ideas of class? How did gender "naturalize" particular meanings of class? How in turn did visions of class as a set of relationships naturally following from economic conditions set in place certain notions of gender? Third, we would ask how and in what ways conceptions of class organized (perceptions of) social experience. Rather than assuming an exact fit between material life and political thought, between experience and consciousness, this approach disrupts that fit, refuses the opposition between them. It argues that articulation, definition—the construction of meaning—must be analyzed as a set of events in itself. Thompson's gestures to traditions of English radicalism account for certain thematic influences or continuities in working-class political expression, but they do not address the cultural, subjective, and textual processes by which such themes acquire meaning.

Thompson insisted that the terms used to express the idea of class were relative to time and place, but he did not ask *how* the meaning of the concept itself was constructed. It is that task of "deconstruction" that some feminists have undertaken in an effort to solve the riddle of women's invisibility, marginality, or subordination in the histories of the working class. If we start by examining how class was represented, however, we relativize assumptions so embedded in our traditions, so naturalized, that they seem to be self-evident even across political and ideological lines. From that relative vantage, canonical texts become particularly valuable targets because their appeal rests, at least in part, on their ability to embody and express those "natural" assumptions, sometimes in new ways, sometimes in comfortably familiar ways. Through analysis of such texts we understand better how a notion such as class operates to construct its own conceptual field and how a text like Thompson's history operates to establish that conceptual field on detailed empirical (and so seemingly incontestable) ground. While the critique of detail with new empirical evidence is important (the addition of new information about women, for example), the concepts that establish the field itself must also be interrogated.

There have been many criticisms among feminist historians of the attention to such interrogations of "traditional" histories because they often focus on men's writings and seem to neglect the importance of establishing women as historical subjects. While there is merit to the argument that we must attend to women in our writings about class, there is also merit to the point that such attention at once takes too much for granted and is necessarily incomplete. Can we write about working-class women without examining the ways the feminine is used to construct conceptions of class? Can we write about any women without asking how their culture represented what they were, as well as how they defined themselves? Can we assume there was no connection between cultural representation and self-definition? How can we construe that connection? Can we assume a pre-existing common self-understanding on the part of all women, or of all women of the same class? Was there an objectively describable working-class women's "interest" in nineteenth-century England? How did politics and the appeals of particular political movements figure in the definitions of such interest?

We cannot write about class without interrogating its meanings—not only its terminology and the content of its political programs but the history of its symbolic organization and linguistic representations. All of this is to say, I think, that in order for feminist labor historians to add women to stories like *The Making of the English Working Class,* we must first figure out how such books work as they are written. That kind of analytic operation makes it possible to theorize a different kind of history of working-class politics, one that recasts our knowledge about gender and class.

III

GENDER IN HISTORY

— 5 —

Work Identities for Men and Women

THE POLITICS OF WORK AND FAMILY IN THE PARISIAN GARMENT TRADES IN 1848

Studies of the working-class movement in nineteenth-century France have stressed the central role of skilled workers who defended craft traditions in their efforts to organize politically and secure economic change. These workers offered association, a cooperative organization of production that regulated economic relationships, as an alternative to the ruthless competition that for them characterized the advent of industrial capitalism. *Fraternité* was the watchword of associationalism and it projected the brotherhood of craftsmen as the basis for a new set of productive relationships.[1]

In attending to the economic bases for the artisans' politics, historians have neglected other dimensions of their discourse, those having to do with gender and the family. This is not because information is scarce or unavailable. On the contrary, the literature of protest of the 1830s and 1840s is full of references to the family and to the roles and traits of men and women. Whether one reads about demands for higher wages or attacks on the cupidity of the bourgeoisie, whether one listens as speakers evoke the depths of worker poverty or as they raise their glasses to toast a future new society, one hears about sexual difference. In the program of utopian socialists of the period, the family was a central theme whether, as with Charles Fourier and the

This essay was first published under the title "Men and Women in the Parisian Garment Trades: Discussions of Family and Work in the 1830's and 40's," in Roderick Floud, Geoffrey Crossick, and Patricia Thane, eds., *The Power of the Past: Essays in Honor of Eric Hobsbawm* (Cambridge: Cambridge University Press, 1984). It has been reconceived and rewritten for this volume; in fact, it has become an entirely new piece. Sections of the original essay are used here with permission of the publisher.

Saint-Simonians, experiments with altered forms of family organization were posed or, as with Etienne Cabet, promises of qualitative improvements in the happiness of traditional couples and their children. The organization of labor and association were only two of the dominant themes in this period of working-class protest; the family was an equally important and interrelated third.

What was the significance of workers' representations of family during the 1830s and 1840s? How did these representations relate to political demands for an equitable organization of labor? How did men and women represent their work identities? How were masculinity and femininity, as well as allusions to women and men, involved in critiques of capitalism? How did gender define the politics of nineteenth-century workers? How did the utopian visions projected in political discourse construct gender?

These questions presuppose an integration of analyses usually carried out separately, for histories of labor, women, and the family have been notably compartmentalized, at least among North American scholars.[2] More important, perhaps, these questions suggest an alternative to reductive theories of causality often used by labor historians. Directing inquiry at discourse permits a more powerful account of human activity than one that insists on opposing material reality and interpretation. The notion that there is a primary causality for economic relationships, for example, is a self-evident fact neither for workers nor for historians; rather it is a way of perceiving or theorizing social organization. One measure of the success of such theorizing is its incorporation into proverbial or common sense wisdom, into generalized cultural understanding far removed from abstract tomes or polemical pamphlets. General belief in monocausal interpretations makes them no less partial or selective. Rather, such interpretations must be understood as part of the apparatus of the cultural production of subjects. So must appeals to "experience" be taken as an aspect of this cultural production, not as a reflection of some pre-existing ground or point of departure.

Nineteenth-century worker protest movements offered analyses of social organization that interpreted "experience" even as they appealed to its objective impact on people's lives. In the process they provided individuals with forms of social consciousness based on common terms of identification and so provided the means for collective action.

Although there can be useful analyses of political discourse at a very general and theoretical level, I am interested in a more contextual reading that taps into politics from a specific and popular perspective. By politics I mean not contests about formal participation in government (although these were surely part of what was at stake in 1848) but contests about power and knowledge that dealt variously and often simultaneously with voting, work, family, and gender. How did representations of the family and sexual difference enter discussions about economics, about the organization of labor in individual trades? What did these have to do with claims about the right to vote? How did strategies for the reform of particular trades also speak to sexual divisions of labor? Did these differ for women and men? These questions assume that occupational identities did not inhere in relations of production, that skill, for example, was a relative rather than absolute description of certain kinds of work. Rather than taking at face value nineteenth-century workers' self-definitions, I ask how these were formulated and in what terms. Were tailors objectively more skilled than dressmakers? Were differences of technical competency as great within male or female trades as between them? Or are there other explanations for the different representations of these trades?

This essay offers a case study of the appeals made to and by men and women in the Parisian garment trades in the 1830s and 1840s. I have chosen the garment trades because many of the basic sewing skills required were shared by men and women, although there were distinctions that involved fitting suits and other garments to size. The garment trades employed the greatest number of Parisian workers during this period (some 90,000 as compared to the next largest, the (exclusively male) building trades, which employed 41,000 in 1847).[3] The trades were in a period of transition as custom-made tailoring and dressmaking faced competition from the growth of the ready-made clothing industry (*confection*). As they decried new commercial and manufacturing practices, garment workers were at the forefront of working-class protest movements. Tailors organized strikes in the 1830s and 1840s; many embraced Cabet's Icarian movement, pioneered in the development of cooperative producer's associations, and swelled the crowds in the revolution of 1848.[4] Dressmakers and seamstresses were among those who responded to the Saint-Simonian gospel, outnumbering other categories of the movement's working-class disciples and contributing importantly to *La Tribune des Femmes*, a newspaper edited in 1832–34 entirely by Saint-Simonian women. Like their male counterparts, politically active seamstresses demanded women's "right to work," successfully organized producer cooperatives, and won contracts from the revolutionary government in 1848.[5] Their leaders joined the chorus of voices proposing cooperative and socialist alternatives to the inequities of the social order, but they added their own feminist verses, thus complicating and sometimes departing from the dominant themes.

The garment trades permit a comparison of the kinds of appeals made to male and female workers, especially the ways in which gender was constructed in these appeals. The emphasis for both groups was on economics, on the ways the garment trades were being transformed by increasingly minute divisions of labor and the employment of large numbers of unskilled workers sewing at home for low piece-rates. Yet the issue of how to control and eliminate the competition raised more general questions about women's wage-earning activity and family responsibilities, appropriate sexual divisions of labor, and political rights. The identities of garment workers were conceived as at once economic, sexual, and political. In this, of course, garment workers were not unique. In defining and formulating their positions, tailors and seamstresses adapted, incorporated, added, and reacted to the ideas of others—workers in various trades, social theorists, republican politicians, and bourgeois moralists. They were participants in a larger culture and a more general political movement. Still, their particular formulations are worth examining closely for they enable us to see in detail how and in what terms gender was implicated in the articulation of a set of specific craft identities.

[I]

During the early months of 1848, in the springtime of the revolution, workers and employers convened at the Luxembourg Palace under the leadership of Louis Blanc to hammer out a new organization of labor. The commission of tailors divided almost immediately between employers and workers in bitter disagreement over the question of the location of work. Tailors insisted that all work be performed at the shop, while employers argued that some home-based production was a vital aspect of the trade's prosperity. According to the tailors, the shop was the only place where work could be divided, "in a regular and equitable manner," and where skilled workers could be trained.[6] The employers disagreed, maintaining that the household of the homeworker was "the first step of the enterprise." Not only would the elimination of these workers interfere with the training of apprentices, there also would be grave moral consequences. For by ending home-based work, the tailors would break "the bonds of the family," separating a father from his wife and children, thus violating "the sacred rights of humanity."[7] The tailors refused to accept this depiction of homework, replying that it undermined rather than enforced morality. It was far better, they said, for everyone if "the household separated for the day" and each family member went to work "as if he were still a worker."[8]

The Luxembourg Commission disbanded before the tailors' dispute could be resolved. It nonetheless exposed one of the ways workers had chosen to challenge rearrangements of work processes. The debate over the location of work is interesting not only as a commentary on the craft but for the link it makes between the organization of labor and the family. In this particular dispute, the tailors equated work in a shop with greater control over conditions of employment, higher wages, and, above all, a long-standing honorable artisanal tradition. Although the history of tailoring, as of many eighteenth- and early nineteenth-century trades, was characterized by a variety of arrangements ranging from lone practitioners to large shops, the protests of the 1830s and 1840s emphasized a single aspect. Changes in the trade were depicted as dramatic departures from a coherent, self-regulating corporate system to a chaotic, competitive one, instead of as intensifications or modifications of processes long underway. The contrast between shopwork and homework, moreover, clarified the nature of the change by offering a highly charged critique of what had occurred. It also established terms for an occupational identity that tied skill as much to the location of work as to practical abilities and it legitimated these definitions through an appeal to gender and to history.

The contrast between shopwork and homework was represented by an opposition between two kinds of workers: honorable craftsmen and miserable *appièceurs*. The first were presented as descendants of the corporation of Parisian tailors whose statues in the eighteenth century stipulated that "all work must be done in the shop, and nothing outside, so that each person can practice his craft and live by his work."[9] These shops employed from 2 to 20 journeymen and were owned by masters who were usually also trained artisans. The shop might be either an independent establishment or some rooms adjoining the master's family lodgings. When the shop was attached to the household, the master's wife lent a hand in the busy season or sewed buttons and hems throughout the year, but the basic unit of production was a team of male journeymen whose livelihood depended on their wages.[10]

The tailors of the 1830s and 1840s overlooked differences between masters and journeymen in their idealized images of the trade of the past. For one thing, journeymen did not belong to corporations in the eighteenth century and their employment was more precarious than descriptions of static systems of organization suggest.[11] But the fact that masters and journeymen had worked together in a shop provided enough of a basis for nineteenth-century tailors to write themselves into the masters' corporate history and thus to distinguish themselves sharply (as skilled artisans) from the increasingly numerous garment workers known as *appièceurs*.[12]

Appièceurs were the home-based workers, paid by the piece and, like women, used sporadically by custom tailors and ready-made manufacturers. Since tailoring was a seasonal trade, intensely busy in spring and autumn, slack for several months in winter and summer, masters used a supplementary labor force to sew seams and finish garments in the busy season. For this they depended on women, who worked alone at home, and on *appièceurs*, men who might come to work at the shop when summoned or who labored at home with unpaid family members or paid assistants. The category of the *appièceur* may have derived from eighteenth-century *chambrelans*, failed masters, inept journeymen, or foreigners whose exclusion from guilds forced them to ply their trade clandestinely from their homes for humiliating prices, and who thereby provided a certain flexibility in the tailoring labor force.[13]

The number of *appièceurs* seems to have increased in the first half of the nineteenth century, a consequence largely of the growth of the ready-made garment industry. Between 1830 and 1848 this sector steadily encroached on the custom market. By 1847, *confection* accounted for over one-third of total sales of men's clothing (by 1860, it had captured half the market).[14] Unlike custom tailoring, which responded to the demands of individual clients, the ready-made industry mass-produced goods in standardized sizes. Cutters prepared parts of a garment in shops and the pieces were then assembled by outworkers. The finished garments were returned to the merchants who either sold them in large shops or sent salesmen off with them to markets and fairs. Some of the first ready-made garments were workers' clothes, since manufacturers assumed that for this kind of garment, high quality was of less importance than a low price.

The manufacture of ready-made goods had enormous advantages over custom tailoring. Cloth could be purchased in bulk and there was far less wasted material. Garments could be produced year round since manufacture did not depend on individual orders. Of course, as ready-made manufacturers expanded their operations for the middle-class market, they had to wait to see what styles were being offered for the next season. But in slow periods they could produce practical items such as work clothes, the styles of which did not change from year to year. The *confectionneurs* had better credit resources, more capital at their disposal, lower overhead, and lower labor costs than did small custom tailors. A large pool of potential workers was available to work and their circumstances—of economic need and isolation—mitigated against collective or individual demands for higher piece-rates. In any case, piece-rates tended to drop during the slack season because, in addition to the men and women who regularly served the *confectionneurs,* shop-based tailors also took on piecework until orders picked up at the shop.

Competition from *confectionneurs* directly affected work arrangements in custom tailor shops. Some employers went bankrupt. A few with reputations for very high quality had enough clients who continued to support them. Still others began to cut labor costs by reducing the number of their shopworkers and turning instead to homeworkers. Some masters became subcontractors and transformed their workrooms into sweatshops; workmen joined the ranks of *appièceurs* and sought jobs where they could, from custom tailors as well as from ready-made garment manufacturers.[15]

Clear lines between job categories are, in fact, difficult to establish. Though offered in the heat of debate between supporters and opponents of homework, assertions like this one seem to have had a measure of validity because they captured the interconnections among various practices in the tailoring trade.

> Married *appièceurs* render a great service; they often perform the most thankless of tasks; apprentices are generally trained by them, for it ought not to be forgotten that the household of the *appièceur* is the first stage of the enterprise.[16]

Those who called themselves tailors *(ouvriers tailleurs)*, moreover, seem to have moved back and forth across occupational designations. Such designations continued to order the tables of statistical inquiries but they no longer neatly or consistently correlated with the work done by individuals.

In their political activities, tailor activists sought to maintain the fast-eroding distinction between custom and ready-made work, a distinction they did not always live out in their lives, but which served both to criticize the present and to design an alternative to it. Strikes and protest movements in this period were aimed at shop-based production. Tailor leaders insisted that employers not use outworkers, that the workshop be the site of all garment production, and that wages be maintained or raised so that individual tailors did not have to resort to *travail à domicile*. Tailors especially resented the masters' attempts to lower rates in the shop because they thought these small entrepreneurs ought to identify with them and they insisted that values of cooperation and association replace the prevailing competitive outlook. Cooperation was exemplified in alternative workshops like the one established during a strike in October 1833, which sought to provide jobs for unemployed strikers and to implement equality between employers and workers. The basis for that equality, it was suggested, rested on shared skill and mutual respect practiced in a single location—the kind, tailors argued, that once existed in precapitalist corporations.[17] During the revolution of 1848, groups of tailors joined with small masters to win back business for the custom trades and guarantee employment for "skilled" workers. Le Travail: l'Association Fraternelle et Egalitaire des Tailleurs won government contracts to produce National Guard uniforms. Those who ran the workshop established standardized pay scales for all positions including outworkers. Though they employed outworkers, they insisted that these were marginal workers, that the shop was the center of the trade's reorganization.[18] *Le Journal des Tailleurs,* a paper addressed to employers and workers in the custom trade, also lauded the worker:

> The *atelier,* well organized, where reciprocal obligations are conscientiously observed . . . The *atelier* has other advantages. . . . for the prosperity of the trade and the well-being of its workers: the power in all seasons, according to needs and circumstances, to divide work in a fair and equitable way, . . . in addition, the *atelier* naturally encourages emulation, which perfects skill and produces that superior elegance that bonds French industry.[19]

In this kind of representation skilled work and the shop became synonymous. Those who worked at home were, by definition, unskilled. From the point of view of organizing protest, of course, *appièceurs* were harder to reach since they were dispersed throughout the city and since their ability to get business depended on their willingness to accept low piece-rates from *confectionneurs* that undercut shop rates. The position of the *appièceur* was antithetical to collective regulation whatever his technical competence, but the tailors' depiction opposed the shop, collective regulation, and skill to the home, chaotic competition, and lack of skill. The opposition depicted two kinds of work and a transformation—a deterioration—of "traditional" trade practices. Home-based production was at once the cause and consequence of the competition experienced by groups of workers and individuals and characterized bitterly in the tailors' political rhetoric as "La concurrence qui nous fait étrangers à notre état."[20]

Inevitably the attack on *appièceurs* and home-based work carried references to women and the family. The goal of the tailors' political organizations was self-regulation of their trade and households were not susceptible to this either informally or formally. The legislation of the revolutionary government made this explicit by exempting family workshops in February 1848 from a proposed law on women's and children's work because legislators objected to the inspection of private households. Not only might privacy be violated, it was argued, but the common interest of the work unit made it impossible to assign responsibility, even to the head of the household, for enforcing the law. If the government refused to regulate the family workshop, members of the trade certainly could not.[21]

The self-exploitation associated with homework was also seen as corrupting the order and emotional fabric of family life. Tailor delegates to the London Exposition of 1862 detailed this situation as they angrily dissented from the claims of a large clothing manufacturer that home-based work increased the "homeloving habits of workers' families."[22] These claims, they said, were "completely contrary to reality":

> No, the practice of the laborer working at home has not improved his lot; no, children are not better cared for and watched over by their parents; no, shared labor does not soften temperaments; on the contrary it sours them more and more. . . . In order to live, a worker toils 16 to 18 hours a day; there are even households where work never stops. . . . While the wife rests, the husband does his share and prepares the wife's tasks; when he finishes or rather succumbs to exhaustion, the wife gets up and the husband takes her place. . . . How can a woman in these deplorable circumstances educate and raise her children decently, when before their eyes are discord and disagreement between father and mother caused primarily by the suffering and forced labor to which parents are condemned?[23]

Tailors' wives had no time for domestic tasks and they endured joyless existences; working "without compensation," they led lives that were "even sadder than their husbands." "When consulted it is rare to find the wife of a tailor who does not curse her fate."[24] By bringing work home tailors disrupted a set of "natural" divisions between day and night, work and rest, parents and children, men and women. The presumed domestic harmony of man and wife gave way to discord and disagreement, which compromised not only present relationships but the future morality as learned by children.

The solution for the tailors involved a clear separation between home and work. And this separation carried with it clarification of all the other issues. Work located at the shop was, by definition, skilled; work performed at home was unskilled, whether the home-worker was female or male. Economic deterioration and deskilling were equated with a move from male to female space. The confusion of spheres inevitably led to the corruption of both home and work; men working at home were demeaned by an implicit association with femininity. In this way, the defense of the *atelier* secured the masculinity of skill *and* the political identity of tailors as skilled workingmen. The utopian vision of cooperation raised the common possession of skill over other differences as a basis for joining owner/workers and their employees in collective regulation of their working life.

The separation of male and female space did not, however, carry with it a division of roles between husband and wife that excluded women from wage-earning activity. The dictum of the *femme ménagère* was absent from the tailors' rhetoric though it had already been articulated by other craftsmen, such as printers.[25] Wives, it is true, were expected to care for children and the household, but their activity was not limited to the domestic realm. Nor was work performed at home thought to be necessarily bad for women. Indeed, according to the document cited above, the sorry situation of the tailor's wife came from the fact that she was not compensated for her work. In a cruel inversion of customary arrangements the husband became the exploiter of his wife. Not only did he fail to contribute to her support, he made it impossible for her to earn her own share of the family wage. The explicit objection to home-based production was that it violated separate types of male and female activity, and that it robbed family members of a control over their distinctive responsibilities. At this moment of their discussion of economic and social reform, tailors worked with concepts of gender that assigned women and men distinctive skills, jobs, and spaces, but they did not endorse a social order that equated women exclusively with domesticity and men with work for pay.

[II]

As the tailors' spokesmen defended the workshop as the site of labor in 1848, seamstress leaders petitioned the republican government for support of their own plans. These were not substantially different in form and ideology from the associations proliferating among craftsmen (though they were numerically far fewer). They shared an emphasis on cooperation and self-regulation and a desire to end the disorder created by capitalist competition. Although seamstresses petitioned for workshops and, indeed, established several cooperative producer associations of their own, the location of work was never as central an issue for them as for the tailors. Work at home was acceptable as long as it neither gave rise to subcontracting nor paid rates below a uniform schedule. Far more important were the wages a seamstress earned, for these were a measure of her skill and the key to her integrity and independence, whether she was single or married. As seamstresses articulated the terms of collective identity, their appeal to women in the garment trades stressed the combined commitments of wage-earning and family.

Unlike the tailors, seamstress leaders defined their potential constituency broadly as all women who sewed for a living. These included dressmakers (*couturières*) and seamstresses (*lingères*), whose different occupational titles conveyed not only different skills but different specialties. (*Couturières* made women's clothing, while *lingères* sewed not only garments of all kinds but other textile products as well.) The leaders looked to the small shops where skilled mistresses trained apprentices and supervised young unmarried workers. They also sought support from older married dressmakers who had either set up a shop or ran a neighborhood "business" from their homes. And they tried to enlist those who did piecework whether regularly or sporadically. This last group included those with both rudimentary skills and long training, those who had established connections to a single shop or manufacturer, and those who took on work wherever it was offered.

Rather than distinguish among levels of skill, seamstresses acknowledged the confusions wrought by a long history of transformation and by the rise of *confection*.[26] Sweated workshops mingled the skilled and unskilled. The ready-made market quickly lured away the clientele of modest means upon whom some independent seamstresses and dressmakers had depended and these women tried to make up for their loss by taking on piecework. Often low piece-rates led them to enlist family members in their work: daughters, sisters, and elderly grandparents might be called upon to help a mother finish her sewing jobs. Girls with aspirations for more highly skilled work might begin by assisting their mothers and then find a better situation, but they might also end up as they had begun.

Although there were surely precedents for craft solidarity in the corporate traditions of female garment makers, that history was not invoked by seamstress organizers in 1848. Instead they spoke of fairness and economic justice and of the special needs and interests of working women. Their analysis located the sources of seamstresses' problems not only in the practices of capitalism (the greed of employers, unfair competition from convents and prisons, the fluctuations of the market) but also in unequal power relationships between women and men. Their socialism, in other words, was mingled with a certain feminism.[27]

When seamstress leaders depicted the crisis in their trade they pointed out that *confection* had two effects. Small producers were undermined and displaced as in tailoring, but this process also involved the substitution of men for women in the ownership of businesses and the control of production. Moreover, the burden of homework fell almost entirely on female family members who nonetheless continued to provide essential domestic services for their husbands and children. In the leaders' rhetoric, their common plight as women who sewed for a living provided seamstresses of all kinds with a basis for collective identification.[28]

In their plans for reform seamstresses stressed above all the need to regulate wages regardless of the location of work; only that way would conflict among women's various activities be resolved. The identity articulated for female garment workers in 1848 assumed that women should be competent managers of their wage *and* domestic labor. Indeed, the validity of women's claims as wage-earners was established by reference to their household responsibilities. When wages were too low and work therefore excessive, complained one militant, "No one makes the soup, there is no dinner for our husbands, there is nothing for ourselves, is that happiness?"[29] By acknowledging women's special connection to household and family, this rhetoric established a distinctively feminine work identity. It employed cultural associations between femininity and domesticity to insist on the authenticity of women who also earned wages, to legitimate their wage-earning as a female activity, and to establish their "interests" as unique to their sex.

The immediate aim of seamstresses' collective political action was to secure greater control over the relationships between work and family. Activists sought this control in a number of ways. They pressured the republican government to establish national workshops for women and then to upgrade wages because they were dissatisfied with the 12 sous a shirt they were being paid. Some deplored the male vanity that led to orders for quilted instead of plain shirts for the National Guard, but it was wages that drew most of their fire. On April 15, two columns of women marched from the women's national workshop to the Luxembourg Palace to demand of Louis Blanc either a daily wage or a rate of 1 franc a shirt. Their petition rejected the existing rate as humiliating, since it amounted to no more than a dole: "What women want," they told Blanc, "is not organized charity, it is properly compensated work."[30]

Among the deputation and, indeed, among the women's associations in this period were a variety of proposals about how work should be reorganized. One seamstress suggested to Blanc that married women be allowed to take work home instead of sitting all day in the national workshops. If the "appropriate rate" were paid and the amount given out controlled, regulation of the trade would be achieved and "households will not suffer."[31] Others suggested that the state open crèches and national restaurants so families would prosper while women exercised their "right to work."[32] A detailed plan called for the establishment of training centers for seamstresses in each *arrondissement* in Paris. Mothers would either leave their children in a crèche near the shop for no charge or, if their skills were such that they needed no supervision, they could take their work home.[33] In the cooperative enterprises set up by custom dressmakers and seamstresses in June and October 1848, everyone earned a standardized *daily* wage; night work, if necessary in the busy season, was paid overtime. The hours for those working in the shop were set from 8 A.M. to 6 P.M. "so that women can take care of their homes and eat with their families."[34]

The seamstresses who articulated and implemented the demands for their trade insisted that women be entirely in charge of their own working affairs. They bitterly resented the fact that a man, one Duclerc, headed the Commission of Women's National Workshops on which their elected representatives sat. And they attributed the intolerably low piece-rates set by the government to male misunderstanding of their interests and needs. Desirée Gay, who agitated for the workshops and then became a delegate to the women's commission from the 2d *arrondissement,* denounced the entire setup as a "deception . . . despotism under a new name . . . a mystification perpetrated by men to rid themselves of women" and their complaints.[35] In contrast to the government-sponsored workshops, the seamstresses' producer associations were run entirely by women, who insisted on setting all policy independent of male interference. The Association Fraternelle des Ouvrières Lingères, for example, returned a government subvention it had won because the terms of support prevented their paying workers the daily wage they deemed was required for a decent life.[36]

The seamstresses organized cooperatives and called for higher wages in the name of "the right to work," the battle cry of workers' movements in 1848. The republican government had endorsed this right in principle in February and on it rested not only social and economic policies but also the new terms of political participation. To seamstress leaders the exclusion of women from universal suffrage was a gross injustice and they sought to expose it by demonstrating that women, too, were producers, holding property in their labor. In the context of 1848, the way to claim political rights for women was to insist on their identity as workers.

> Women ought to work . . . it is better for women to have a trade than a dowry. . . . If men and women both furnish the means of existence, they will help one another and be united.[37]

> The working woman will contribute her share to the family income and we, who have demanded the right to work for all, will dare also to believe in equality, the religious and fraternal expression of the two sexes.[38]

To assert equality with men these women stressed wage-earning, the lowest common denominator of comparability. While the rhetoric of skill consolidated alliances within the male world of work, it served no such purpose for women. For relations among women were not at stake; rather it was their likeness to men as producers that would win them the political rights they had been denied. At the same time as they argued for women's and men's similarity as producers, however, women offered a notion of "worker" that was always specified, modified by an explicit feminine designation. They insisted that women workers' definably different interests and needs (related to their domestic roles) were grounds for their inclusion in politics. In democratic governments, they reasoned, all interests must be represented by those who knew and understood them. "We ask not to be citizens," they insisted, "but citizenesses *(les citoyennes)*. If we demand our rights it is as women that we do so . . . in the name of our sacred family obligations, of the tender services of the mother."[39] Obviously mothers could not be subsumed in the category of the (male) citizen or worker. For this reason, Desireé Gay maintained that women must hold special meetings of their own to define their interests and then join men's meetings. Only then could a collective vision emerge:

> Women and men can enlighten one another and agree on their common interests, so that it cannot be said that association disunited those whom God united, and so that in the future we wish to create [there will not be] two separate camps, with men in one and women in the other.[40]

Gay's version of the social republic was shared by her associates at the feminist-socialist newpaper, *La Voix des Femmes*. They called for a new society in which women could obtain divorce, control their own wages, refuse the domination of a "selfish husband," and care for their children and households as well as enjoy the "right to work." As autonomous individuals, women could then contribute fully as social beings: "Emancipated in the family and the state, mistresses of ourselves, we will be so much more painstaking in the fulfillment of our responsibilities."[41]

The feminist appeal to equality rested on a double vision of men's and women's similarity as wage-earners and their different, but complementary, interests and responsibilities. Their rhetoric invoked republicanism and Saint-Simonianism; it contained demands for political rights in the present and a vision of the future. From one perspective, the appeals made to seamstresses were remarkably similar to those made to tailors. Both stressed the rights of producers and divisions of labor between the sexes, divisions that, although they associated women with home and family, did not make domesticity the antithesis of productive society. There were, however, important differences of meaning and emphasis. While feminist seamstresses offered wage-earning as proof of the fact that women qualified as producers (and thus as citizens), political tailors premised their collective identity on the possession of (historically transmitted) skills. These separated them from other workers, unskilled and mere wage-earners. The tailors' representation demeaned exactly what the seamstresses prized; it provided grounds for including in a collective worker movement members of other skilled trades, but also for excluding simple wage-earners and therefore women. The tailors' acceptance of wage-earning as an activity for women thus did not necessarily challenge either the masculine image of skilled work or the hierarchical reading tailors offered of shop and home, work and family. Unlike the seamstresses, the tailors' belief in the complementarity of these places did not mean equality between masculine and feminine, male and female.

In 1848, as in the two decades before the revolution, workers tied redress of their economic grievances to reform of the political system. The work identities they elaborated included a political dimension, in the formal, legal sense of participation in government. The existing terms of this participation were different for men and women, albeit within the working classes both groups were excluded before 1848. Men faced distinctions based on wealth and property; women as a category were explicitly and repeatedly denied citizenship. Claims for rights took this prevailing gender difference into account. Republican and socialist male workers reinterpreted the meanings of property and asserted that skilled labor qualified them for the vote. Feminist workers, in contrast, put forth two arguments. One had to do with their likeness as producers to men as a category; the work identity they elaborated thus lacked the craftsmen's refinements and particularities, stressing the homogeneity of wage-earners, not the distinction of skill. The other had to do with their difference from male workers, the reasons that as a category *women* had an interest in securing the vote. The asymmetrical relationship of men and women to politics, the different assumptions about them in the political discourse of the period, were contained in the different work identities developed by and for seamstresses and tailors, female and male workers, as a basis for collective action in 1848.

[III]

As tailors and seamstresses formulated trade strategies, they located themselves within a broader discourse aimed at criticizing capitalist political economy and refuting the arguments of bourgeois moralists. Within the body of critical social(ist) theory, there were different emphases and programs but there were also common uses of images of the family and of references to gender. The family was projected as an abstract entity, a place of complete human fulfillment, in opposition to the alienation of capitalist society. The resolution of conflict and competition was depicted in the heterosexual couple: a harmonious reconciliation of the opposites masculine and feminine. Whether masculine/feminine were equal or hierarchically arranged within the unit was ambiguous in the vision; the ambiguity permitted the different interpretations developed by tailors annd seamstresses, and also a certain inconsistency in usage. Idealizations of the family coexisted, for example, with women's attacks on the structure of patriarchal law and their demands for political equality, or with men's denunciation of household labor and their celebration of fraternity and skill.

The formulation of trade strategies does not seem to have followed a single theoretical program. Rather it variously invoked images available, in Paris at least, in the growing worker press and political movements. These images were contained in writings of Cabet and his associates at *Le Populaire,* in Saint-Simonian seminars and street corner lectures, in republican banquet speeches, and in the pages of the feminist *La Voix des Femmes*. They were incorporated into street songs and serialized melodramas. The images were general ones in the culture of the period, but their usage in workers' rhetoric inverted what we now think of as standard bourgeois themes.

The workers' representation of the family as an alternative to capitalism associated femininity with love and emotional bonds. Women embodied and expressed human feeling. What they did was less important than what they stood for. Cabet described the loving qualities of women in a glorious romantic vision that stressed their distinctive contribution, at the same time assuming that femininity did not contradict participation in productive activity. In Icaria, he wrote, all women will work "in workshops and practice the trade of their choice; but their work will be moderate, the workday short."[42] The Saint-Simonian feminist Jeanne Deroin, one of the organizers of seamstresses in 1848, shared Cabet's view of the feminine, although her version of male/female relationships was more egalitarian than his. For Deroin, Christ's mother embodied the loving, maternal, innocent, and devoted traits of the female character: "Woman must fulfil . . . her mission of sacrifice and devotion. She acts because she loves. Love of humanity is eternal love."[43]

Capitalism's destructive impact was its corruption of love, depicted as the downfall of a young girl. Usually a seamstress, this working daughter faced the impossible choice of starving to death because her earnings were insufficient or of becoming a prostitute. "Poverty or shame" was a different side of the same coin. Wrote Cabet of the "daughter of the proletariat": "She must work for her family to survive but under conditions in which she is brutalized, loses her beauty and health, and is threatened constantly by the plague of libertinage."[44] The story of the seamstress was recounted again and again, becoming a folk tale or morality play with a predictable plot and outcome. The theme of the destruction of innocence by rape or death served as a stark physical analogue for capitalism's impact. By defiling or destroying a young female's life, the "social order" attacked not only the existing generation but the next one. In addition, the tragedy of the young seamstress involved a perversion of all that was natural and human. Purity and innocence were synonymous with female virginity. Prostitution represented the antithesis not only of virginity but of its natural loss as well, for women sold for money what ought to have been given for love.

In the most shocking rendition of one of these tales, a young girl, the sole support of her family when her artisan father loses his job, in desperation becomes a prostitute. One night she approaches a man who turns out to be her father. Her only recourse, the only way to preserve her decency after this incident, is suicide.[45] What makes this story so awful is that against her will and by force of circumstances a young girl becomes her own antithesis: innocence becomes promiscuity, familial devotion almost leads to incest, the natural becomes the unnatural, culminating in suicide. The symbol of the destroyed seamstress consciously evoked middle-class idealizations of young womanhood, to show the measure of bourgeois hypocrisy and class oppression. Working-class "reality" was shown to be a far cry from bourgeois ideals and was, indeed, caused by capitalist egoism, embodied usually in a young fop who takes advantage of a working girl's straitened circumstances. Furthermore, bourgeois ideals were shown to be contradicted by their own practices, for not love but the cash nexus exemplified in dowry and inheritance dominated bourgeois family relationships. In contrast stood the impoverished workers *communauté,* based on nothing more than affection. At a banquet in 1848, citizen Legre, a tailor, rose to toast the family. He followed two other workers whose toasts played on the bourgeois themes of property and order. They hailed those two ideas, but inverted their customary meaning. Work was equated with property and the toast to property became an endorsement of the artisans' inalienable right to work. Order was redefined as cooperation and association, a new harmony that would replace the disorder sown by capitalist competition. Legre raised his glass "to the human family, based on love and not money . . . [in which] solidarity replaced individualism." The so-called defenders of the family, he went on, were charlatans; they were debauched and their daughters and wives sold themselves in return for luxury. The true friends of the family were not speculators but those who, "mocked by the old society, nonetheless sought in the bosom of the family the refreshing balm of love to heal their wounds."[46] The family in this vision was not an organizational structure but a fulfilling human experience, the collective happiness of utopian socialism that reconciled differences and harmonized opposites as exemplified by a marriage. Saint-Simon first offered a reconciliation of the individual and the collectivity and he was regularly quoted by his disciples: "The social individual is the man and the woman. Without their union nothing is complete, moral, durable, or possible."[47]

In a play on those bourgeois notions that offered a sharp division of labor between men and women and that posited the spatial and temporal coexistence of aggression and love, competition and association, this utopian vision of the family encapsulated a total transformation of human relationships in a new social order. The family projected in this vision could not coexist with capitalism; it was meant as its critical antithesis. For political tailors and dressmakers in 1848, the symbol of the distressed seamstress and the emotional fulfillment embodied in the family articulated the misery of life and a dream of its opposite. To offer specific proposals about the organization of the family or to endorse a role for women exclusively concerned with domesticity would have been to accept the bourgeois view that the ideal family could somehow exist apart from and indeed resolve capitalism's alienating effect. The utopian socialist vision accepted no such possibility; rather it insisted that families under capitalism could not be fully happy, that until French society was transformed no institution could realize the fulfillment depicted in idealized visions of the family.

The utopian theorists' idealization of the family rested unequivocally on an elevation, a ringing positive endorsement, of characteristics associated with the feminine. Nevertheless, the uses of the feminine and its implications for women were neither singular nor clearcut. As an abstract counter to capitalist alienation, the model of the loving, unified family need not suggest anything about how workers ought to live, how the sexual division of labor ought to be implemented. It was simply a dream, something to aspire to, something by which to expose (and rally against) the drawbacks of the present society. Then again, the idealized family could serve as a standard against which to measure the exploited family and lead, as it did in the tailors' rhetoric, to demands for the immediate protection of the household (and the moral and emotional relationships it contained) from the exactions of sweated labor. Yet another interpretation stressed the regenerative powers of women and the need to grant them full influence in social and political life. In this (feminist) logic, protection of a family's source of love and emotion in the present required not only glorification of maternity but rights for women.[48]

Utopian visions of the family were sufficiently ambiguous to permit a spectrum of interpretations and these coexisted and conflicted in the debates of the labor movement in 1848. Yet they also shared a common ground because of their opposition to certain bourgeois representations of social order.[49] The uses of gender in the garment workers' discourse variously opposed masculine and feminine, male and female, but not in the ways customarily generalized by historians from bourgeois discourse. On issues of skill, character, and emotion, men and women were thought to be different, but the dichotomy did not neatly or consistently oppose work and family, producer and childbearer, economic and domestic, public and private, husband and wife. The ways in which these oppositions did work, however, shows how crucial gender was to the formation of work identities and political appeals. With concepts of gender, workers construed and acted on their "experience," putting into play the terms according to which debates unfolded in 1848 and, ultimately, their history was written.

6

A Statistical Representation of Work

LA STATISTIQUE DE L'INDUSTRIE À PARIS, 1847–1848

L'examen qui place les individus dans un champ de surveillance les situe également dans un réseau d'écriture; il les engage dans toute une épaisseur de documents qui les captent et les fixent.

MICHEL FOUCAULT, *Surveiller et Punir*

Statistical reports were weapons in the debate on the "social question" that preoccupied French domestic politics under the July Monarchy. Private and public inquiries (*enquêtes*) were undertaken with increasing frequency during the years 1830–48 as conservatives and social reformers alike collected evidence to support their positions. Analyses of social problems and programs for reform (relating above all to the situation of workers in cities and new industrial centers) rested on claims to scientific truth displayed and categorized in numerical tables. This approach looked to Enlightenment ideas about the power of objective science and drew on methods of data collection and analysis developed in the late eighteenth century.[1] Even as debates about how to gather information and how to use it revealed the problematic and contingent nature of such statistical truth, the parties to the debates nonetheless invoked its objectivity and authority. The discourse of social reform in early nineteenth-century France established legitimation through the presentation of supposedly incontrovertible statistical facts.

Statistics established an unprecedented sense of certitude and so worked to legitimize the claims of bourgeois administrators and their aristocratic and working-class critics; rarely was its status as objective science called into question. When the director of the prefecture of police, Louis Frégier, wrote in 1840 about Paris's dangerous classes, he offered statistics that he expected would correct exaggeration and

This essay was first delivered as the John Lax Memorial Lecture at Mt. Holyoke College in October 1984. It was subsequently revised and published under the title "Statistical Representations of Work: The Politics of the Chamber of Commerce's *Statistique de l'Industrie à Paris, 1847–48*," in Steven Laurence Kaplan and Cynthia J. Koepp, eds., *Work in France: Representation, Meaning, Organization, and Practice* (Ithaca, N.Y.: Cornell University Press, 1986) pp. 335–63. It is used here with permission of the publisher, Cornell University Press.

error and "put enlightened minds on the road to truth."[2] Alexandre Parent-Duchâtelet, author of a study of prostitution published in 1836, insisted on expressing his findings numerically: "In collecting and editing all material I have made the greatest effort to present numerical results for every point I have treated, because at present a judicious mind cannot be satisfied with expressions such as many, often, sometimes, very often, etc. . . . especially in circumstances when it is a question . . . of serious determinations and grave consequences."[3] When asked for advice about how best to promote reform, the novelist Eugène Sue urged the founders of the workingman's paper *La Rûche Populaire* to "expose the situation of the working classes by facts and incontestable figures."[4] And the editors of another workers' newspaper, *L'Atelier,* sought to refute the "false allegations" of a member of the legislature by compiling information on wages, hours, and the cost of living in various trades. Facts and figures served as a kind of self-evident truth. "Our figures," they warned the erring politician, "will certainly be well worth your consideration."[5]

The legacy of all this investigation is volumes of statistical information on various aspects of economic and social life. Historians have used them as invaluable sources for reconstructing the world of work and the lives of workers—the irrefutable quantitative evidence upon which rests the revision of old and the formulation of new interpretations. In a sense we have accepted at face value and perpetuated the terms of the nineteenth-century debate according to which numbers are somehow purer and less susceptible to subjective influences than other sources of information. Even though the language of some social historians, with its hierarchical oppositions between quantitative and qualitative sources, numerical data and literary evidence, scientific and impressionistic analyses, hard and soft documentation, is less compelling than it was several years ago, there remains the tendency to treat numbers as significantly different from words. Accounts by French doctors who detailed the miseries of workers in new industrial centers are assumed to contain presuppositions, opinions, and political positions that must be decoded and explicated, whereas the figures they cite—wages, family size, number of employees per establishment—are accepted as essentially unproblematic (except perhaps from the purely technical points of view of thoroughness, methods of collection and calculation, etc.). This is even truer for statistical reports. After their purposes and specific contexts are duly noted, these are rarely considered part of the interest of the source. Instead we have plucked out the numbers without questioning the categories into which they are arranged, and we accept as equally objective the explanations that accompany the tables, rarely feeling the need to situate the authors of these texts within particular discursive contexts.[6] This procedure has at least three results: it presumes to divide an indivisible or integral problem, that of the nature of reality and its representation; it denies the inherently political aspects of representation; and it simply underutilizes the sources.

It is not my intention here to dispute the utility of statistical reports that detail the growth of populations, the size of households, or the gender of a labor force. Rather, I want to argue against a simple positivist use of them and for a fuller and more complicated conceptualization of the "reality" they represent; for a reading of statistical reports that problematizes and contextualizes their categories and conclusions; for an end, in other words, to the separation of statistical reports from other kinds of historical texts.

Statistical reports are neither totally neutral collections of fact nor simply ideological impositions. Rather they are ways of establishing the authority of certain visions of social order, of organizing perceptions of "experience."[7] At least since the eighteenth century, numbers have been used to establish the authenticity of interpretive or organizational categories. Thus the collection of population statistics according to households (rather than, say, villages or places of work) reveals and constructs a certain vision of social organization based on a particular idea of the family that is "naturalized" in the course of presenting the data. To take another example, the world of work and workers was not merely reflected in the statistical inquiries of the 1830s and 1840s, but was defined and given meaning by them. Who would represent workers and in what terms was an issue of considerable political contest. Representation was not only a matter of the franchise or the delegation of civic rights; it was a question of the power to define reality itself—hence the proliferation of debates about the contents and methodologies of statistical inquiries and the articulation in any particular *enquête* of some meanings in opposition to others.[8]

Statistical reports exemplify the process by which visions of reality, models of social structure, were elaborated and revised. If, in its final form, a statistical volume seems fixed and absolute—somehow true—its contents in fact suggest questioning and flexibility. Implicit in its pages are a series of debates and discussions on which its authors seek to have the final say. The fascinating aspect of reading these reports lies, in fact, in their method of argumentation, for statistical reports are constituted as, and in, political discourse. As such they provide valuable insight into the processes by which relationships of power are established, exemplified, challenged, and enforced.

My focus in this essay is on one such report, the *Statistique de l'industrie à Paris, 1847-1848,* prepared by the Paris chamber of commerce and published in 1851.[9] The figures presented in it have permitted historians to gauge the size and describe the organization of a range of trades on the eve of the revolution of 1848. What has not been explored is how the document construes the world of workers and their work. My purpose is to pursue that exploration, and I have attempted to analyze not only the contents of the *Statistique* but the form of its presentation and the rhetorical structure of its argument. I begin by placing it in its historical and political context, as part of an ongoing debate about the condition of workers in the 1830s and 1840s. Then I examine the categories of classification employed in the presentation of data and show how these drew on current theories of political economy and how they invoked the authority of science to make their case. Finally, I analyze how the authors of the report, by literal and metaphoric uses of sexual references, attempted to persuade readers of the necessity of accepting their interpretations. I conclude that the *Statistique* used statistics and science to legitimate its particular political argument. The exercise, then, is less about what the *Statistique* says, for the terms of its argument will be familiar to students of nineteenth-century French history, than it is about *how* it operates as political discourse.

[I]

Il faut aujourd'hui arracher les populations ouvrières à ses idées fausses et les ramener dans le cercle des réalités.

LE MONITEUR INDUSTRIEL
JULY 2, 1848

The Paris chamber of commerce was an elite group of businessmen, manufacturers, and economists. It was founded in 1803 when the prefect of the Seine established an assembly of sixty businessmen to elect fifteen of their number to watch over economic matters in the capital city. Thereafter, the membership varied (between fifteen and twenty); new members were recruited by those on the board, and each year one-third of the group was replaced or reappointed. The chamber was a semiautonomous body, responsible ultimately to the minister of interior. It represented and permitted close collaboration between business and government during the period we are concerned with, the first half of the nineteenth century.[10]

The chamber of commerce began work on the *Statistique de l'industrie* in the second half of 1848, in an atmosphere charged with social tension. Although the introduction to the volume offers no explanation for the timing of the inquiry, it seems to have been the chamber of commerce's contribution to the "reestablishment of moral order, so profoundly troubled in our country."[11] There had been a revolution in February 1848 whose leaders wrestled with the establishment of a republic. In June an insurrection had revealed to the nation's leaders the extent of the danger of social revolution: "family, property, nation—all were struck to the core; the very civilization of the nineteenth century was menaced by the blows of these new barbarians."[12]

The "new barbarians" were the Parisian workers who had taken to the streets to protest the closing of government-sponsored national workshops, organizations designed to provide relief to the unemployed. In the eyes of the protesters the closing of the workshops signaled the government's betrayal of the principles of the revolution they had helped to make in February, a revolution that replaced a monarchy with a republic. The government considered the protests a threat to the republic and sent troops, under the direction of General Louis Eugène Cavaignac, to restore order.

In the weeks that followed his quelling of the uprising, General Cavaignac, now head of the government and equipped with emergency powers, sought the aid of businessmen, politicians, and social scientists in the permanent restoration of order. He met with manufacturers in the various *arrondissements* of Paris and had them submit their analyses of the causes of the June Days;[13] he asked the government committee on labor to look into ways of stimulating economic recovery and to propose plans for relief of the unemployed;[14] and he requested cooperation from the Académie des sciences morales et politiques, the semiofficial body of learned men who studied social questions and made policy recommendations.[15] These groups all recognized that the material conditions of workers had to be improved, but they also stressed the importance of ideas. In the words of *Le Moniteur Industriel,* a newspaper representing commercial and manufacturing interests, there had to be a concerted attack on the "false ideas" that had stimulated "uncontrolled ambitions," on the "thirst for reform so imprudently excited" by the extravagant promises of certain socialists, formerly members of the government. If the image of workers was of besotted, deluded savages whose passions had been stimulated beyond control, there was nonetheless the possibility of imposing discipline. An exposure to "reality" would restore the lost sense of balance. Workers had to be shown that their condition was not lamentable, that industry had not inevitably engendered poverty—indeed, that the personal efforts of the "intelligent" and "laborious" resulted in individual progress and collective improvement: "It is time to return to a more decorous language and a healthier estimation. Our society, thank God, does not merit all the curses it has received. Without doubt, it still has a way to go in ameliorating [social conditions] and it will do that . . . what has to be fortified today, however, is the sentiment of duty and the dominion of conscience."[16]

In the *Statistique de l'industrie* the chamber of commerce offered a blueprint for the "reality" of Parisian economic organization. The title word *statistique* identified the report with official compilations of information regularly prepared for administrative use and distinguished it from the highly politicized *enquête* of May 1848.[17] The authors placed the report in historical context explicitly to establish its superiority to earlier efforts; implicitly, they evoked the range of highly charged questions previously addressed.[18] This permitted them to speak to these issues, to offer opinions and answers, without having to acknowledge that an argument about causality and a set of political positions informed their own research. Under the guise of objectivity, the *Statistique* sought to have the last word in a long-standing series of political debates about how to evaluate the impact of industrial capitalism on the lives of French workers.

The debate involved at least three groups in French society. The first consisted of private social investigators, the most famous of whom were doctors attached to the Académie des sciences morales et politiques, whose practiced scientific eyes assessed and recorded the details of the moral and physical degeneration of industrial workers. They attributed the crime, vice, and ill health they found in industrial centers to specific kinds of working conditions and employer practices. Thus Dr. Louis Villermé, in an 1840 study, cited three "pernicious practices" as fundamental causes of social disorder. These were the mixing of the sexes in factories, which led to the corruption of morals; the long day for child workers, which destroyed their health; and the practice of certain employers of advancing wages as loans to their workers, which led to improvidence and poverty.[19] The point of most of these treatises was to argue for reform—philanthropy, savings banks, education, sanitary housing, or protective legislation—the child labor law of 1841, for example, which limited to ten the working hours of children in large factories. But while they insisted, often successfully, on the need for reform, the social investigators writing in the 1830s and 1840s also developed a powerful image of the working class: morally vulnerable, socially dependent, easily drawn to corruption and vice. Various influences were said to separate the dependable laboring classes from the dangerous classes; these were particularly geographic stability and intact family or familylike structures—at home and in the workplace.

The second group consisted of representatives of workers, who began through their newspapers in the 1830s to demand that the facts of working-class poverty be exposed by those who experienced them firsthand. The details of working-class life could not be understood by outside observers. Instead, they argued, accurate information and interpretation had to come in the form of testimonies by those who lived the experience. This group attacked the concentration of capital as the source of the deterioration of skilled trades, increased competition among wage laborers, and lower wages and greater suffering for families. Not moral failure, they insisted, but capitalism had degraded the work and lives of skilled craftsmen. From the columns of *L'Atelier* and *Le Populaire,* from the pages of Flora Tristan's *Union ouvrière* and Louis Blanc's *Organisation du Travail,* came the call for government attention to these problems and political representation for the interests of labor.[20]

The third party in the debate about the "social question" was made up of government investigators who tried to collect statistics (usually from employers or chambers of commerce) on patterns of industrial growth, wages, and employment. Their stated concern was to keep track of economic activity because it established national prosperity. In this endeavor the condition of workers was not a primary concern; indeed, it was assumed that everyone ultimately benefited from economic growth. In the 1820s, information on workers was gathered as part of the computation of costs of production (the "price of manpower" headed columns of figures that would later be designated "wages").[21] The ambitious *enquête industrielle* conducted fitfully and imperfectly by the minister of commerce over the period 1839–47 planned to count all enterprises, document numbers of workers and their wages, and provide a comprehensive view of the state of the economy—presumably, at least in part, as a way of evaluating and responding to the cries for economic reorganization or reform.[22] Still, the concentration on industry denied the centrality of the problems of workers and the organization of labor.

That problem seemed to grow in significance during the 1840s, as reports on the poverty or danger of the working classes were published and as strikes increased in size and frequency. In the political campaigns for reform that intensified during this period, advocates of republicanism took up the cry for government attention to labor. They denounced the bias or ignorance of existing economic and social data and called for official recognition of workers' problems in the form of a government inquiry into work and working conditions. "The enquête will not be the *how* of social reform, but the *why* of political reform."[23] Republican and socialist spokesmen likened the *enquête* to the *cahiers de doléances,* the lists of grievances articulated by various social groups on the eve of the French Revolution of 1789.[24] And they insisted on the self-evident truth contained in such documentations: it would dispel the image of a morally depraved working class and establish the case for recognizing the connections between workers' economic and political rights.

The success of this appeal became apparent in February 1848, when crowds demanding the "right to work" helped overthrow the July Monarchy and bring in the Second Republic. For the leaders of the new government, however, universal manhood suffrage was enough of a reform, and they sought to limit rather than increase the influence of labor in the administration of the country. Argument turned especially on the inclusion in the government of a minister of labor, who would presumably have power to implement fundamental economic change. The majority consistently refused this demand, substituting largely symbolic gestures. Thus Albert, a worker, and the socialist Louis Blanc were included in the first provisional government of the republic, and the "right to work" was proclaimed a fundamental principle. Louis Blanc was assigned to preside over the Luxembourg Commission, a body devoted to examining labor/management disputes but that had no legislative or budgetary powers. Another commission allotted funds to cooperative worker associations, while the minister of public works directed the national workshops, a stopgap measure to relieve the massive unemployment that followed the revolution.

The final gesture was made in May 1848. After a demonstration on May 15 that included thousands of dissatisfied members of the national workshops, Louis Blanc repeated the demand for a minister of labor. A cabinet member with information and power would deal positively with economic and social questions and fulfill the promise of the revolution, he argued. The conservative Constituent Assembly refused his request and instead voted to launch an *enquête* on agricultural and industrial labor. The inquiry into work—a radical demand under the July Monarchy—became in May 1848 a conservative ploy to deny government standing and thus political influence for the interests of workers. In addition, some thought it might provide information to refute the most extravagant of the workers' complaints.[25]

Still, the *enquête* was a political compromise, and as such it embodied divergent approaches and methods. Though it was designed to thwart the most radical of labor's political demands, its questions, categories, and plan of implementation nonetheless acknowledged the existence of a definable working class whose interests conflicted with those of its employers. Its twenty-nine questions focused almost exclusively on the conditions of work and the lives of workers in 1848. There were no questions about the capital resources of manufacturers, the organization of production, the volume of trade, or the value of commercial activity. There were questions about how new jobs might be created, about whether convent and prison manufacturing competed unfairly with artisanal production, and about what measures might be taken to ameliorate the lot of poor working families. More striking (especially when contrasted with the later chamber of commerce *Statistique*) was the absence of self-conscious exercises in definition. It was assumed that anyone (whether worker or employer) answering the questions about apprenticeship, earnings, cost of living, housing conditions, religious and moral education, and the like knew what a worker was. In addition, the committee of inquiry assumed that, despite shared categories, there would be different responses to its questions from workers and employers. Precisely because it represented a compromise the *enquête* acknowledged the class conflict that had emerged in the course of the revolution of 1848.[26]

The committee charged with conducting the *enquête* (the committee on labor) was acutely aware of the volatile nature of its work, and it sought to avoid disastrous political consequences. It deliberated carefully about how to choose local representatives from whom to gather information, and it seriously considered the warning of the mayor of Paris that if elections were held among workers the gatherings might become a pretext for more street demonstrations. Committee members listened to delegations of angry workers who perceived them as heading a forum for airing and resolving grievances rather than as a neutral body devoted to gathering information. And they sought to influence the conduct of these workers by publicly praising the decorous and respectful and denouncing the hostile and impetuous. An *enquête* that recognized the potential bias of its sources was bound to be perceived as an instrument of political influence. For this reason the committee had moved slowly at first; after the June Days it stopped work on the *enquête* altogether. Instead it turned its attention to other matters—providing workers with clean housing and savings institutions; creating agricultural colonies for abandoned children, orphans, and delinquents; revising the child labor law of 1841 to increase the permissible hours of work—all measures designed not to deal with workers' demands but to offer alternative solutions in the form of moral tutelage and social control.[27]

This, then, was the historical and political context for the chamber of commerce's *Statistique*. Government-sponsored research on work and working conditions had acquired enormous political significance, indicating not simply a desire for information but the intention of acting on labor's demands. The chamber was determined to repudiate this connection between information and politics, so it prepared what it deemed a neutral report on an objective situation that would stand outside all political disputes. Its schedule of questions differed from those developed in May 1848. Neutral, paid investigators visited factories, workshops, and households to collect data. They asked for no opinions about how things might be improved; they simply wanted descriptions. The focus of their questions was industry, not labor. Indeed, although the bulk of the information sought treated workers (three-fourths of the tabulated figures dealt with them), the structure of the *Statistique* seemed to subordinate them—to place them where they belonged—in the economy, which was the ostensible focus of concern.

Somewhat surprisingly and without real explanation, the chamber's committee decided to compile retrospective information for 1847. A report, designed in June 1848 and carried out over the next months, might have been aimed at gauging the effects of the revolution, but this seems not to have been its purpose. Indeed, there were only occasional comparisons offered in the text of the report between the data for 1847 presented in the tables and the actual state of employment in particular trades in 1848. Rather, the point seems to have been to capture a more normal situation to which things could be returned. From this perspective the *Statistique* offered a plan for economic reconstruction and a way of demonstrating to frightened investors that the turmoil of recent months was an aberration, uncharacteristic of the basic organization and relationships of the Parisian economy.

The format of the report conveyed a sense of stability and control. Indeed, the visual impression as one turns page after page is of precision and order. There were thirteen sections representing the different types of industry in Paris (clothing, food preparation, chemicals, construction, etc.). Within each section particular enterprises were described. Figures were given for the average value of businesses of different sizes, the number of "employers," the age, sex, and number of their workers, the location of work, and the average daily wages paid. Underneath the tables, written explanations amplified the description. For each kind of enterprise the text was divided into informational sections beginning with a discussion of the technology and organization of work, followed by details about apprenticeship practices, average wages, and seasonal variations in employment. The final section dealt with the "morals and customs" of workers. This last section examined traits of character and patterns of behavior that explained the prosperity or lack of it of any particular group of workers. The tone of this final section had the same impartiality as the discussions of technology and wages. References to workers' improvidence and dissipation, although we might see them as interpretations, were presented as facts, identical to the various numerical facts.

The classificatory scheme of the *Statistique* arranged all information according to the kinds of manufactured goods produced or sold and the types of manual services performed (repairing shoes or laundering, for example). *Industrie* denoted entrepreneurial as well as productive activity. Indeed, the authors of the report carefully defined and justified their depiction of the world of work as a world of entrepreneurs. Listed as heads of "enterprises" were (1) all self-employed individuals; (2) all individuals making goods to order who employed one or more workers, whether or not these were family members and whether or not they were paid; (3) all individuals making goods to order for "bourgeois clientele" (this category included tailors, dressmakers, and even washerwomen); and (4) all individuals making goods to order and working for several different manufacturers. The authors of the report recognized that the last two categories particularly could also be deemed "simple homeworkers," but they argued that precise counting required the entrepreneurial designation. Whereas workers employed in a shop or at home by a single employer would be enumerated by their bosses, those working for more than one employer might be counted twice or perhaps not at all. The solution was to define them as heads of businesses, however small their businesses were.[28]

The effect of this categorization was to reduce significantly the number of people who had come to think of themselves as workers in the Parisian population. The *Statistique*'s definitions denied the class identification that had from February to June joined impoverished masters, independent craftsmen, and skilled employees at large establishments—all calling themselves workers or proletarians—in clubs, demonstrations, and producer associations. By referring to both workers and bosses as *industriels*—industrial producers—the *Statistique* refused the socialist terminology that sharply distinguished workers and bosses; it moved the focus away from the relations of production to the simple fact of productive activity. In this way the neutral terms of classification presented a particular picture of economic organization; one, moreover, that was associated with a set of conservative political beliefs.[29]

Instead of the conflict depicted in the socialist rhetoric, a conflict that had been acted out in the June uprising, the report presented a seemingly neutral picture in which hierarchical relationships (of ownership, management, skill, sex, and age) were part of the order of production itself, the guarantee of high quality and efficient adaptation to the market. Conflict was absent from the descriptions. It was depicted as an unnatural aspect of the arrangements; its causes were extraneous to the system. The economy of Paris was portrayed as a busy world of *petites entreprises*. With pride the authors pointed to the art, ingenuity, and skill of these *industriels:* "Their infinitely varied products are known the world over. . . . The manufacturers often guide, and follow in their turn, the caprices of fashion and taste of the elegant world. The lively and intelligent workers adjust with marvelous skill to all changes of design."[30]

The *Statistique* retrieved from 1847 and presented in carefully categorized and enumerated form the "reality" of Parisian economic life. Implicitly, it disputed the radical claims of socialist revolutionaries, showing them to be misapprehensions, if not dangerous fantasies. The *Statistique* constructed and justified a model different from that offered by socialists and according to which economic, political, and moral order would be restored. In this effort it invoked the science of political economy as its methodological and theoretical guide, the guarantee of accuracy and of truth.

[II]

La statistique est une verification de l'économie politique par les faits.
E. BURET, *De la misère, 1840*

To direct its research effort the chamber of commerce chose the leading spokesman for the science of political economy. By his name alone, Horace Emile Say (1794–1860) embodied the French liberal school. His father, Jean-Baptiste Say, introduced France to Adam Smith's theories and added his own interpretations of the role of markets in economic development. Indeed, if there was one name in France that immediately denoted political economy, it was that of the scion of a leading Protestant family, Jean-Baptiste Say. Horace Say studied in Geneva and worked for a large commercial company for a number of years, traveling to the United States and Brazil. In 1831 he was appointed as a judge to the commercial tribunal of the department of the Seine, and in 1834 be became a member of the Paris chamber of commerce. He served on the municipal council of Paris and in 1846 published a book on the administration of the city of Paris. In 1848 he was secretary of the chamber of commerce. Identified with the liberal Parisian bourgeoisie, Say joined the Conseil d'état in 1849 and left it after Napoleon III's coup d'état in 1851. His experience mingled business and administration, and he exemplified the close ties between commerce and politics that existed under the July Monarchy and persisted into the Second Republic.

Horace Say was committed to propagating the teachings of his father. In 1842 he founded the Society of Political Economy, and throughout the 1830s and 1840s he published numerous editions of his father's books, adding his own revisions and commentaries. Of his own publications, the *Statistique* was probably Horace Say's greatest accomplishment. It won the statistical prize of the Académie des sciences morales et politiques in 1853, which conferred on it enormous prestige at a moment when the economic policy of the empire was still being formulated, and which probably also contributed to Say's election to the academy in 1857.[31]

Assisting Horace Say was his son Jean-Baptiste Léon (1826–96). Léon Say served as an administrator for the railroads after attending the Collège Bourbon, and he too was an active proponent of his grandfather's theories. He worked on the *Dictionary of Political Economy* and wrote in defense of free trade and individual liberty. After February 1848 he joined the Paris National Guard, and he participated in the suppression of the June insurrection. A loyal supporter of Cavaignac, he campaigned for the general's election to the presidency of the republic in December 1848 against the more reactionary forces supporting Bonaparte. Léon Say became prefect of the Seine in 1871 and a minister of finance during the 1890s. In those years a conservative republican, he continued to follow the family doctrine in his policies.[32] In a funeral address in 1878 for the liberal economist Frédéric Bastiat, Léon Say recalled the sense of ideological embattlement he had felt in 1848: "In 1847 all of political economy's efforts were directed against the system of protection; in 1848 it was obliged to confront new adversaries. It found itself struggling against the socialists. . . . [These were] serious battles; liberty of commerce, protectionism became incidents; the central doctrine was that of the liberty of the individual; we had to save the individual from the new pantheism that would have absorbed all humanity into the state."[33]

The *Statistique* was part of the struggle being waged against socialism. It was framed according to the terms of political economy, a doctrine that claimed the status of science, and thus a truth value that stood outside human construction or control. J.-B. Say had written: "The general laws of the political and moral sciences are beyond dispute. . . . They derive from the nature of things as surely as the laws of the physical world; one does not imagine them, one discovers them."[34]

His followers accepted this reasoning, finding in the certainty of their science the explanations they needed for otherwise contradictory or confusing detail. Indeed, their procedure in the *Statistique* was to examine information closely, discussing it even when it did not seem to fit the general scheme, and then to resolve any tensions between information and categories of explanation by invoking the principles or laws of the theory. This was the case for the informing concepts of the report: the definition of productive activity as *industrie* and the designation of various kinds of producers, including some workers, as entrepreneurs or *chefs d'industrie.*

The focus of the report on *industrie* followed directly from J.-B. Say's writings. In the *Traité d'économie politique* he explained that *travail,* or labor, was too restrained a concept for describing production. Labor denoted only manual work or physical force, without including the knowledge of nature and the economy and the implementation of that knowledge (organizing production and selling goods or services) that were also required to create value.[35] Those engaged in industry were entrepreneurs, even if, like a tailor or shoemaker, a dressmaker or washerwoman, they performed manual labor and earned very little. The training, talent, and skill required of craftsmen almost by definition meant they were self-employed or potentially so and that they engaged in the thinking and commercial activities that distinguished *industrie* from *travail.* For Say, entrepreneurs served a critical function at the center of networks of production and exchange. When "events seconded their skill" they profited handsomely, and many "acquired large fortunes."[36] If upward mobility and the possibility of steady improvement were synonymous with being an entrepreneur, then the larger the number of entrepreneurs, the more valid the association of capitalism's promise with individual economic progress. In contrast, being a worker (*ouvrier*) meant inhabiting an essentially stagnant position. Those called workers were unskilled; they executed their tasks under the direction of others, and they forfeited their part of the profits yielded by production in exchange for a wage.[37] Although there might be collective improvement for workers as civilization advanced, individual mobility was not held out as a goal.

Using Say's terminology, the *Statistique* listed three categories of *chefs d'industrie* in its columns. There were those who employed more than ten workers; those employing between two and ten workers; and those employing one or no workers. The last category included as workers the family members who assisted the "head" of the enterprise. Husbands of washerwomen "working with their wives," children, relatives or wives of shoemakers or tailors, all were counted as *ouvriers*.[38] The family work unit, whether genuinely an independent business (as were bakeries, butcher shops, and dairy stores) or a collectively of wage-earners (as were shoemakers or garment workers paid by the piece) became in this account a *petite entreprise*.

If the tables fixed an impression of small businesses, the accompanying text recognized the problems inherent in applying the concept to certain categories of enterprise. Again and again, usually in the section on wages, the authors conceded that the term "employer" or "head of the business" was not an accurate rendering of the situation of many tradesmen and tradeswomen. Although counted as employers, these self-employed individuals were—and the language used is the same over and over again—"really workers."

> The caners and upholsterers of chairs working by themselves are really workers.[39]
>
> The "employers" who make custom-made shoes are themselves really workers.[40]
>
> The "employer" dressmakers working alone are really workers.[41]
>
> The manufacturers of shawls are really master workers.[42]

The case of seamstresses was so confusing that a separate count was established by a house-to-house visit, and the reporters gave up trying to separate workers and the self-employed, presenting instead a table headed *ouvrières lingères* (seamstresses).[43] For tailors, a series of footnotes in effect withdrew the "employer" categories for those tailors, piecers, and used-clothing dealers who worked alone, assimilating them into the worker category for the purposes of calculating wages. Thus the report counted piecers as heads of their own businesses in one section: "The piecers (*appièceurs*) working at home alone or with their wives are listed in the tables as *industriels* and not as workers."[44] But for purposes of listing average wages, the report redefined their status: "Employer-piecers are really workers. The product of their labor is the best proof of it."[45]

The statistics on wages might have called into question the prosperity and the entrepreneurial nature of many small trades and disputed the charts that fixed the numbers of manufacturers and their workers. By the authors' own admission, "worker" was a more appropriate term for many of the impoverished craftsmen and craftswomen who, in effect, sold their labor and not the goods they produced. But since the terminology of classification was held to stand outside human definition, the "facts" had to be interpreted within the given theoretical framework of political economy. Any other approach—modifying the model in light of the facts, for example—would have compromised the utility of this science for establishing the indisputability of the *Statistique*'s claims. So the authors dealt with the ambiguity of the situation of some producers only as a problem of methodology for the calculation of wages and not as a major challenge to their vision of economic organization.

As it presented its information, the *Statistique* addressed, but without acknowledging them, a series of alternative interpretations of the plight of workers. These interpretations were dismissed by simply asserting the axioms of political economy. One such interpretation, for example, suggested that hundreds of small producers had been driven into poverty by an unregulated economic system. The *Statistique*'s reply was that state and corporate regulation necessarily hindered prosperity. "Private interest," J.-B. Say had written, "is the most skillful of masters."[46] Another interpretation cited excessive subdivision in the organization of production, particularly the subcontracting practice associated with ready-made garment manufacture and building construction. Workers' groups in 1848 had successfully lobbied for laws outlawing subcontracting, so convinced were they that these practices undermined the structure of their trades.[47] The authors of the *Statistique* referred obliquely to the debates of 1848 when they invoked Say's theory of markets to reject the idea that the "distress" of certain groups of workers could be attributed to subcontracting. Say had argued that the multiplication of enterprises always happened in response to consumer demand and inevitably stimulated production and employment.[48] In similar terms the authors of the *Statistique* observed: "It is difficult to accept the idea that the condition of workers has really been worsened by the presence of new industrial entrepreneurs [who] have augmented the demand for labor and offered a new resource during periods of unemployment; without doubt we must attribute the distress of these workers to other causes."[49]

The "other causes" ultimately had to do with the family, the "natural" organization within which people lived and that determined such economic phenomena as the law of wages. The *Statistique* explained that the "distress" of seamstresses followed not from subcontracting in the ready-made garment industry but from the fact that the conditions of female employment violated the law of wages. J.-B Say had explained the law of wages in the *Traité,* and he pointed out that there was a different calculus for women than for men. A man's wages had to maintain the worker and provide for the subsistence of his children as they accumulated the physical "capital" that would fit them to be the next generation of unskilled manual labor. For men, then, the costs of the reproduction of the labor force were included in the "price" paid for labor power. Women and children, in contrast, were "natural dependents" and so never had to be entirely self-supporting. Those women who for some reason had to be self-sufficient were always at a disadvantage, since they faced competition from other women who needed only to supplement a family's income. This was the permanent state, the "law" of the female labor market.[50]

Neither J.-B. Say nor the reporters for the *Statistique* found wage-earning itself a contradiction of female status. Women engaged in "occupations of which they are capable," and these might even include some tasks traditionally performed by men. (In the *Statistique* the authors noted that Parisian compositors prohibited women from working with them although this was "work that they appear capable of performing without fatigue and that is permitted them in other towns, at Senlis, for example.")[15] The problem was rather that too many women "had the misfortune" to live outside their "natural" setting—the family—which in fact was the only economically viable context for all workers, women as well as men.[52]

The family was critical to the *Statistique*'s analysis not only of wages but of all economic and social life. The authors located in the family not only a model for organizing production but the sources of individual moral development. The family was the natural environment that fostered those qualities of individual discipline and orderliness necessary for the health and prosperity of society. Drawing on Say, but also on the writings of the reforming doctors of the 1840s, the authors of the *Statistique* used the family as the governing conception for all social relationships. The focus of their analysis, moreover, was the worker and the extent to which he or she was embedded in family structures. If the stated subject of the report was industry, the preoccupation of its authors was with the morality of workers. Morality or its absence, of course, had political as well as economic consequences; the discussion of morality then permitted the authors to allude to the politics of 1848 in the context of a purely objective economic report.

In the *Statistique* the terms that established moral contrasts linked work discipline and personal comportment. Good workers were orderly, hard-working, assiduous, punctual, law-abiding, and thrifty. Bad workers were turbulent, difficult to govern, lazy, dissipated, and improvident, indulging a taste for pleasure and frivolous conduct. These qualities were developed in the interlocking worlds of family and work. The analysis offered by the *Statistique* played back and forth across the organization of work and the condition of family life, using one to explain the other. The more closely the structure of work resembled a family, the more enmeshed in families the workers, the better behaved was the work force. Although a bad family could transmit the "original sin" that forever tainted the morality of a worker, families were also influenced by the nature of the work their members performed.[53] The small shop, headed by a benevolent and fatherly employer with a stable group of married skilled workers, practicing a trade they had acquired by formal apprenticeship, was the ideal workplace. Workers were inevitably well paid and well behaved, replicating in their private lives the orderly relationships of the shop. If the natural substances they worked with had the right qualities, the positive effects were further enhanced. Thus, of all those working with metals, the craftsmen who used precious metals were best off. Gold and silver somehow developed in jewelry workers a civilized taste for good things, as water stimulated in those who worked with it—washerwomen and tanners, for example—an unfortunate and excessive thirst for alcoholic drink.[54] These references established a clear equation between material substances and the family. All were "natural," and their effects could be studied in similar ways.

Jewelry workers provided the exemplary case for the authors of the *Statistique*. They offered an idealized account of the "experience" of these workers in the form of a descriptive life history:

> In general the jewelry workers, who earn good wages, like to be well dressed; the vulgar pleasures of the cabaret attract them less than those of the dance, the theater, a walk in the country. It thus comes about that they prefer the domestic life to a disorderly existence (*une existence de désordre*). They marry the more willingly because they can find work for their wives to do at home, without abandoning the care of the household. . . . Later the wife can take on as apprentices one or two young girls; the [worker's] children can also be initiated early into tasks suitable for their ages; order

and comfort characterize the home, and the worker's household is transformed into a small shop.[55]

This rendition dissolved the line between family and workplace; the orderliness of one constructed the order of the other and led to the (self) improvement of the worker and his emergence as an entrepreneur: "It is easy for those with intelligence to become manufacturers on their own account if they want to."[56] As if to underscore the influences that led to such success, the authors closed their account by returning the jewelry worker to his place, naturally subordinated to his employer: "Relations between employers and workers have always been rather good. Reciprocal relations of politeness were generally observed, at least until the revolution of February; many employers even followed the practice of holding a joyous repast annually for their workers; and when a worker married, he invited his employer and his wife to sit at the banquet table."[57]

The authors of the *Statistique* emphasized the importance of the small shop by comparing it with other kinds of workplaces: the *chantiers* with constantly shifting labor forces (as in the building trades); factories with large numbers of workers and with no traditional boundaries of age and sex separating them; and individual rooms, where pieceworkers toiled in isolation, unsupervised and therefore subject to no codes of professional or moral conduct.[58]

According to the report, the great disadvantge of the *chantiers* was that hiring took place outside; workers presented themselves at certain spots—the Place de Grève for the building trades, the Cloître-Saint Jacques-l'Hôpital for washerwomen—and waited for an offer of employment. The line between lounging and looking for work was hard to maintain, and the sexual overtones (waiting in the street for a proposition) were impossible to avoid. For building workers, "many occasions for mutual stimulation arise, and the hiring place is often the starting point for pleasure trips by men of irregular conduct."[59] Washerwomen often had to listen to "vulgar propositions" and face the temptations of prostitution.[60]

The report pointed out that in the large factories employers could not vigilantly supervise their workers and "penetrate benevolently into their intimate lives."[61] Instead of apprenticeship, young workers learned by example; the imitation of their elders respected no differences of age and status and therefore was "often harmful to their morality."[62] The "vie commune" of the factory, the mixing of the sexes in the same workroom, relaxed moral restraint so much that "energetic men in these conditions easily become turbulent."[63] Overstimulated (the sexual metaphor was unmistakable), they were now open to "unfortunate illusions," to ideas that inevitably disrupted industrial production and political order.

Finally, on the *Statistique*'s list of negative examples there were the isolated workers, living on their own in the furnished rooms of the city. These *logements garnis* were temporary quarters for Paris's itinerant and migrant populations, for those outside the order of family or workshop. Having neither vigilant employers nor parents to train and supervise them, these workers, said the report, had a "tendency" to misconduct, promiscuity, and, if they were women, prostitution.[64]

Although according to the *Statistique* conditions at work were critical to engendering good morals, the authors also suggested that an orderly family life might act as a corrective to a dangerous kind of workplace. Here building workers, and particularly masons, were an example. They were itinerant workers, but the report pointed out that theirs was a tight craft organization and apprenticeship was still in force. Although masons lived in furnished rooms in Paris, these residences struck the investigators as decent places since they were organized by trade and supervised by elders. Although temporarily living outside families, the masons were closely bound by family ties: "They have a family residence in their villages to which they contribute all their savings."[65]

Similarly, the *Statistique* drew a distinction among homeworkers. Those living in their own residences, married, and owning some furniture were, however poor, described as upright and honorable. And the investigators assumed that even those in furnished rooms had "good conduct" when they were married or when lodging was somehow organized by trade. In the marginal world of the *logement garnis,* which had been for Frégier in 1840 the breeding ground of the "dangerous classes," the authors of the *Statistique* found four categories of workers: those with good, passable, bad, or very bad moral conduct.[66] The determining factor was family ties *or* a trade structure with some vestige of hierarchy or regulation among its members. Regulation, moreover, was expressed ultimately as sexual repression. In the orderly and thrifty workers praised in the *Statistique,* all "turbulence," lust, passion, and excitement had been disciplined.

The proponents of free trade and individual liberty thus made a case for discipline and regulation. But unlike the socialists, whom they attacked for wanting to regulate the economy, Horace Say and his collaborators did not seek to impose artificial laws on what they defined as natural phenomena. Instead, they attributed a natural regulatory function to the family, whose existence and well-being it was then the function of the state to promote. The role of moral science was to find ways to nurture and protect this natural, hierarchical, and repressive institution. If for political economy "protectionism" had been anathema as economic policy, as social policy it was the order of the day.[67]

The analysis of the family and of morality served several functions in the *Statistique*. It permitted the authors to endorse small-scale artisanal forms of organization without seeming to call for intervention in the economy, and it moved the causal explanation for the revolution of 1848 away from the economic system and toward the working-class family. As such, it served the polemical purpose of a reply to the socialists, in the guise of a scientific report. The terms of its science were powerful and persuasive, presented as descriptions of the workings of natural phenomena—the family and the economy. The ordering of its information in numerical tables appealed to a general belief that quantitative evidence could resolve politically inspired disputes. From this perspective the *Statistique* worked as documentation of an externally existing reality; its format and mode of presentation made an eloquent case for its status as fact.

[III]

La criminalité de la femme est plus dangereuse que celle de l'homme parce qu'elle est plus contagieuse.
C. LUCAS, *De la réforme des prisons, 1838*

The *Statistique* also offered a political argument, veiled in discussion of sexual disorder. The argument rested on the invocation of a dangerous and disorderly "reality" that competed with and threatened the "reality" the authors endorsed. The introduction of the second and antithetical "reality" made clear the necessity for accepting the authors' economic blueprint. For us, it also calls into question the document's status as objective scientific description.

The *Statistique* presented the world of work in terms of oppositions between good and bad, orderly and turbulent, domesticated and dissipated workers. Although there were precise accountings of the numbers of men and women in the work force and in every branch of manufacturing, the attributions of types of moral conduct were specific to neither sex. According to the report, men and women were to be found in both the good and bad categories, often sharing similar traits in the same trades. Yet in their portrayal of family and morality the authors played on themes of unregulated female sexuality, using the image of the prostitute to conjure up visions of a (working-class) world dangerously out of control.

The report used women to refer to either limit of the possibilities of moral behavior. "Naturally" associated with the family, they embodied and transmitted all its virtues: "Good conduct is often hereditary, especially from a mother to her daughter."[68] Like a mother, a vigilant (female) employer kept her young employees in line, screening out those with reputations or habits of "easy virtue." At the head of an enterprise (sewing garments or selling food) that they conducted in a family setting, married women exhibited impressive managerial and commercial traits. As workers, they were also more reliable when married, having accepted in the power and protection of a husband "the natural law" of their own dependency.[69]

In the *Statistique* the situation of the married working women represented that of the "good" working class in relation to its employers—in exchange for a certain dependency (on the intelligence and resources of a boss), the worker relinquished his right to profit and accepted a wage. His good behavior, like a wife's sexual fidelity, acknowledged his place in a system of subordination and domination. Accepting the rules meant channeling one's desire, obeying the law one had not written and could not alter.

Women who lived outside a family lived outside the law, and this had worse consequences for some than for others. Old women living alone were miserable; unable to provide for themselves because they had lost their supporters, they had no control over their lives. The victims of circumstance (and beyond sexual corruption), they could only be pitied for their fate.[70] In contrast, young women on their own were dangerous, and their condition was synonymous with unfettered sexuality. Among milliners, for example, everything depended on

> the condition in which the workers are placed. Thus almost all those who live with the milliners who employ them display upright, orderly conduct, they are accustomed to thrift and order. . . . It is not the same for those women working in rooms and for those who are free to do what they wish at the end of the day; it is among them that one finds dissipation and hardship. In general, paid by the day or the piece, they earn wages sufficient for subsistence; the difficult position into which they too often fall must be attributed to their lack of thrift and their disorderly conduct.[71]

The authors of the *Statistique* developed the association between women and sexual indulgence by pointing out that women living alone exhibited worse conduct than men. Among groups of tumultuous workers the women were typically cited as being "even more" turbulent or dissipated.[72] Lacking internal correctives, young women indulged passion and vice, and prostitution was inevitably the result. Inherently repugnant because they accepted and exploited sexuality, prostitutes also developed a taste for luxury that further corrupted their behavior. (J.-B. Say had warned that while consumption was important for the economy, luxurious tastes distorted its smooth processes.)[73]

> One notices sometimes the traces of a well-being that their avowed occupation cannot justify.[74]

> A great number of workers exhibit a doubtful conduct and have wages insufficient to support the style of life they lead. They are part of the personnel of public balls and are rarely assiduous at their work.[75]

The word "doubtful" (*douteuse*) recurred in references to single working women's conduct. It conveyed not only a negative judgment about dubious behavior but a sense of duplicity and deception as well. The investigators could never be sure what these women really did; appearances might not be accurate, self-designated occupational titles might be a ruse. The double check the investigation designed to count seamstresses (taking information from employers and visiting all households where seamstresses might be living) represented not only the genuine difficulty of counting the numbers of homeworkers in a trade open to any women with rudimentary sewing skills, but the difficulty of knowing what the truth really was: "The method of doing a census of seamstresses in their homes appears a more certain one."[76]

In many cases this method meant two visits, because the seamstresses lived in lodging houses that received exhaustive and detailed treatment in a separate section of the *Statistique*.[77] The count of seamstresses also involved a more thorough attempt to ascertain information about their moral conduct: "Information on the living conditions of these workers came from the impressions the census takers had, . . . from answers the workers themselves supplied, and from their neighbors."[78] Even then, "it was difficult to evaluate the conduct of these workers" or even to decide if they were workers:

"For a certain number the occupation of seamstress is clearly only a means of concealing their real sources of income."[79]

These workers subverted the precision of the *Statistique*'s count of Parisian workers; they called into question the ability of the objective observers to "see" the facts, and they refused to fit into the established categories. The uncertain character of these so-called workers suggested the larger problem of determining the status of any single woman who lived outside the normal contexts of family, work, economy, and exchange. The hint of prostitution conveyed this sense of irregularity and corruption. Workers but not workers, these women were marginal to, yet part of, the world of Parisian industry. In their behavior lay the threat to moral order, the destruction not only of work discipline but of all social relationships. Lacking proper appreciation of their subordination to a parent or husband, these women lived as outlaws. The very ambiguity of their situation, the fact that they defied categorization, was the measure of their dangerousness.[80]

The prostitute represented sexuality—male as well as female—corrupted, inverted, or simply unregulated, out of control. Women, in their "natural" subordination and dependency, represented the working class in relation to capital.[81] In the text, representations of class and sexuality were displaced onto one another; the figure of the single working woman carried both references. In the *Statistique*'s obsessive preoccupation with women of "doubtful" conduct one finds encoded a set of observations and warnings about another "reality"—the dark and dangerous side of the working class (indeed of the human personality), which must be known if only to be contained.[82] This "reality" always lurked below the surface; it was the underside of the busy, artistic, prosperous world of work the authors had proudly extolled in the introduction to the volume. It was, as the insurrection of June 1848 had shown, a dangerous and chaotic universe in which ordinary rules of conduct and natural hierarchies were overturned, in which the fatherly surveillance of employers could no longer contain the "turbulence" of their sons. The only corrective to this situation, the only way to prevent its reemergence, was to reimpose the terms of patriarchal law.

The authors of the *Statistique* thus offered both a vision of "reality" and an argument about why it had to be accepted as a framework for economic life. In so doing, they produced a text that reveals something about their own political relationship to "reality": it is a reality contingent rather than absolute, constructed rather than discovered, imposed for clear political ends rather than lived naturally or inevitably. As the numerical tables ordered a mass of information into categories of understanding that conveyed a certain model of social structure, so the law imposed and enforced—made real—the desired relationships of social and political life.

[IV]

In the years that followed the design and publication of the *Statistique,* the Second Empire's tough censorship laws and vigilant police informers prevented the appearance of alternative versions of the reality of the world of work. The terms of the *Statistique*'s analysis thus maintained a certain official status. The chamber of commerce continued to employ the *Statistique*'s categories in subsequent studies; the investigation into *Industrie à Paris* in 1860 followed the same format used in 1848. Under the Third Republic new techniques of investigation and a far different political climate spawned new kinds of statistical inquiries with different constructions of the world of work.[83] The histories of these efforts cannot preoccupy us here; when they are written, however, they will surely uncover not simply the organization and structure of the world of work but the extent to which its very depiction was a matter of intense debate and political contest.

It is in terms of politics as power and knowledge that we can finally assess the uses for historians of the *Statistique de l'industrie* of 1847–48. Written in the wake of 1848, it was intended to dispute the revolution's most radical economic and political claims and to reassert a vision of economic organization that had been severely challenged, especially by socialist theorists. Encoded in the documentation was the analytic framework of political economy and an argument about what might happen if it was not accepted. The scientific claims of the investigators and the tabular presentations of their information fixed the report's meaning and reinforced its status as authoritative description. This, and the political climate of the period that permitted no challenges to be heard, gave the authors the final word not only for the moment but for posterity. When the *Statistique*'s administrative and polemic uses had long been outdated, historians searching for unimpeachable data took the report at face value, incorporating its documentation without questioning its categories and interpretations. This procedure perpetuates a certain vision of the economy and of statistical science as an essentially objective enterprise; it makes the historian an unwitting party to the politics of another age. An alternative approach situates any document in its discursive context and reads it not as a reflection of some external reality but as an integral part of that reality, as a contribution to the definition or elaboration of meaning, to the creation of social relationships, economic institutions, and political structures. Such an approach demands that the historian question the terms in which any document presents itself and thus ask how it contributes to constructing the "reality" of the past.

— 7 —

"L'ouvrière! Mot impie, sordide . . ."

WOMEN WORKERS IN THE DISCOURSE OF FRENCH POLITICAL ECONOMY, 1840–1860

L'ouvrière! Pour tous ceux qui, comme Jules Simon, ont lu dans le grand livre de la vie réelle, ce mot sonne aux oreilles comme le synonyme, comme le résumé des choses cruelles: douleurs, privations, misères, prostitution.

HIPPOLYTE DUSSARD
Le Journal des Economistes, 1861

At the Paris Salon in 1861 Auguste-Barthélemy Glaize exhibited a painting called "Misère la Procuresse." The picture is dominated by an old hag, shredded rags exposing an ugly drooping breast and bare leg. She drags a walking stick (her stance recalls figures of Death) and points or beckons with crooked fingers to the lights of a distant city. Behind her, working assembled around a candle, are some earnest young women in rural clothing. One holds a spindle; beside her is a spinning wheel. In front of the hag are a group of vuluptuous, naked women, spilling out of or on to a horse-drawn chariot that is moving rapidly toward the city. The painting depicts not so much a static contrast as a narrative of transition: from country to city, from traditional to modern society, from order to disorder, from appropriately female attire and behavior to sensual degradation and corruption. The transformation of wise into foolish virgins is effected by the old woman, whose hideousness warns us, but somehow not her victims, of the fate that awaits them. For the artist, it was also important that his subjects were workers. "How many young women," he wrote in the catalogue, "giving up work, throw themselves into all the vices brought on by debauchery in order to escape this spectre that seems always to pursue them?"[1] The spectre was, of course, poverty, defined in the words of one critic of the time as "the mother of despair and infamy, of prostitution of all kinds." But Glaize's

This essay was published in Patrick Joyce, ed., *The Historical Meanings of Work* (Cambridge; Cambridge University Press, 1988) and is reprinted here with permission of the publisher. The comments of Albert Hirschman, Laura Engelstein, Michael Fried, and Ruth Leys were particularly helpful to me.

words were as ambiguous about causality as was his painting. For the abandon of the young women seems to emanate from themselves; rather than being driven to a horrible fate, they rush off with a certain pleasurable eagerness to embrace it. Poverty is as much a warning about the consequences of unleashing women's (natural? inevitable?) tendencies as it is the cause of their fall.

This ambiguity about women and poverty characterized much of the debate about women workers during the nineteenth century, a debate that captured public attention in 1858–60 (the very years Glaize was painting his canvas) with the publication of a number of studies including Julie-Victoire Daubié's "La Femme Pauvre au XIXe siècle," which won the Academy of Lyon's competition in 1859, and Jules Simon's *L'Ouvrière* (1860). Indeed, the acclaim Glaize's painting received probably stemmed in part from the fact that he captured so well the terms of his contemporaries' discussion. Maxime du Camp said as much in his comment; he found the painting "absolutely fantastic and nevertheless fantastically real, comprehensible to all."[2]

The publication of these studies placed the issue of *l'ouvrière* at the forefront of debates on morality, economic organization, and the situation of the working classes. It also linked the concerns of political economy with the general debate on women that raged in this period—what one historian has called "La Querelle des Femmes of the Second Empire." The years 1858–60 saw an outpouring of books specifically on Woman: Proudhon's *De la justice dans la Révolution et dans l'église* (1858) foreshadowed his more virulent diatribe, *La Pornocratie ou les femmes dans les temps modernes* (published posthumously in 1871); Michelet's *L'Amour* (1858) and *La Femme* (1860); and the feminist reponses to these works by Juliette Lamber Adam, *Idées anti-proudhoniennes sur l'amour, la femme et le mariage* (1858), and Jenny d'Héricourt, *La Femme Affranchie* (1860).[3] The question of the working woman served to focus some concerns about independence, legal status, and appropriate female social roles, although it was not central to all aspects of the debate on the woman question.

For economists the theme of *l'ouvrière* was not new in 1858–60, although the subject itself was central as never before. References to women had long figured in the discourse of political economy in nineteenth-century France, if only implicitly or as part of a general discussion of the working classes. That discourse included the voices of theorists propounding a new economic "science," and critics of all kinds—protectionists who attacked the notion of a free market, moralists who feared that economic development undermined social order, socialists who railed against individualism and competition, and feminists who questioned the effects of new divisions of labor.

It is inaccurate to place these voices in clear opposition to one another as in a formal debate for they overlapped in important ways, forming what Denise Riley in another context has dubbed a "web of cross references," intersecting at some points, diverging sharply at others.[4] One of the important points of intersection was the representation of working women; through different conceptions of femininity, sexuality, and social order contemporaries exchanged opinions about the effects of industrial development on French society.

In this essay I want to approach the discourse from one perspective, that contained in or directly referred to by political economists. These were the men (and a few women) who took it upon themselves to define the terms of a new science of economics (the workings of the market and of the organization of the production and distribution of wealth), to codify its laws and discipline its practitioners. They addressed themselves to "public opinion" and to legislators as they aggressively sought to translate their views into policy. Through public addresses, a journal (*Le Journal des Economistes,* founded in 1842), and an organization (La Société d'Economie Politique) they announced their views to the world. They had an eminent representative in the academy—the holder of the chair of Political Economy at the Collège de France—as well as members in the Académie des sciences morales et politiques, chambers of commerce, and local and national government offices. However beleaguered political economists felt as they urged unwilling governments to institute free trade in the 1840s and 1850s, they had a crucial impact on the articulation of the new economic order. For, having established the intellectual and institutional power of their science through control of knowledge and access to government, political economists were able to provide the conceptual framework within (and against) which those addressing economic questions had to work.

[I]

References to working women in the writing of nineteenth-century French political economists were direct and indirect. The figure of the working woman served both as an explicit topic in discussions of poverty, wages, occupations, and the family and as a way of signifying disorder. It is often impossible to separate these usages for, as we shall see, they refer to one another, as is the case in Glaize's painting. Most of the discussion of working women also involved considerations of cities; two kinds of cities and two kinds of problems were constantly evoked. The first was the situation of young women on their own in urban centers such as Paris (*femmes* or *filles isolées*), working for a pittance and so swelling the ranks of the urban poor. The second concerned the denizens of new manufacturing centers, women who worked long hours tending machines, and who lived in households as members of units that only barely resembled normal families.

The term used to refer to independent women workers was ambiguous. In the regime of the policing of prostitution, *femmes isolées* referred to candestine prostitutes who were not registered in one of the houses where the trade was permitted.[5] In surveys of workers, such as the *Statistique de l'industrie* prepared by the Paris chamber of commerce in 1848, *femmes isolées* denoted women wage-earners (usually seamstresses or dressmakers), living alone in furnished rooms where they sewed garments at piece rates for the ready-made clothing trades.[6] The fact that the term was the same was not coincidental. Ever since Parent-Duchâtelet's massive inquiry into prostitution in 1836 it was generally recognized that casual prostitutes came from the ranks of working girls.

> Of all the causes of prostitution, particularly in Paris and probably in other large cities, there is none more active than the lack of work and poverty, the inevitable result of insufficient wages. What are the earnings of our dressmakers, our seamstresses, our menders, and in general all those who occupy themselves with the needle? . . . let one compare . . . the price of their labor with that of their dishonor and one will cease to be surprised to see such a great number fall into a disorder that is, so to speak, inevitable.[7]

Parent's analysis also included explanations that were not strictly related to wages or working conditions. He thought that, in addition to poverty, "vanity and the desire to glitter in sumptuous clothing, along with laziness, is one of the most influential causes of prostitution, especially in Paris."[8] Such desires could run rampant when young women lived and worked outside the surveillance of employers or parents. As the authors of the *Statistique* of 1848 noted, "dissipation" and "disorderly conduct" were associated with "women working in their rooms and . . . those who are free to do what they wish at the end of the day."[9] In fact, the occupational status of such women was, in the eyes of the *Statistique*'s authors, "doubtful." It was never clear whether their wages came from respectable work or from prostitution: "One notices sometimes the traces of a well-being that their avowed occupation cannot justify."[10] The condition of independence, whether it unleased insatiable desires or brought misery and unemployment, led to prostitution.

The luxury and wastefulness associated with prostitution provided a striking contrast both to forms of necessary (and self-regulating) consumption that kept economies functioning and to appropriate (and self-limiting) forms of sexuality. An article in *Le Journal des Economistes* in 1842 made the connection between consumption and sexuality explicitly. Its author located criminality not in poverty but in passion, in "moral poverty" brought on by "immoderate desires." He warned against too rapid an increase in the standard of living of "the lower orders" that might overstimulate desire: "We must take care, in seeking to accelerate their progress, not to set in motion a disordering of their passions."[11]

The interchangeable usages of *femmes isolées* suggested that all such working women were potential prostitutes, inhabiting a marginal and unregulated world in which good order—social, economic, moral, political—was subverted. Rhetorically, then, the use of the term *femmes isolées,* with its ambivalent references, had a double effect: it conflated certain types of working women with prostitutes and it also identified sexual license with poverty. The ambivalent causality (poverty or bad morals?) was less important than the association itself because there was only one cure for sexual license and that was control.

Commentaries on women workers acknowledged various categories and forms of female employment, but the situation of *femmes isolées* preoccupied those writing about women workers. Political economists lauded workshops in which skilled mistresses supervised and instructed apprentices (the analogy was to mothers and daughters) and they granted the necessity and the utility for married women to earn eages by combining homework with domestic chores. But inevitably their writings passed over these instances to the question of poverty and thus to the dilemma of the *femmes isolées.*[12] This was because *femmes isolées* revealed the stark reality of women's economic status; in their pathological condition one understood the "natural laws" of women's wages.

What were these laws? As articulated by Jean-Baptiste Say, one of the early theorists of French political economy, and repeated by his followers, there was a fundamental difference between the calculations of men's and women's wages. A man's wages had to maintain the worker and provide for the reproduction of the labor force; his wages included subsistence costs for his children and wife, "natural dependents" who could never be entirely self-supporting.[13] Women's wages, like men's, were set by the laws of supply and demand, but an additional factor operated in the competition for women's jobs. Those women who for some reason had to be self-sufficient always faced competition from women in the natural state, that is those who needed only to supplement a family's income and who therefore were willing to work for less than a subsistence rate. Say recognized that the inverse might be logically true in the male labor market—that unmarried men with no dependents might seem less costly to employ than those married and could therefore drive wages down below family subsistence rates. But he reminded his readers of the long-run consequences of this system: workers would not reproduce, future supplies of labor would diminish, and wages would have to go up.[14] ("Wages go up when two employers run after one worker; wages go down when two workers run after one employer" was the maxim cited in treatise after treatise on theories of wages and profits.) The solution was to set male wages—for those single or married—to include costs of reproduction. For according to political economy, reproduction was an economic concept not a biological function. It had to do with the provision of supports for life, the accumulation of capital, not the production of life itself. As Say pointed out, "The difficult thing is not to be born, it is to subsist."[15] Subsistence prepared a child for manhood, built up the strength and skill eventually required for work: "This capacity . . . can be considered a capital that is formed only by the annual and successive accumulation of sums [by the parents] assigned to develop [the worker]."[16]

What we now refer to as "human capital" was acquired and measured solely in monetary terms as the "sums" allocted to rearing a child or the "wages" paid to an adult man. For this reason the worker's wage had to be set higher than that required for his individual maintenance; the additional amount represented an employer's investment in the next generation of workers. A woman's labor in childbirth and her activities caring for children did not figure in these calculations. Childbirth and childrearing were rather the raw materials on which economic forces acted, the elements of nature with which human societies were built. Say defined production as the activity that gave value to things, that transformed them from simple matter into exchangeable items of recognized value.[17] In his lexicon reproduction was a synonym for production:

> Sometimes production is called reproduction because it is, in effect, nothing more than the reproduction of materials in another form which gives them a value. . . . The word production is more precise because the wealth in question does not come from the material itself but from the value given to the material.[18]

This definition of reproduction subsumed and made irrelevant a more exclusively biological reference. Whether the capital was human or not was beside the point, the emphasis was on how value was created and by whom. By a kind of circular logic, fathers were deemed the agents of transformation of babies into adults since their wages included subsistence costs. These wages, which in theory recognized and reimbursed workers for their part in the creation of value in the shop, became in relation to the household a means of conferring on the father the status of value-creator. By attaching a monetary value to human development and imputing it all to the father's wages, women's contribution, both as domestic workers and wage-earners, was rendered irrelevant.[19]

In part this had to do with a certain level of abstraction—the man's wage subsumed all social labor costs including his particular expenditure of labor power. But the representation of production-reproduction as a male activity came also from a conception of the economy that depended on nature at once as its analogue and its antithesis. The economy was said to be a natural phenomenon with laws akin to those in the physical world; the status of political economists as scientists rested, after all, on their claim to observe in human activity the autonomous laws of the economic order. If the economy was a natural phenomenon, its activities nonetheless involved the transformation of matter, of nature's bounty, by humans into things of value. The distinction between natural matter and the creation of value was defined in the oppositions: birth/subsistence, raw material/products of value, nature/worker, mother/father. In this scheme women's contributions to the social value acquired by children were both acknowledged and obscured because men's wages were seen as covering or reimbursing these costs. At the same time women's wage work was denied the kind of value-creating status attributed to men's. Women were by definition inferior workers, and so incapable of creating the same kind of value. The workers' newpaper *L'Atelier* put it precisely in a preface to a discussion of the problems of women wage-earners: "Although women's work is less productive for society than that of men . . ."[20]

The asymmetry of the wage calculation was striking: men's wages included subsistence and reproductive costs, women's wages required family supplements even for individual subsistence. In both cases, membership in a family was assumed (and encouraged), but the results were quite different. Men could live on their wages whether single or married; women could not. Men embodied the possibilities of individual liberty advanced by theorists of political economy, women became the dependent social beings with obligations and duties to others that the theory assumed them to be. Although critics of political economy argued that all wages should minimally guarantee male and female workers' subsistence, the theorists replied that this was impossible since women's wages were incomplete without some contribution from a man. Or, as Eugène Buret put it in his 1840 study of *The Poverty of the Working Classes:*

> Woman is, industrially speaking, an imperfect worker. If a man doesn't add his earnings to the insufficient wage of his partner, sex alone constitutes for her the cause of poverty (*le sexe seul constituera pour elle une cause de misère*).[21]

Buret used "sex" in a double sense: as a reference to women's socially acceptable activities—what we now call gender—and to denote the physical act that beyond certain boundaries led to depravity and corruption. *Femmes isolées* demonstrated that outside the context of the family neither work nor sex could bring women acceptable returns.

But women could work within family structures. The issue in these discussions of *femmes isolées* was not that women were unfit for work or that work unfitted them for maternity. For studies of wages and the distribution of wealth assumed the importance of women's contributions to household budgets, while descriptions of women workers pointed out how well-behaved were employees doing work appropriate to their strength and sex, and subjected to careful supervision in familylike settings. Good behavior, moreover, led to financial well-being, for those who practiced thrift and moderation somehow managed quite well despite low wages. The corrective to women's low wages was, in fact, not only financial support from men but the decorum associated with the repression of desire—the desire to live beyond one's means and the desire for sexual indulgence both associated, of course, with prostitution. Here political ecnomists implicitly took on their socialist critics, some of whom had used the figure of the prostitute to symbolize the plight of all workers under capitalist exploitation. They did not argue the question directly, but simply asserted a contrary definition grounded in the authority of their science. If socialists had pointed out that the sale of labor power was no different from the sale of women's bodies, that economic and sexual exploitation were of a piece,[22] political economists established a careful distinction between the productive and disciplined use of "muscular force" and the wasteful, self-indulgent aspects of sexual activity. By locating sexuality in women's bodies, furthermore, they established a gendered contrast: between work and sex, productivity and wastefulness, discipline and indulgence, male and female. This had the effect of denying men's part in the exchange that established prostitution and so of proposing a solution seemingly untainted by it. If economic productivity and moral order were to be maintained, the male principle must prevail. This meant that the patriarchal family—a hierarchical, interdependent entity—had to be the school for and embodiment of order. The ambivalent figure of the *femme isolée,* by linking poverty and sexuality, demonstrated the consequences of all lives lived outside regulated contexts.[23]

The implications of the discussion went well beyond references to the reality of women's lives. *Femmes isolées* represented the domain of poverty, a world of turbulent sexuality, subversive independence, and dangerous insubordination.[24] They embodied the city itself.[25] For some writers they exemplified urbanization's worst efforts ("the blasts of unspeakable exhalations, the pell-mell of fumes, of evil emanations and bad dreams that hover above our darkened cities"[26]); for others they were the source of the working-class demoralization so evident in large urban centers. Cause and effect were usually not clearly sorted out in the political economists' writings. The figure of the *femme isolée* instead functioned evocatively. In their association with prostitution, these women carried the "moral leprosy" that made large cities "permanent centers of infection"; they permitted expression of or simply expressed those "tumultuous passions" that, in time of political upheaval—as in the revolution of 1848—threatened to overturn the entire social order.[27] *Femmes isolées* signified economic and social deviance. The political threat posed by their situation underlined the need for some kind of government intervention and it brought into sharp relief what the desirable alternative ought to be.

In the presentation of the problem of the *femmes isolées* we see political economy's incorporation of moral science into its discourse on the production of wealth. This process has been well described by Giovanna Procacci, who notes that the "grafting of morality onto economics" in the first half of the nineteenth century made "possible the elaboration of a whole set of technical instruments of intervention."[28] What those were and how they operated are not our concern here, but it is important to note that intervention was addressed to the family and not the economy.[29] The family was seen as the natural regulator of morals, whereas the economy was self-regulating in a realm outside human control. Yet the laws of each were interconnected and—in the language of political economy—discoverable by scientific observation as were "the laws of [magnetic] attraction or gravity."[30] It is impossible to separate moral from economic considerations in the writings of these political economists.[31] Analyses of wages linked gender and economics: the "natural dependency" of women on men within families explained the differential between male and female wages; the "natural laws" of supply and demand explained why women would always have to depend on men. One set of "natural" laws articulated and constructed the other. And any discussion of the plight of *femmes isolées* assumed and reasserted the "fact" of women's inferior or, in Buret's formulation, "imperfect" standing as wage-earners and the consequent necessity of keeping them within a family structure.

[II]

Two themes, integrally related, are evident in political economy's discussions of women workers in manufacturing cities. One had to do with the impact of machinery on work itself. The new division of labor brought a regime of interchangeability—of product parts and workers. When mechanical power could be substituted for human strength, at least one of the marks of difference between men's and women's work could be erased. The other had to do with the physical space of factories, city streets, and workers' homes where the "promiscuous intermingling" of the sexes took place. This implicitly referred to the leveling of differences at work, but was presented as a separate concern. The issue of women's employment in factories, then, involved a consideration not only of wages and working conditions but also of the relationship among industrialization, urbanization, and the sexual division of labor.

With the introduction of machinery, jobs had acquired a certain homogeneity. In fact, in the 1840s and 1850s, machines were used only in a limited number of places in France, mostly in textile production. Even in the textile industry, the labor market remained sexually segregated. Yet political economists recognized that the potential of machinery was to dissolve all differences among workers. Among political economists, critics of the new division of labor objected to the worker's loss of individuality—"he can be replaced by whoever comes along"[32]—and of skill, the mark that distinguished between "les bons et les mauvais ouvriers";[33] proponents claimed that machines had so simplified work that those who could not be employed before because of weakness or lack of training—women and children—now had opportunities to earn wages.

> [Machines] create jobs simple enough to trust to those who until now have not been able to work, to children and women, and, in general, to the weakest part of the population.[34]

This resulted in a more productive use of socially available labor power. But it also had ambiguous implications. Since differences of "muscular strength" were no longer required, and since such strength had been a factor in male and female wage differentials, a certain equality between the sexes might be achieved. The labor market might as a result be more open, demonstrating the virtue of "liberté du travail." More ominously, of course, machines could feminize all work by dissociating production from human physical effort, from the value-creating activity recognized by the wage and associated in political economy with masculinity.

Interestingly, it was (male) workers who raised the spectre of feminization, not political economists.[35] At least in the 1830s and 1840s, political economists addressed the question of mechanization as a matter of morality, of a threatened disruption of "natural" distinctions between the sexes. Commentaries noted, for example, that machines had wreaked havoc in all-female trades, such as spinning, by dissociating them from feminine skill and household locations.[36] But the question of the impact of machinery on job distinctions was taken up most often in discussions of morality framed in terms of the consequences of the spatial mixing of the sexes. This, and not the nature of work itself, was the preoccupation of the major accounts of factory life published in the 1840s and 1850s.

There were many accounts of factories written in this period by investigators affiliated with the Académie des sciences morales et politiques, among them Louis Villermé, Louis Reybaud, and Armand Audiganne. Like travelers in foreign lands, these men journeyed from city to city, recording in minute detail the new and strange sights they had seen.[37] Their reports were reprinted in *Le Journal des Economistes* or *La Revue des Deux Mondes,* and then in book form. They attained wide circulation and acquired tremendous authority, and their views were cited as scientific evidence for various analyses and programs put forth in the period. These accounts, providing as they did the moral dimension for economic science, fed into debates on the future of French industrial development that raged in the 1840s and 1850s and they were used by both sides—those who urged unfettered economic growth, mechanization, and free trade and their opponents who advocated restricted growth, small-scale production, and protective tariffs. What is striking is how important sexual difference was in the construction of the terms of the debate.

Dr. Louis Villermé's sensational accounts are typical of the genre and his preoccupation with sex has already been noted by historians.[38] Villermé compared the poverty and disorder of the various cities he visited in terms of their relative levels of sexual disorder. In the worst cases, certain neighborhoods of Lille, for example, promiscuity, incest, obscenity, and prostitution were rampant and they were evident both at work and at home.

> What! you mix the sexes in your workshops when . . . you could so easily separate them? Are you then not ignorant of the licentious discourses which this mixture provokes, of the lessons of bad morals which result . . . and of the driving passions which you encourage as soon as their voice begins to make itself heard?[39]

Even in factories where men and women worked at different tasks, the fact that everyone arrived and left at the same time led to promiscuity and fostered the practice of young girls working a "fifth quarter" of their day as prostitutes.[40] The mingling in the streets continued in households:

> I would rather add nothing to this description of hideous things which reveal, at a glance, the profound misery of these unhappy inhabitants; but I must say that in several of the beds of which I have just spoken I have seen individuals of both sexes and of very different ages lying together, most of them without nightshirts and repulsively dirty. Father, mother, the aged, children, adults, all pressed, stacked together. I stop. The reader will complete the picture, but I warn him that if he wishes it to be accurate, his imagination must not recoil before any of the disgusting mysteries performed on these impure beds, in the midst of obscurity and drunkenness.[41]

The publicist Theodore Fix, writing on the condition of the working classes in *Le Journal des Economistes* several years after Villermé's study had appeared, cited the "grave disorders" (which indicated political disturbances as well as moral offenses) that followed from the situations the doctor had described. In opposition to those who argued that manufacturing itself was responsible for the disorder apparent in factory towns, Fix insisted that moral corruption caused poverty. He called for a "police des manufactures" as a way of raising living standards in factory towns. Fix offered examples of employers who had taken measures to regulate their workers' conduct, even at some financial cost. They rigorously separated the sexes, regulated hours so that men and women did not mix in factory corridors or on the streets, and expelled anyone who engaged in obscene conduct. "These sacrifices . . . are always largely compensated and their factories are among those that prosper most."[42] Whether others shared Fix's solution or not, they shared his description of the symptoms.[43] "Pell-mell" was the recurrent phrase used to designate the irregularities that existed, a random scattering that defied natural hierarchies and separations, that made home and workplace indistinguishable, that dissolved the meanings of the differences between men and women.

Women workers were emblematic of the problem. Their fate in factory towns was regularly contrasted with the situation of women in all-female workshops or of those working for wages at home. Although it was often acknowledged that women workers earned good wages in factories—better than in any other female work—the moral effects outweighed these economic gains. Factory women were said to be exposed to vulgar company, seduced, torn from the cares of household and children, or, alternatively, allowed to discover in the company of others the pleasures of sensuality, the taste for luxury, the possibility of fulfilling sexual and material desire. In contrast, women employed in all-female workshops (usually of relatively small scale) or at home were depicted as chaste, orderly, and well prepared for the responsibilities that marriage and motherhood entailed.

What is striking about these purported descriptions of factory towns is how exaggerated they were. For one, other accounts tell us that men and women were not usually indiscriminately mixed in factories; they describe jobs and workrooms that tended to be segregated by sex. Moreover, men and women shared space on the streets of small towns, on farms and in households, in much the way they did in manufacturing centers. A characteristic feature of any family or household was, after all, the mixing of age and sex in the same physical space.[44] How can we explain the contradictions? By attending to the rhetorical as well as the literal functions of these writings, by examining the contrasts used to constitute meaning. These accounts try to render as physical detail what were in fact abstract qualities. In Villermé's descriptions the effect is achieved by lining up obscene conversation, incest, darkness, and filth in implied opposition to decorous language, private marital intercourse, light, and cleanliness. The graphic portrayal of promiscuous mingling stood for the absence in industrial cities of the defining characteristics of good order: hierarchy, control, stability, all expressed as a matter of the customary relationship between women and men. "Public morals are profoundly relaxed in the big cities," wrote the authors of a book on abandoned children, ". . . they are especially so in the industrial cities where a very great number of workers of both sexes live together in one place."[45] Somehow the equivalency—workers of both sexes, not men and women united in families—illustrated and explained the problem. The disorder of unregulated sexuality flourished where the social lines of sexual difference had become blurred.

If the absence of distinctions between the sexes indicated "grave disorder," then the moralization of the working classes required that sexual difference be articulated and enforced. It was in these terms that a new generation of moralists examined the impact of wage work on women's domestic responsibilities and began to describe maternity as woman's primary "natural" labor. The metaphoric use of female sexuality to talk about working-class poverty or disorder implied for them a literal solution—attention to the lives and activities of working-class women.

[III]

The long discussion of the condition of the working classes in terms of women's disordered sexuality culminated and changed (but did not end) in 1858–60, in the context of negotiations for and then passage of the free trade treaty with England. Concluded in January 1860, this document doomed all attempts to stop the progress of urban industrial growth. Critics and proponents agreed that France could meet the English challenge only with further mechanization and by intensifying the pace of economic change. What would the moral effects of this kind of development be? That question called forth reponses that spoke at once to the "querelle des femmes" and to economic issues, explicitly spelling out the terms of sexual difference, particularly as they applied to women's "natural" roles.

Moralists who identified themselves with political economy explored questions of morality through detailed investigations into women's work and wages: Jules Simon (professor, publicist, member of the Société d'Economie Politique) published his articles on "Le Travail et Le Salaire des Femmes," first in *La Revue des Deux Mondes* and then combined in a book called *L'Ouvrière,* which appeared in 1860. Julie-Victorie Daubié, a young governess and virtually unknown until she submitted her winning entry to the Academy of Lyon's competition in 1859, published parts of her essay first as "Quels Moyens de Subsistence Ont les Femmes" in *Le Journal des Economistes* in 1862–63 and then as a book, *La Femme Pauvre au XIXe Siècle,* in 1866. Both Simon's and Daubié's studies were about the facts of women's manual work (there was no talk of professions or jobs requiring high levels of education) and some reviewers read them only as that.[46] But they were also moral statements less preoccupied with economic matters than with general questions of order and justice.

These two studies were addressed to popular audiences, to that informed readership known as "public opinion," but they also belonged broadly to what I have referred to as the discourse of political economy. They drew on and spoke to the knowledge and ideas propounded by political economists; Simon accepting their precepts, Daubié taking a critical position.

Although their subject was more narrowly construed as working women, these studies were situated in the tradition of earlier scientific reports on the condition of the working classes. Simon explicitly evoked the method of firsthand observation used by his predecessors (Audiganne, Reybaud, Villermé):

> I have not seen everything and I have not told everything I have seen; but there is not a single misery recounted that I haven't witnessed and that still doesn't oppress my heart.[47]

Daubié took a somewhat different tack, for she had neither reputation nor standing nor membership in a learned scientific society. She achieved the authority of her text by muting her own voice and instead citing historical documents, informed sources, and government reports. Yet at crucial moments she introduced dramatic anecdotes that, though she did not claim firsthand experience of them, made her appear a witness to the stories she told.[48]

Like their predecessors these were self-consciously moral works that assumed that economic laws had been accurately described and instead concentrated on moral (and what we would call social) science. Simon's first line announced his intention: "The book you are about to read is a book about morality."[49] Daubié insisted there ought to be "treatises of moral justice as prologues to treaties of commerce" and clearly saw her own work in those terms.[50] Simon and Daubié established the need for moral considerations in an overly materialistic age by citing (sexual) disorder. Both books evoked the same images of prostitution, incest, and debauchery apparent in earlier studies; it is clear that they assumed readers were already familiar with those studies. Yet the tone and emphasis of Simon's and Daubié's books contrasted sharply with the earlier works in their concentration on positive solutions. While prostitution and incest had been Villermé's focus (and titillation), Simon worshiped at the altar of an idealized motherhood and Daubié, more practically, sought ways to improve the position of working mothers. If the older investigations understood working-class disorder in terms of women's unregulated sexuality, these studies focused on mothers as the key to orderly family and social life. If the older studies detailed the breakdown of order in terms of a loss of sexual difference, these studies imposed a grid of sexual difference as a means of achieving or maintaining order in social and economic organization. If before, women's sexuality posed the entire problem of a disruptive working class, now maternity (depicted as an asexual female physical function) seemed to indicate a potentially more manageable working class; calls for the protection of maternity, moreover, implied a new vision of the relationship between laboring classes and middle classes, workers and the state.

In effect, Simon and Daubié simply reversed the emphasis of earlier constructions, making explicit what had before been implicit (that modest women and good mothers were the antitheses of prostitutes, that discipline and domestic order were the opposite of poverty). The effect on representations of women workers was striking: they were now portrayed more often as victims torn by economic necessity (poverty) from their "natural" labor as mothers and wives, or from the work and workplaces appropriate to their sex. The real danger to be avoided was not so much uncontrolled sexual passion but lost maternal sustenance—the key not only for the proper education of children but for the support and strength of family life. If the explicit focus had moved, however, from negative to positive representations, sexual difference was, as earlier, established not as a systematic comparison between women and men but solely in terms of the "natural" purposes and physical characteristics of women's bodies.

Simon and Daubié had different agendas. He was prominent commentator on social affairs who would later become one of the Third Republic's important legislators. She was a self-defined feminist, who would earn the first baccalaureate awarded to a woman (in 1862) and who would lead campaigns against government regulation of prostitution and for women's suffrage in the early years of the Third Republic. Simon wrote his book in the name of society, citing and endorsing Michelet's views on the female character; Daubié wrote in the name of women, making a claim for the importance of women's (economic) independence. The differences of argument and intention between them were crucial, but the similarities were also revealing. In both cases discussions of women workers converged on the question of motherhood, viewed as the defining quality or characteristic of femininity.

L'Ouvrière began with a dramatic contrast between advances in technology and science and the degradation of family life. Mechanization had substituted women for men in industry because "according to the law of wages" women were cheaper to employ. This employment in itself actually improved women's material situation because the wages they earned in factories were higher than those paid elsewhere. What then was the problem? Simon cited Michelet's anguished cry:

> *L'ouvrière!* impious, sordid word that no language has ever known, that no age ever understood before this age of iron, and that holds in balance all our supposed progress![51]

And then added his own explication: "The woman who becomes a worker is no longer a woman."[52]

The contradiction woman/worker had several manifestations. Women did what was formerly men's work; they left the "hidden, sheltered, modest life, surrounded by warm affection, that is so necessary to their happiness and ours"[53] for the factory where they mingled all day with women of "doubtful morality" and men, some of whom "dominated" them (the sexual innuendo seems intended) as supervisors; they exerted more physical force at work than was appropriate for their bodies;[54] and they earned wages that might lead them to question their husband's authority at home.[55] Distinctions within the family were leveled: there was no longer a mother and father, but two workers; there was no longer a family to return to at the end of the day, only a dirty lodging where children were abandoned and deprived of a mother's love. Factory shifts even ignored the differences between day and night—all that was natural and once taken for granted had been disrupted.

According to Simon there were still models of normality and these, interestingly, involved women earning wages, but in domestic settings or very small workshops where natural differences could be respected (silkspinning and weaving in the region around Lyon were exemplary). For Simon, the ideal was a family enterprise in the countryside, where women worked at delicate tasks suited to their weaker condition, interrupting production to care for children and husband, to infuse the household with loving spirit, to embody and "personify" the family.

> It is necessary that women be able to marry and that married women be able to remain at home all day, there to be the providence and the personification of the family.[56]

Women at home guaranteed the kind of behavior that conserved resources and prevented the poverty that followed from (men's) tendency to wastefulness and dissipation. (Here the danger of luxurious self-indulgence has been attached not to prostitutes but to working-class men.) Men's wages were designed to support families if carefully managed and used in the kind of "moral" atmosphere only women could maintain. Those who argued that raising men's wages would restore women to their rightful place at home misunderstood the causality, according to Simon. It was necessary first to implement morality, then men's wages would be adequate for family support.[57] The economy, this argument assumed, was not susceptible to intervention, nor was the family. But while political economy had provided the insights according to which institutions might be molded to economic "laws," moral science had not sufficiently detailed the importance of the "natural" roles of men and women for the organization of family life.

Simon rarely referred to men, though when he did he assumed they did hard labor, outside, away from the household. The evocation of men—as at once productive wage-earners and amoral characters—came through implicit contrasts with women. Simon's most eloquent (and memorable) descriptions elaborated his idealizations of women:

> Woman grows only with love, and love develops and strengthens only in the sanctuary of the family.[58]

> If there is one thing that nature teaches us with evidence it is that woman is made to be protected, to live as a young girl close to her mother, as wife, under the protection and authority of her husband.[59]

> We can write books and invent theories on duty and sacrifice, but the true teachers of morality are women. It is they who softly counsel the right, who reward devotion with a caress. . . . All material improvements will be welcome; but if you want to improve the condition of women workers and at the same time guarantee order, revive good sentiments, make the country and justice understood and loved, do not separate children from their mothers![60]

What was at stake was the essence of femininity and that had to do with love, morality, and maternity. Wage-earning as an activity undertaken by women was not harmful as long as it did not distract them from their "natural vocations"; indeed, it kept them from boredom and periods of useless inactivity. But it was not by wage-earning that women created social value, it was by exemplifying and enforcing family morality.

I have used the term "social value," but Simon did not. References to the creation of social value, indeed of any value by women, were absent from Simon's conceptual vocabulary. He seems to have relegated the language of value to matters of technical economics, which was not appropriate for discussing what women were or did. Rather, Simon's entire text was constructed in opposition to material, monetary concepts: women were associated with a secularized spirituality, with love and feeling; they lived in a domain outside the economy and their behavior was detached from it; their qualities were inherent in their physical make-up, linked, above all, with the functions of motherhood. Women effected the transformation of others: under their tutelage children became moral, loving beings; men became responsible, disciplined husbands and fathers; even wages achieved their true value when "morale" prevailed in a household. But this was not value—creating activity precisely because it could not be recognized in monetary terms. To do so, in fact, would be to undermine women's effectiveness, to reduce to cash an activity of literally unmeasurable importance. What women created, after all, had no quantifiable exchange value in the market for it was not the physical force or the capacity for labor of children that mothers produced. Those qualities still depended on subsistence as provided by the father's wage. Rather, women inspired those behavioral characteristics on which depended not so much a society's productive capacity or its wealth as its stability and the bases of its social organization. All of this left in place, indeed took as axiomatic, political economy's earlier definition of production, and of men as value-creating (and therefore wage-earning) producers. While Simon brought to light and to social relevance the domestic and childrearing activities of women, he did so without challenging the calculus of political economy. Instead, he constructed the meaning of his text with a new set of oppositions: economic/noneconomic, workplace/household, factory/family, material/spiritual, physical growth/moral education, wage-earning/moralizing, economy/society, worker/mother, male/female.

To recognize in these contrasts the "ideology of domesticity" or "the doctrine of separate spheres" is at once to get and miss the point. There is, of course, in Simon's work a theme now familiar to historians of nineteenth-century Europe and North America, thanks largely to research by historians of women. But to label the theme and assume we therefore know what it means is to miss the chance to see when and in what contexts these kinds of ideas were articulated as well as how, specifically, they worked. In Simon's case it seems fair to conclude that he drew on (and preempted) the views of earlier critics of capitalism (those of romantic Catholics and Christian socialists, for example) who argued from the Bible that woman's destiny was the labor of childbirth and the responsibility of maternity and that wage labor was therefore an unnatural activity.[61] But the timing of the publication of his work is also crucial and it helps explain his equivocation on the question of whether or not industrial growth could be stopped. Clearly Simon thought not, and at every point he threw up his hands about the impossibility of saving less efficient small workshops instead of building new factories. Indeed, his book offers no economic solution, no way of turning back the clock. One critic was so annoyed at Simon's refusal to suggest policy that he deemed the book "a long moan uttered by a man of sensitivity and talent" and wondered what the impact of such a study could be.[62] The impact seems to me to have been ideological, not immediately programmatic. For it provided a kind of compromise with opponents of free trade who had warned that rapid industrial and urban growth would sap the (moral and physical) vitality of France and who, in 1860, hysterically denounced the treaty with England as the fruition of their worst fears. In his discussion of women workers, Simon accepted some of the critique offered by protectionists, but he also pointed out (reluctantly, his tone suggests) that history could not be reversed. Simon's discussion of the true nature and mission of women set forth an alternative way to understand the future. He developed and endorsed a vision of moral order and social organization detached from, unaffected by, and yet perfectly compatible with an economy of unlimited industrial growth.

Simon's book was offered as a study of the facts of working women's lives but it was above all an exercise in prescription and idealization. His most urgent and exhortative statements were about femininity, not about work, and he eschewed all discussion of practical solutions to the problems he described. Simon insisted that neither legislation nor coercion could change the direction of social organization, but he did suggest that a process of "education and institutions" might eventually have some effect.[63] In no small way his book constituted part of that process of education by offering a normative statement about womanhood as a goal to be attained. The idealized family with woman at its center was the model according to which people might increasingly choose to live. The remedy to be hoped for was "the return of the mother to the family . . . to family life . . . to the virtues of the family."[64] Indeed, once the natural bases and the salutary social impact of the family were explained, it would achieve in reality its theoretical promise: "It is always to be wished," Simon wrote, "that facts be made to accord with institutions."[65] The title of Simon's book, then, represented dismal facts that were contrary to the institutional necessities of the family: "L'ouvrière" was the antithesis of "la mère."

Julie Daubié approached the study of women workers differently from Simon, but she began with many of the same assumptions. Like him, she equated immorality and disorganization with the loss of clear lines of sexual difference. One of the destructive impacts of industrial wage labor, she argued, had been to erase certain institutionalized sexual distinctions, thereby depriving women of legitimate economic activity and moral protection. Men or machines (or both) had usurped women's traditional trades—spinning, embroidery, lace-making—leaving them with only unskilled menial occupations. The loss of exclusive rights to practice these trades meant for women the loss of customary skill, of work appropriate to their "natural aptitudes" of legal and moral protection, of jobs, and of wages that contributed significantly to subsistence.[66] The regime of industry erased the lines of differences:

> Today the mother is forcibly torn from her family, the wife from her husband, her household, the work of her sex; childhood has become the prey of the most avid speculation; the young girl . . ., the weak, and the strong, all riveted to the same chain as slaves of industry, have to perform equal labor.[67]

This system produced irresponsible men who monopolized all advantages, and exploited women who bore without compensation the burdens of "civilization."[68]

These burdens took their toll on the physical constitution of women—the bodies of young girls were martyred to debauchery and seduction, the bodies of mothers were unable to suckle infants so worn out were they with fatigue. Daubié graphically painted the losing struggle of women against steam-driven machines in terms of physical violation:

> The woman who competes with machines, struggling for speed against wheels and gear, has squandered her life to industry without receiving in exchange the certainty of her daily bread. But it is not enough that industry has slain her body, industry also has killed her soul.[69]

She underscored this image by citing doctors who concluded that, "from the point of view of health, the condition of working women is much more deplorable than that of prostitutes."[70]

Prostitution represented the physical and moral abuse of women, the perversion of their proper vocation, which was motherhood. Wrote Daubié, "In all well-constituted societies, the woman ought to be above all wife and mother and her most beautiful work will be to bring a man into the world."[71] As bearer of children and director of the household, women personified the family; when men agreed to support their wives and children, they acknowledged their social duty to protect the family (and, by extension, the country).[72] In effect, they enacted toward the institution of the family the same maternal solicitude mothers naturally expressed for their children. Daubié's vision of an ideal moral order, then, echoed Simon's: morality rested on a sense of responsibility to others developed in families at whose center was a woman.

Like Simon, Daubié did not refer to maternity, to the example women set, the moral instruction they gave, as having "value." She accepted political economy's equation of value with wage-earning and so assigned domestic functions to a separate sphere. At the same time, however, she thought it possible for women to create value in the labor market and to use their wages, if necessary, for the sole support of their children. In a clear disagreement with political economists, she saw nothing inherently different about women's and men's productivity, and for that reason she insisted on equal wages for both sexes. She argued that women's social status would be enhanced if only they had access to decent paid labor. But she also thought that work, though it might be necessary, was not a desirable solution for married women.

Daubié addressed as separate issues what for Simon and others were inherently contradictory concepts—wage labor and motherhood—in an effort to provide practical solutions to the pressing problem of women's poverty. In her view, this problem had two related causes: the monopoly by men of previously all-female trades or of trades perfectly suitable for women, and the selfishness of men (embodied in the Le Chapelier Law of 1791) who pursued individual rights (seducing and abandoning young women, drinking away family resources, refusing to contribute to household expenses) instead of fulfilling their social duties.

> I have searched in vain for man's duty in social organization; I have found only his right to the unlimited liberty to oppress. That, if I am not mistaken, is the node of all questions of work and political economy.[73]

If the poverty of women was caused by men, then women must be given the power to seek redress of their grievances. Simon's solution of simply returning women to the home would be futile in the absence of laws that could limit oppression or force men to recognize their duty. Daubié agreed that the long-term remedy was a "moralization" of men (both workers and employers), but she maintained that this would only be achieved by strengthening the position of women. That would come neither from a return to the past nor from idealized pronouncements, but from the implementation of equality—equality before the law, equal participation in making laws, equal access to training and apprenticeship in all jobs, and equal hourly pay.

Equality, in Daubié's view, would not eradicate sexual difference; it would put women in a position to protect themselves. First, equal access to jobs would enable women to break unjustified male monopolies of trades perfectly suited to women (such as printing) and to enter those trades "that bring out naturally the attributes fitting" to their sex.[74] Second, equal pay would remove the pressure for women to work to excess in violation of their natural inclinations and it would permit single women to support themselves without having to depend on (and thus become sexually vulnerable to) men. Here Daubié implicitly rejected the asymmetrical wage calculus of political economy, assuming instead that women were, like men, "naturally" independent and that wages ought to provide any individual worker's subsistence. Women's natural physical limits ought not to disqualify them from wage-earning because the wage conferred the status of producer, it did not reflect inherent capacities. Third, legal rights would enable women to force seducers to acknowledge paternity and recalcitrant husbands to recognize their financial obligations to their families. Equality before the law would give women the power to enforce normative rules of family organization in very much the same structural terms that moralists and political economists envisioned them.

In effect, Daubié addressed two problems and offered two apparently different solutions to them. The first problem was economic in origin and had to do with the pressing fact that women needed to work and that existing jobs and wage scales made subsistence impossible. The effects of this situation were both material and moral. For single women the result was "poverty or shame"—both of which led to debauchery and death—for married women the result was not only individual poverty but the sacrifice of children. The second problem was moral in origin and had to do with the fact that men had abandoned their families, pursuing individual liberty instead of fulfilling their duties. This had an economic effect especially on married women and made it necessary for them to supply the subsistence their husbands should have provided; it also had a moral effect, disrupting family organization and social order. Despite the fact that she pointed out that material and moral causes and effects were related, Daubié offered two separate solutions for the two problems she had described: the first—for single women—equality in the job market; the second—for married women—the legal power to enforce paternal responsibility.

In a sense, the second solution canceled the radical import of the first, for it suggested that equality was a compensatory measure for women who had not yet married, or who could not marry, or whose husbands were delinquent providers. By endorsing political economy's view of men as the major source of subsistence (economically responsible for the reproduction of the labor force), Daubié left in place the theoretical formulation that defined women (as a category, whether single or married) as "imperfect" wage-earners. Though her practical solutions were a far cry from Simon's and though gender power relationships were the cornerstone of her analysis, Daubié remained within the conceptual boundaries earlier set by political economy, accepting the notion that work and family (economics and morality) were separate spheres when in fact it was precisely the relationship between them that lay at the heart of wage calculation.

[IV]

In the discourse of political economy women workers were a prominent topic; they served at once as an object of study and a means of representing ideas about social order and social organization. Political economists focused attention on women workers because they seemed to reveal something of the problematic of urban/industrial development, especially its moral dimension. Through that act of observation, women workers became an essential part of the conceptual vocabulary of moral science, the means by which normative rules were articulated and applied. This involved a double move that at once set women workers apart from the larger world of work as a distinctly deviant case and made their situation central to the resolution of the problem posed by the urban working classes.

The marginalization of women workers rested on and reinforced political economy's presentation of its economic and moral science in terms of the "natural" qualities of women and men; the invocation of nature legitimized certain precepts and put them beyond the bounds of dispute. This was the case for the discussion of women's lower wages as a result of their "natural" dependency (a function of motherhood) and the projection of a desirable moral/social order in terms of sharp lines of sexual difference, spatially divided between home and work, physically divided between men's "muscular force"/productivity and women's maternity/domesticity.

The discourse of political economy with which I have worked here was clearly idealized and it tells us little about what work meant to the women who performed it. Nonetheless it did not take place in a realm apart from the material, economic, or political. Rather it established the definitions according to which policy was debated and programs enacted and even fundamental critiques—such as those of socialists—were developed.[75] Political economy provided the terms by which relations of production and sexual divisions of labor were established and contested.

The marginalization of women workers was, then, a historically produced effect that must itself be critically examined. Historians who treat women workers as marginal to processes of urbanization and industrialization perpetuate uncritically the terms of the nineteenth-century discourse and so miss the opportunity to analyze its operation. It is precisely by studying the production of women workers' marginality that we can discover some of the central issues of public policy and political debate in mid-nineteenth-century France. Through such an approach, we not only see a new dimension of history but we put ourselves in a position to identify—and perhaps to change—one of the ways in which the meaning of work has been constructed.

IV

EQUALITY AND DIFFERENCE

8

The Sears Case

In the past few years "equality-versus-difference" has been used as a shorthand to characterize conflicting feminist positions and political strategies. Those who argue that sexual difference ought to be an irrelevant consideration in schools, employment, the courts, and the legislature are put in the equality category. Those who insist that appeals on behalf of women ought to be made in terms of the needs, interests, and characteristics common to women as a group are placed in the difference category.[1] In the clashes over the superiority of one or another of these strategies, feminists have invoked history, philosophy, and morality and they have devised new classificatory labels: cultural feminism, liberal feminism, feminist separatism, and the like.[2] Recently the debate about equality and difference has been used to analyze the Sears case, the sex-discrimination suit brought against the retailing giant Sears, Roebuck & Company by the Equal Employment Opportunity Commission (EEOC) in 1978, in which historians Alice Kessler-Harris and Rosalind Rosenberg testified on opposite sides.

There have been many articles written on the Sears case, among them a recent one by Ruth Milkman. Milkman insists that we attend

This essay was first written as an article for a special issue of *Feminist Studies* on the influences of post-structuralism on feminism. This version is a rewriting of that essay, "Deconstructing Equality vs. Difference; or, The Uses of Post-Structuralist Theory for Feminism" (Spring 1988), Vol. 14, No. 1. Material from the original essay is used here with permission of the editors of *Feminist Studies* who hold the copyright. Discussions with Tony Scott first helped me formulate the argument, the thoughtful suggestions of William Connolly, Sanford Levinson, Andrew Pickering, Barbara Herrnstein Smith, and Michael Walzer sharpened and improved it.

to the political context of seemingly timeless principles: "We ignore the political dimensions of the equality-versus-difference debate at our peril, especially in a period of conservative reaction like the present." She concludes:

> As long as this is the political context in which we find ourselves, feminist scholars must be aware of the real danger that arguments about "difference" or "women's culture" will be put to uses other than those for which they were originally developed. That does not mean we must abandon these arguments or the intellectual terrain they have opened up; it does mean that we must be self-conscious in our formulations, keeping firmly in view the ways in which our work can be exploited politically.[3]

Milkman's carefully nuanced formulation implies that equality is our safest course, but she also is reluctant to reject difference entirely. She feels a need to choose a side, but which side is the problem. Milkman's ambivalence is an example of what the legal theorist Martha Minow has labeled in another context "the difference dilemma." Ignoring difference in the case of subordinated groups, Minow points out, "leaves in place a faulty neutrality," while focusing on difference can underscore the stigma of deviance. "Both focusing on and ignoring difference risk recreating it. This is the dilemma of difference."[4] What is required, Minow suggests, is a new way of thinking about difference and this involves rejecting the idea that equality-versus-difference constitutes an opposition. Instead of framing analyses and strategies as if such binary pairs were timeless and true, we need to ask how the dichotomous pairing of equality and difference itself works. Instead of remaining within the terms of existing political discourse, we need to subject those terms to critical examination. Until we understand how the concepts work to constrain and construct specific meanings, we cannot make them work for us.

A close look at the evidence in the Sears case suggests that equality-versus-difference may not accurately depict the opposing sides. During testimony, most of the arguments against equality and for difference were, in fact, made by the Sears lawyers or Rosalind Rosenberg. They constructed an opponent against whom they asserted that men and women differed, that "fundamental differences" —the result of culture or long-standing patterns of socialization— led to women's presumed lack of interest in commission sales jobs. In order to make their own claim that sexual difference and not discrimination could explain the hiring patterns of Sears, the Sears defense attributed to the EEOC an assumption that no one had made in those terms—that women and men had identical interests.[5] Alice Kessler-Harris did not argue that women were the same as men; instead she used a variety of strategies to challenge Rosenberg's assertions. First, she argued that historical evidence suggested far more variety in the jobs women actually took than Rosenberg assumed. Second, she maintained that economic considerations usually offset the effects of socialization in women's attitudes to employment. Wages were an incentive to take new, demanding, or atypical positions. And third, she pointed out that, historically, job segregation by sex was the consequence of employer preferences, not employee choices. The question of women's choices could not be resolved, Kessler-Harris suggested, when the hiring process itself predetermined the outcome, imposing generalized gendered criteria that were not necessarily relevant to the work at hand. The debate joined then not around equality-versus-difference but around the relevance of general ideas of sexual difference in a specific context.[6]

To make the case for employer discrimination EEOC lawyers cited obviously biased job applicant questionnaires and statements by personnel officers, but they had no individuals to testify that they had experienced discrimination. Kessler-Harris referred to past patterns of sexual segregation in the job market as the product of employer choices, but mostly she invoked history to break down Rosenberg's contention that women as a group differed consistently in the details of their behavior from men, instead insisting that variety characterized female job choices (as it did male job choices), that it made no sense in this case to talk about women as a uniform group. She defined equality to mean a presumption that women and men might have an equal interest in sales commission jobs. She did not claim that women and men, by definition, had such an equal interest. Rather Kessler-Harris and the EEOC called into question the relevance for hiring decisions of generalizations about the necessarily antithetical behaviors of women and men. The EEOC argued that hiring at Sears reflected inaccurate and inapplicable notions of sexual difference; Sears argued that "fundamental" differences between the sexes (and not its own actions) explained the gender imbalances in its labor force.

The Sears case was complicated by the fact that almost all of the evidence offered was statistical. The testimony of the historians, therefore, could only be inferential at best. Neither historian had much information about what had actually happened at Sears; rather each of them sought to explain small statistical disparities by reference to gross generalizations about the entire history of working women. Moreover, in a kind of parody of positivism they were forced to swear to the truth or falsehood of these generalizations that had been developed for purposes other than legal contestation and they were forced to treat their interpretive premises as matters of fact. Reading the cross-examination of Kessler-Harris is revealing in this respect. Each of her carefully nuanced explanations of women's work history was forced into a reductive assertion by the Sears lawyers' insistence that she answer questions only by saying yes or no. Similarly, Rosalind Rosenberg's rebuttal to Kessler-Harris eschewed the historian's subtle contextual reading of evidence and sought instead to impose a test of absolute consistency. She juxtaposed Kessler-Harris's testimony in the trial to her earlier published work in an effort to show that Kessler-Harris had misled the court.[7] (In court, Kessler-Harris argued that history showed a profusion of job choices by women; her book suggested that women "preferred" work that could be combined with domestic responsibilities.)[8] Outside the courtroom, however, the disparities of the Kessler-Harris argument could also be explained in other ways: in relationship to a labor history that had typically excluded women, it might make sense to overgeneralize about women's experience, emphasizing difference in order to demonstrate that the universal term "worker" was really a male reference that could not account for all aspects of women's job experiences. In relationship to an employer who sought to justify discrimination by reference to sexual difference, it made more sense to deny the totalizing effects of difference by stressing instead the diversity and complexity of women's behavior and motivation. In the first case, difference served a positive function, unveiling the inequity hidden in a presumably neutral term; in the second case, difference served a negative purpose, justifying what Kessler-Harris believed to be unequal treatment. Although the inconsistency might have been avoided with a more self-conscious analysis of "the difference dilemma," Kessler-Harris's different positions were quite legitimately different emphases for different contexts; only in a courtroom could they be taken as proof of bad faith.[9]

The exacting demands of the courtroom for consistency and "truth" point up the profound difficulties of arguing about difference. Although the testimony of the historians had to explain only a relatively small statistical disparity in the numbers of women and men hired for full-time commission sales jobs, the explanations that were preferred were totalizing and categorical.[10] In cross-examination, Kessler-Harris's multiple interpretations were found to be contradictory and confusing, while the judge praised Rosenberg for her coherence and lucidity.[11] In part, that was because Rosenberg held to a tight model that unproblematically linked socialization to individual choice; in part it was because her descriptions of gender differences accorded with prevailing normative views. Kessler-Harris, in contrast, had trouble finding a simple and singular model that would at once acknowledge difference *and* refuse it as an acceptable explanation for the Sears employment pattern. So she fell into great difficulty maintaining consistency in the face of hostile questioning. On the one hand, she seemed to be assuming that economic opportunism equally affected men and women (and thus that men and women were the same). How then explain the gender differences her own work had identified? On the other hand, she was tarred (by Rosenberg) with the brush of subversion, for implying that all employers might have some interest in sex-typing the labor force, for deducing from her own (presumably Marxist) theory a "conspiratorial" conclusion about Sears's behavior.[12] If the patterns of discrimination that Kessler-Harris alluded to were real, after all, one of their effects might well be the kind of difference Rosenberg pointed out. Caught within the framework of Rosenberg's categorical use of historical evidence, Kessler-Harris and her lawyers relied on an essentially negative strategy, offering details designed to complicate and undercut Rosenberg's assertions. Kessler-Harris neither challenged the theoretical shortcomings of Rosenberg's socialization model nor offered an alternative model of her own. That would have required, I think, either fully developing the case for employer discrimination or insisting more completely on the "differences" line of argument by exposing the "equality-versus-difference" formulation as an illusion.

In the end the most nuanced arguments of Kessler-Harris were rejected as contradictory or inapplicable and the judge decided in Sears's favor, repeating the defense argument that "an assumption of equal interest was unfounded" because of the differences between women and men.[13] Not only was the EEOC position rejected, but Sears's hiring policies were implicitly endorsed. According to the judge, since difference was real and fundamental, it could explain statistical variations in Sears's hiring. Discrimination was redefined as simply the recognition of "natural" difference (however historically or culturally produced), fitting in nicely with the logic of Reagan conservatism. Difference was substituted for inequality, the appropriate antithesis of equality, becoming inequality's explanation and legitimation. The judge's decision illustrates a process literary scholar Naomi Schor has described in another context: it "essentializes difference and naturalizes social inequity."[14]

The Sears case offers a sobering lesson in the operation of a discursive, that is a political, field. It provides insight not only into the manipulation of concepts and definitions but also into the implementation and justification of institutional and political relationships. References to categorical differences between women and men set the terms within which Sears defended its policies *and* the EEOC challenged them. Equality-versus-difference was the intellectual trap within which historians argued not about tiny statistical disparities in Sears employment practices but about the normative behavior of men versus women. Although we might conclude that the balance of power was against the EEOC by the time the case was heard and that, therefore, its outcome was inevitable, part of the Reagan plan to reverse affirmative action programs of the 1970s, we still need to articulate a critique of what happened that can inform the next round of political encounter. How should that position be conceptualized?

When equality and difference are paired dichotomously, they structure an impossible choice. If one opts for equality, one is forced to accept the notion that difference is antithetical to it. If one opts for difference, one admits that equality is unattainable. That, in a sense, is the dilemma apparent in Ruth Milkman's statement cited at the outset of this essay. Feminists cannot give up "difference"; it has been our most creative analytic tool. We cannot give up equality, at least as long as we want to speak to the principles and values of a democratic political system. But it makes no sense for the feminist movement to let its arguments be forced into preexisting categories, its political disputes be characterized by a dichotomy we did not invent. How then do we recognize and use notions of sexual difference and yet make arguments for equality? The only response is a double one: the unmasking of the power relationship constructed by posing equality as the antithesis of difference, and the refusal of its consequent dichotomous construction of political choices.

Equality-versus-difference cannot structure choices for feminist politics; the oppositional pairing misrepresents the relationship of both terms. Equality, in the political theory of rights that lies behind the claims of excluded groups for justice, means the ignoring of differences between individuals for a particular purpose or in a particular context. Michael Walzer puts it this way:

> The root meaning of equality is negative; egalitarianism in its origins is an abolitionist politics. It aims at eliminating not all differences, but a particular set of differences, and a different set in different times and places.[15]

This presumes a social agreement to consider obviously different people as equivalent (not identical) for a stated purpose. In this usage, the opposite of equality is inequality or inequivalence, the noncommensurability of individuals or groups in certain circumstances, for certain purposes. Thus, for purposes of democratic citizenship the measure of equivalence has been, at different times, independence, or ownership of property, or race, or sex. The political notion of equality thus includes, indeed depends on, an acknowledgment of the existence of difference. Demands for equality have rested on implicit and usually unrecognized arguments from difference; if individuals or groups were identical or the same there would be no need to ask for equality. Equality, therefore, might well be defined as deliberate indifference to specified differences.

The antithesis of difference in most usages is sameness or identity. But even here the contrast and the context must be specified. There is nothing self-evident or transcendent about difference, even if the fact of difference—sexual difference, for example—seems apparent to the naked eye. The questions always ought to be, What qualities or aspects are being compared? What is the nature of the comparison? How is the meaning of difference being constructed? Yet in the Sears testimony and in some debates among feminists, (sexual) difference is assumed to be an immutable fact, its meaning inherent in the categories male and female. The Sears lawyers put it this way: "The reasonableness of the EEOC's a priori assumptions of male/female sameness with respect to preferences, interest, and qualifications is . . . the crux of the issue."[16] The point of the EEOC challenge, however, was never sameness but the irrelevance of categorical differences.

The opposition men-versus-women, as Rosenberg employed it, asserted the incomparability of the sexes and, though history and socialization were the explanatory factors, these resonated with categorical distinctions inferred from the facts of bodily difference. When the opposition men-versus-women is invoked, as it was in the Sears case, it refers a specific issue (the small statistical discrepancy between women and men hired for commission sales jobs) back to a general principle (the "fundamental" differences between women and men). The differences within each group that might apply to this particular situation—the fact, for example, that some women might choose "aggressive" or "risk-taking" jobs, or that some women might prefer high- to low-paying positions—were excluded by definition in the antithesis between the two groups. The irony is, of course, that the statistical case required only a small percentage of women's behaviors to be explained. Yet the historical testimony argued categorically about "women." It thus became difficult to argue (as the EEOC and Kessler-Harris tried to) that, within the female category, women typically exhibit and participate in all sorts of "male" behaviors, that socialization is a complex process that does not yield uniform choices. To make the argument would have required a direct attack on categorical thinking about gender. For the generalized opposition male-versus-female serves to obscure the differences among women in behavior, character, desire, subjectivity, sexuality, gender identification, and historical experience. Kessler-Harris's insistence on the specificity (and historically variable aspect) of women's actions seemed like so many special cases, so many ultimately irrelevant exceptions, because she did not present a fully theorized alternative to Rosenberg's insistence on the primacy of sexual difference.

The alternative to the binary construction of sexual difference is not sameness, identity, or androgyny. By subsuming women into a general "human" category, we lose the specificity of female diversity and women's experiences; we are back, in other words, to the days when "Man's" story was supposed to be everyone's story, when women were "hidden from history," when the feminine served as the negative counterpoint, the "Other," for the construction of positive masculine identity. It is not sameness *or* identity between women and men that we want to claim, but a more complicated historically variable diversity than is permitted by insisting that male and female are antithetical categories, a diversity that is also differently expressed for different purposes in different contexts. In effect the duality this opposition creates draws one line of difference, invests it with biological explanations, and then treats each side of the opposition as a unitary phenomenon. Everything within each category (male or female) is assumed to be the same; hence differences within either category are suppressed. In addition, the relationship between the categories is presented as one between positive (male) and negative (female) poles. In contrast, our goal is to see not only differences between the sexes but the way these work to repress differences within gender groups. The sameness constructed on each side of the binary opposition hides the multiple play of differences and maintains their irrelevance and invisibility.

Placing equality and difference in antithetical relationship has, then, a double effect. It denies the way in which difference has long figured in political notions of equality and it suggests that sameness is the only ground on which equality can be claimed. It thus puts feminists in an impossible position, for as long as we argue within the terms of discourse set up by this opposition we grant the current conservative premise that since women cannot be identical to men in all respects, they cannot expect to be equal to them. The only alternative, it seems to me, is to refuse to oppose equality to difference and insist continually on differences—differences as the condition of individual and collective identities, differences as the constant challenge to the fixing of those identities, history as the repeated illustration of the play of differences, differences as the very meaning of equality itself.

Alice Kessler-Harris's experience in the Sears case shows, however, that the assertion of differences in the face of gender categories is not a sufficient strategy. What is required in addition is an analysis of fixed gender categories as normative statements that organize cultural understandings of sexual difference. This means that we must open to scrutiny the terms "men" and "women" as they are used to define one another in particular contexts—workplaces, for example. The history of women's work needs to be retold from this perspective as part of the story of the creation of a gendered work force. In the nineteenth century, for example, certain concepts of male skill rested on a contrast with female labor (by definition unskilled). The organization and reorganization of work processes was accomplished by reference to the gender attributes of workers, rather than to issues of training, education, or social class. And wage differentials between the sexes were attributed to fundamentally different family roles that preceded (rather than followed from) employment arrangements. In all these processes the meaning of "worker" was established through a contrast between the presumably natural qualities of men and women. If we write the history of women's work by gathering data that describe the activities, needs, interests, and culture of "women workers," we leave in place the naturalized contrast and reify a fixed categorical difference between women and men. We start the story, in order words, too late, by uncritically accepting a gendered category (the "woman worker") that itself needs investigation because its meaning is relative to its history.

If in our histories we relativize the categories man and woman, of course, it means we must also recognize the contingent and specific nature of our political claims. Political strategies then will rest on analyses of the utility of certain arguments in certain discursive contexts, without, however, invoking absolute qualities for women or men. There are moments when it makes sense for mothers to demand consideration for their social role, and contexts within which motherhood is irrelevant to women's behavior; but to maintain that womanhood is motherhood is to obscure the differences that make choice possible. There are moments when it makes sense to demand a reevaluation of the status of what has been socially constructed as women's work ("comparable worth" strategies are the current example), and contexts within which it makes much more sense to prepare women for entry into "nontraditional" jobs; but to maintain that femininity predisposes women to certain (nurturing) jobs or (collaborative) styles of work is to naturalize complex economic and social processes and, once again, to obscure the differences that have characterized women's occupational histories. An insistence on differences undercuts the tendency to absolutist and, in the case of sexual difference, essentialist categories. It does not deny the existence of gender difference, but it does suggest that its meanings are always relative to particular constructions in specified contexts. In contrast, absolutist categorizations of difference end up always enforcing normative rules.

It is surely not easy to formulate a "deconstructive" political strategy in the face of powerful tendencies that construct the world in binary terms. Yet there seems to me no other choice. Perhaps as we learn to think this way solutions will become more readily apparent. Perhaps the theoretical and historical work we do can prepare the ground. Certainly we can take heart from the history of feminism, which is full of illustrations of refusals of simple dichotomies and attempts instead to demonstrate that equality requires the recognition and inclusion of differences.[17] Indeed, one way historians could contribute to a genuine rethinking of these concepts is to stop writing the history of feminism as a story of oscillations between demands for equality and affirmations of difference. This approach inadvertently strengthens the hold of the binary construction, establishing it as somewhat inevitable by giving it a long history.[18] When looked at closely, in fact, the arguments of feminists do not usually fall into these neat compartments; they are instead attempts to reconcile theories of equal rights with cultural concepts of sexual difference, to question the validity of normative constructions of gender in the light of the existence of behaviors and qualities that contradict the rules, to point up rather than resolve conditions of contradiction, to articulate a political identity for women without conforming to existing stereotypes about them.

In histories of feminism and in feminist political strategies there needs to be at once attention to the operations of difference and an insistence on differences, but not a simple substitution of multiple for binary difference, for it is not a happy pluralism we ought to invoke. The resolution of the "difference dilemma" comes neither from ignoring nor embracing difference as it is normatively constituted. Instead it seems to me that the critical feminist position must always involve *two* moves: the first, systematic criticism of the operations of categorical difference, exposure of the kinds of exclusions and inclusions—the hierarchies—it constructs, and a refusal of their ultimate "truth." A refusal, however, not in the name of an equality that implies sameness or identity but rather (and this is the second move) of an equality that rests on differenc*es*—differences that confound, disrupt, and render ambiguous the meaning of any fixed binary opposition. To do anything else is to buy into the political argument that sameness is a requirement for equality, an untenable position for feminists (and historians) who know that power is constructed on, and so must be challenged from, the ground of difference.

— 9 —

American Women Historians, 1884–1984

Histories of the progress of democracy, of the expanding participation of individuals and groups in social and political life, often assume a kind of mechanical model for change. The emphasis is placed on gaining access to resources, spaces, institutions. Access has a physical connotation—approaching, entering, using. The idea of access is represented metaphorically as passages through doors and gates, over obstacles, barriers, and blockages. Accessibility is most often measured quantitatively—the number of individuals or members of groups who gain entry. While this kind of discussion has been useful and important for detecting discrimination or democratization, it has also drawn attention away from certain qualitative issues. How are those who cross the thresholds received? If they belong to a group different from the one already "inside," what are the terms of their incorporation? How do the new arrivals understand their relationship to the place they have entered? What are the terms of identity they establish?

These questions assume that entry alone does not solve all the

This essay has a long history. I began to do research on American women historians in preparation for a talk at the Berkshire Conference on The History of Women in June 1981. That talk was published as "Politics and the Profession: Women Historians in the 1980's," in *Women's Studies Quarterly* (Fall 1981) IX. I continued my research for another talk, this time at the American Historical Association in December 1984. The version printed here was written expressly for the special issue of *Daedalus,* "Learning about Women: Gender, Politics and Power" (Fall, 1987), and was published as "History and Difference." I am grateful to Jill Conway and Jacqueline Goggin for their critical readings of the first draft of this essay, and to Goggin for generously providing me with information she has gathered in her own extensive work on the subject of American women historians.

problems of discrimination, that organizations and institutions are hierarchically differentiated systems, that physical access is not the end of the story. The questions are relevant generally for the study of social organization, but they have been posed most forcefully by those interested in gender and race. That ought not to be surprising, since our culture has embodied difference in generative organs and skin color. The experience of the bearers of these marks of difference poses a challenge to physical models of access, for it belies the conclusion that all that matters is getting in the door.

The question of difference is often posed sociologically, but it is also conceptual or cultural. The social practices of the members of a craft or profession are intimately related to the ways they interpret the meaning of their work. The knowledge said to be vested in a profession, such as medicine or history, also helps to inform its structure, organization, and membership. In history, for example, the notion of an archetypical actor, a universal human agent, was usually embodied in a (white) male. Although it was assumed that Universal Man stood for all humankind, in fact this representation created hierarchies and exclusions. Women, blacks, and various others were either invisible as historical subjects or somehow depicted as less central, less important than white men. Until recently, most history written exemplified the centrality of white men and the marginalization of most others. As in written history, so in the organization of the historical profession, white men predominated; women, blacks, and others occupied a clearly secondary place. Since the 1960s, there have been changes both in written history and in the historical profession and these are related. Both developments involve what might be called the fall or, better, the particularization of Universal Man. It has become less possible to subsume historical subjects under a single category of Man, and simultaneously women, blacks, and others have become visible and increasingly important both as subjects of history and as professional historians.

It is through an examination of the articulation of difference, of the hierarchical and unequal relationships among different groups, that the interdependencies of knowledge and organizational behavior are most evident. We can better understand the full meaning of occupational identities when we see not only who is included in them but how differences among practitioners are dealt with, which differences matter, how they are understood, and whether and how they change over time. Difference then provides insight into what might be called the culture of a profession, or the politics of a discipline.

My focus in this essay is on a particular kind of difference—gender or sexual difference. I examine the women historians who, by virtue of holding the Ph.D. in history, an academic position, and membership in the American Historical Association, were recognized as members of the profession of history. Having accepted the discipline in its double sense—as a system of training and a system of rules—they qualified from the beginning as professionals. Their inclusion in an elite body of professionals, however, was not without complications. For while they assumed that access ought to give them full entitlement to professional identity, they regularly encountered reminders of their difference. Their perceptions of and reactions to different treatment varied over time and in accordance with many factors, not the least of which were their understandings of history (their conception of the knowledge they professed) and their definition of who was included as a historical subject. The experience of women historians as they grappled with the problem of difference points up the powerful obstacle to equality posed by concepts of history that posit a unitary process experienced by a representative Universal Man.

[I]

When the American Historical Association (AHA) was founded in 1884 women were explicitly included as members. The Executive Council resolved that "there is nothing in the Constitution . . . to prevent the admission of women into the Association upon the same qualifications as those required of men."[1] In the effort to organize the discipline, women were acceptable especially if they had some university training and self-consciously practiced the scientific method considered so crucial to the new professional history. The fact of holding an advanced degree granted women nominal membership in the tiny elite of scholars who constituted the AHA.[2] Even those who did not hold the Ph.D. were considered eligible; for the shared goal of founders such as J. Franklin Jameson and Herbert Baxter Adams was to disseminate history throughout the nation with the help of talented researchers and teachers. Despite this seemingly open policy, however, women were treated differently once admitted to the AHA. The treatment was sometimes subtle, sometimes quite explicitly discriminatory, and it rested always on the assumption that, ultimately, visible bodily difference mattered.

Recruiting women to the Association fit with the larger democratic mission of the organization's founders. They were determined to wrest history from the gentlemen antiquarians whose practice they felt undermined the tenets of science.[3] Indeed, they constructed the image of the new professional history in direct opposition to romantic antiquarianism. To an earlier focus on picturesque traditions and romantic incidents, what medieval historian Nellie Neilson referred to scornfully as "the praise of ladies dead and lovely knights," they opposed the more difficult study of institutions and politics.[4] And they attacked as elitist and somehow unscientific the notion that good historians must have classical training and literary sensibility. Jameson articulated the issue clearly in 1891:

> Now it is the spread of thoroughly good second-class work . . . that our science most needs at present; for it sorely needs the improvement in technical process, that superior finish of workmanship, which a large number of works of talent can do more to foster than a few works of literary genius.[5]

By including women in the AHA, the founders underscored their democratic and leveling impulse, their desire to "bring all the historical resources of the nation within the purview of [the] Association," and their belief that their science could be mastered by any intelligent person.[6] There was, indeed, an important point made by the fact that women practiced scientific history: the power of objective investigation was such that it overcame any feminine predisposition to pursue quaint or esoteric topics. There was as well a complicated symbolic dimension that relied on the oppositions masculine/feminine and male/female. Whatever the sex of its practitioners, the old history was represented as feminine, the new as masculine. By enlisting women on the side of scientific history, its proponents demonstrated that they had vanquished what aristocratic and romantic tendencies remained in their newly organized discipline.

There were, to be sure, also quite straightforward reasons to bring women into the new Association. They represented an important institutional constituency for the creation of history departments and the implementation of standardized history curricula in the high schools, academies, and colleges of the nation. If the new history were to triumph, it must be properly taught; AHA founders therefore approached teaching with missionary zeal. In the 1880s and 1890s, women's colleges represented a significant component of the academic world and (although headed by men) they were increasingly staffed by female teachers. Women members of the AHA could thus serve the particularly useful function of bringing history into their separate strongholds—the women's academies and colleges. Nellie Neilson fulfilled that task at Mt. Holyoke College; Lucy Maynard Salmon, whose field was American History, did the same at Vassar. When she was hired in 1887, President James Taylor wrote to Herbert

Baxter Adams that the "inadequate provision" for history at his institution would soon be remedied. "The recent appointment of Miss Salmon . . . will doubtless result in the satisfactory reorganization of the entire department."[7]

At one level, AHA spokesmen insisted on a uniform history curriculum, making no distinctions between what was to be taught to women and what to men. They saw no irony in the practice of teaching history, employed in the 1880s and 1890s at Wellesley as at Johns Hopkins, that assigned to students the roles of members of the English House of Commons and had them debate major issues of constitutional and legislative policy.[8] (That women had no vote and no formal political role in either the United States or England was apparently irrelevant to the substance and method of this pedagogy.) In addition, women were not excluded as objects of historical interest. Adams, for example, urged that history's scope go beyond a focus on great men, reminding his colleagues of

> The unnumbered thousands, yea millions, of good men and true, and of faithful, devoted women . . . [who] support good leadership and carry humanity forward from generation to generation. It is often the biography of some plain man, like Abraham Lincoln, or some self-sacrificing woman, like Florence Nightingale, that affords the greatest encouragement and incentive to ordinary humanity. But we must remember that no man, no woman is worthy of biographical or historical record, unless in some way he or she has contributed to the welfare of society and the progress of the world.[9]

Despite some gestures in the direction of symmetry, however, the history promoted in these years treated men and women asymmetrically. This followed from the way history was conceptualized; from its assumption that processes of change were evolutionary, linear, and unitary. Welfare and progress were essentially political concepts and progress was measured as movement toward democratic self-government. Adams advocated the study of "towns, plantations, parishes and counties" as well as states and nations. Large and small, the units of analysis were polities and the conception of study was unitary and integrated.[10] The small units echoed the large; they provided ways of understanding how political organization worked and under what circumstances it progressed.[11]

The notion of history as the study of progress toward democracy assumed a linear and universal process applicable at different rates and in different forms to all people. The assumption of unity and universality made it possible to include all sorts of different groups in history, but it also made specification of their difference unnecessary. A single, prototypical figure represented the historical subject: white, Western man. The study of history for Adams and his colleagues was the study of politics and this meant the study of "man in organized society." The purpose of such study was self-knowledge, which "leads to self-determination and self-control." Beyond that, the teaching of history had important political consequences, for it led to "self-government . . . the highest and best result of the experience of man in society."[12] In pointing to these examples of Man as the subject of history, I do not mean to say that historians like Adams excluded women from their conception; they did not. Rather they subsumed women, included them in a generalized, unified conception that was at once represented in the idea of Man, but was always different from and subordinate to it. The feminine was but a particular instance; the masculine a universal signifier.

The consequences of such thinking were at once to deny and to recognize difference—to deny it by refusing to acknowledge that women (or other Others such as blacks and Jews) might have a fundamentally different historical experience; to recognize it by somehow disqualifying for equal treatment those different from the universal figure. This double effect was evident in the way history was written: (middle-class) white men were the typical subjects, acting to make things happen, while women were represented (if at all) as "devoted" and "faithful," ensuring generational continuity through timeless reproductive roles that were outside history. It was also evident in institutional and organizational arrangements, in the leadership structure, for example, of the AHA. For despite the AHA's gestures of formal inclusiveness, it was simply taken for granted that the members who really mattered, as well as the leaders, were white men. The language of universality rested on, contained within it, differentiations that resulted in unequal treatment for women in relation to men.

Adams worked hard to keep women as members of the organization, but it was always clear that they were women, special individuals differentiated not by achievement or training but by their presumed "natural" endowments and by their association with women's colleges. At AHA meetings, for example, there was an annual smoker for "the men of the Association." The ladies—wives of historians and female historians—attended a Colonial Dame's Tea. Women protested against this practice, but their objections were ignored. Lucy Salmon wrote in 1905, for example, "We do not care for afternoon teas where we meet society women, and deprecate entertainments that separate the members into two classes, men and women."[13] The AHA never went beyond tokenism when it came to including women in leadership positions. Lucy Salmon was the sole woman to serve on special committees (including eventually the Executive Council) in the early period, but when she urged Adams to include another woman on the Committee of Seven (the group concerned with the teaching of history), he wrote to a friend that he was "inclined to think that one woman is enough!"[14] In 1919, then a member of the Council, Salmon lamented her inability to increase the numbers of women sharing power in the AHA:

> I do not wish to seem to press the names of women for membership on any of these committees; and yet, as I think I have written more than once before, I can but feel that the Association has by self-denying ordinance been deprived of the services of a good many women.[15]

This situation, so evident at the outset, continued well into the 1960s. Arthur Link has noted that for most of the AHA's history "women were given short shrift in positions of leadership and governance." He cites as evidence the facts that only five women were included among the 96 members of the Executive Council before 1933 and that women were represented on committees in a ratio of about one to nine, an underrepresentation in relation to female membership in the Association.[16]

Although there were high and low points for women in the AHA, these never resulted in a clear end to discriminatory treatment. The 1920s and 1930s, for example, saw an increase in the numbers of women receiving the Ph.D. and employed in history departments (especially in women's colleges). Yet as the prestige and power of research universities increased in this period, women were increasingly marginalized by their confinement to undergraduate faculties and female institutions.[17] Within the AHA they constituted about 19 percent of members in 1920, but not 5 percent of the leadership.[18] The prevailing tone was of an elite male club whose formal structure and informal social practices marginalized women. The patterns continued with little variation into the postwar period. Howard K. Beale, writing in 1953, noted that "discrimination against women is persistent," and he linked it to a larger set of biases "against Negroes, Jews, Catholics, women, and persons not 'gentlemen' " that operated throughout the profession of history.[19] The effects of these biases were systematically documented as they affected women, by a special committee set up in 1970 in response to demands by women historians for a change in treatment. These women argued that the recruitment of large numbers of women to the field of history, in process since the mid-1960s, would not itself guarantee equality; rather there had to be explicit attention to eradicating discrimination.[20] The committee report, known as the Rose Report (for its chair, Willie Lee Rose), provided extensive evidence of the long history of the systematic underrepresentation of women within the AHA and the profession as a whole, and it recommended the creation of a standing Committee on Women Historians to provide advocacy and to monitor statistics in an effort to "secure greater equity for women as prospective students and teachers of history."[21] By appointing this committee, the AHA formally acknowledged the persistence of gender differentiation and the need to attend to it as a long-term structural problem.

In the history of women in the AHA, one moment does stand out as a distinct exception to otherwise exclusionary practices at the leadership level. In 1943 a woman became President of the Association. Yet the election of Nellie Neilson to the AHA presidency did not signal the beginning of a new era. Instead it indicated the brief triumph of what seems to have been a coalition of "progressive" historians and organized feminists, in the larger context of coalitions and popular-front mobilizations against fascism on the eve of America's entry into World War II. Neilson's nomination as second vice-president (putting her automatically in line for the presidency) came in 1940, a year that was particularly auspicious for its attention not only to women but to other previously neglected groups. Under Merle Curti's chairmanship the program committee arranged several sessions on the theme of the "Common Man." Selig Perlman spoke on "Class in American Labor History," W. E. B. DuBois chaired a panel on "The Negro in the History of the United States," and Mildred Thompson, of Vassar College, presided over a session on women in history—the first time a full session was devoted to women's history at an AHA conference.[22] The attention to women's history and the election of Neilson came as a result of years of lobbying by women, some of them organized in the Berkshire Conference of Women Historians (founded in 1929), others simply acting on deeply held feminist commitments. They were active enough in 1939 for the chair of the Nominating Committee to note in his report the existence of a "feminist block [*sic*]."[23] Their pressure coincided with the determination of "progressives" like Curti and Beale to practice democracy within the Association, symbolically and actually to assert history's connection to the democratic processes it chronicled—at the very moment that constitutionalism and liberalism were under seige in Europe. The committee was explicit about its goal of including women and wrote to all AHA members in May 1940 urging them to nominate and vote for "women of distinction" who "have not had sufficient recognition among the Association's officers."[24]

The election of Neilson, however, did not constitute or even set in process an evolution toward equality for women. The general pattern of underrepresentation persisted even under her presidency and, as the war came to an end, it was intensified by a decline in the numbers of women receiving Ph.D.'s and jobs in history.[25] In addition, a new discourse emerged that emphasized the masculine qualities of the historian, associating them with the preservation of national traditions and democracy, scholarly activities that evoked renewed commitment to the heroism of the war effort, though now in time of peace and Cold War. Calling for greater appreciation of businessmen's efforts to build America, Allan Nevins suggested in 1951, for example, that historians abandon "feminine idealism" and portray businessmen in "their true proportions as builders of an indispensable might."[26] (The contrast between idealism and materialism, sentimentality and "might" was presented as a contrast between femininity and masculinity; and, although it did not speak about women directly, it had clear implications for the association of Cold War ideology and gender in the depiction of the typical historian.)

"I have seen in my generation the rise, and now the beginning of the closing of doors to women," wrote Beatrice Hyslop, a historian of the French Revolution, as she contemplated retirement from Hunter College in 1969.[27] Hyslop's comments referred to the 1950s and early 1960s in contrast to the years of her doctoral work in the early 1930s. Ironically, she wrote just as a great transition began, but it would still be many years before women were regularly included in positions of power in the AHA and not until 1987 that a second woman assumed the office of President.[28]

[II]

The AHA formally endorsed inclusiveness and spoke a language of universality that nonetheless rested on differences. Representing the typical historian and the typical historical actor as a (white) male made women a particular and troubling exception. Their likeness to the universal type could not be taken for granted; rather it had to be demonstrated, proven, in the behavior of any individual woman. Thus, whatever their skills and training, women had the further challenge of repudiating the disabilities assumed to attach to their sex. This was no easy task, whatever strategy was adopted. One could choose to ignore systems of differentiation, accepting their limits and operating within them; but this, of course, left the systems in place and often placed a great burden on the individual woman, who attributed the treatment she received to her own failings. One could attribute specific instances of discrimination to individual misogyny, and thus avoid a systemic analysis. One could acknowledge the way gender differences led to unequal treatment and condemn them as violations of democratic principles either individually or collectively. One could affirm the difference of women and elevate it to a position of complementarity or even superiority to men. Either in the name of equality or in the name of difference, collective action by women could be politically extremely effective; but it carried with it the potential for underscoring the fact of women's separate and different identity, of pointing up rather than playing down the contrast between historians and women historians.

The history of professional women historians since 1884 illustrates all of these strategies. Sometimes, in fact, individuals used combinations of them in the course of their lives. It is interesting to examine some of them in detail because they provide another way of grasping the operations of a profession as a differentiated system and we can understand the effects of such a system on the individuals perceived to be different. Here I will focus on those strategies that recognized and sought to combat discrimination; they enable us to see how professional women historians formulated their critiques in relation to prevailing concepts of history.[29]

Lucy Salmon's strategy was to insist that women be included in the universal idea of humanity. If this were the case, then the practice of excluding women contradicted notions of universality and equality and led, as she made clear to the AHA, to a waste of available talent. She believed firmly in coeducation (she held her bachelor's and master's degrees from the University of Michigan), though she always taught at a women's college. While she accepted the limits of available employment, she constantly battled President Taylor's attempts to regulate women faculty members' lives at Vassar.[30] Women, she felt, ought to be treated no differently from men. They were, after all, meant to be included in the universal figure of Man; any other interpretation was irrational or unjust.

It was precisely because Salmon considered women part of the definition of the human that she actively campaigned for the vote. For her, suffrage would be a way of furthering equality, of granting women full membership in society. In fact, society would be the ultimate beneficiary because so many more talented and able people would be formally involved in the business of politics. Once won, the vote would guarantee the full participation of women in a variety of political institutions, including, undoubtedly, professional associations.

Salmon based her argument on her general belief (shared with her professional colleagues and evident in all the history she wrote) that history meant progress toward democracy and equality. She saw prejudice against her sex as a matter of individual attitudes, the relic of a less civilized past destined eventually to disappear, or the result of insufficient experience, intelligence, or education. Thus, she wrote of Woodrow Wilson, with whom she had studied for the Ph.D. at Bryn Mawr, that his life was governed by narrow and self-serving ambition. Furthermore, he did not like teaching and

> he was singularly ill-adapted to teaching women. He had apparently never had any of the normal relationships of life with women, he assumed that women were quite different from men, and he made, I felt, no effort to understand them. He always assumed that they were intellectually different from men and that, therefore, they would not interest him. I am quite sure that he never whole-heartedly believed in college education for women. He once said to me that a woman who had married an intellectual, educated man was often better educated than a woman who had had college training. All of this used to amuse me and I never presented any other side of the subject to him or stated my own views—it would have been useless to do so. I felt that his opinions were simply derived from a limited educational and social experience and hoped he would some time learn better![31]

Like many of her contemporaries, Salmon participated in professional life assuming (even as she recognized discrimination) that equal treatment was her due. For her, "progress lay in the direction of obliterating rather than emphasizing the differences between men and women."[32] Salmon's biographer notes that she "distrusted any movement which recognized a special 'woman's sphere' " and she refused to acknowledge it in her writing, in her professional and political activities, and in her personal deportment.[33] Such recognition would only perpetuate the false idea that biological differences between the sexes could be the basis for educational or professional distinctions. Individual efforts to remove prejudice were, in Salmon's view, preferable to collective action because such action inevitably accepted difference. "Do not think," she wrote to a colleague, "that . . . I am not interested in the work that women are doing, I am intensely interested in all good work, but not specially because it is done by women." She conceded that women labored under many disabilities, but insisted that these "must be removed . . . by women individually rather than collectively."[34]

Lucy Salmon succeeded in gaining professional prominence during her lifetime; by her own standards she had individually removed obstacles that lay in a woman's path. She increased the participation of women on AHA committees and she also encouraged women students to become historians, relying on a women's network of contacts to nurture and support them. When she died, she was eulogized as an "original" thinker by Edward Cheney, who urged the publication of an unfinished manuscript of hers because "we ought not to allow anything she wrote to disappear."[35] Arguably her work was more serious and profound than that of many of her male associates, including Herbert Baxter Adams. Yet her name virtually disappeared from accounts of the history of the profession, such as John Higham's celebrational *History,* published in 1965. Indeed Higham's *History,* a story of the discipline from its institutionalization in 1884, demonstrates the workings of gender difference and the limits of individualized strategies to deal with it. Not only is Salmon absent from these pages devoted to the leading historians in America, but so are virtually all women (and blacks). No works by women are included in any of the summaries of historiographic debates; Mary Beard appears in two footnotes as the author of a book about her husband and as a co-author with him of a book entirely credited to him in the text; and Nellie Neilson's presidency is not so much as acknowledged even in passing.[36] The invisibility of women in this book is not the result of their absence from the ranks of practicing historians and active AHA members; rather it follows directly from the assumption that a universal male figure (white, Anglo-Saxon) can be used to typify the historical subject and that those different from him are insignificant, less important, because at once represented and excluded by him. To insist, as Salmon did, on the irrelevance of gender difference in the face of this kind of thinking was to attack the effects but not the source of differentiations, exclusions, and discrimination.

Another set of strategies involved explicit reforms of the institutional exclusion of women, sometimes by individuals, sometimes by collectively organized groups. These emerged most forcefully in the 1920s and 1930s, a period of great ferment nationally and within the discipline of history.[37] There were, for example, chairs for women endowed at the research universities in attempts to rectify the virtual absence of women faculty in these male strongholds. George Herbert Palmer was probably following his wife, Alice Freeman's, wishes when he left money to establish a full professorship for a woman in the University of Michigan History Department. Similarly, Florence Porter

Robinson, herself employed to teach Home Economics at Beloit College though she held the Ph.D. in History, left her estate to the University of Wisconsin for a chair in History for a woman. In both cases, the donors stipulated salaries and terms of employment identical to men's.[38]

The issue of positions for women at universities was also taken up by the Berkshire Conference, an organization founded in 1929 by professors at East Coast women's colleges, who wished that "we scattered women historians could get together oftener to exchange ideas." Returning on a train together from an AHA meeting, a group of women discussed the possibility of creating a "greater sense of comradeship in our craft." According to Louise Loomis's recollection, the point was to provide an informal opportunity for discussion and "social contact" among themselves.[39] There was also resentment against a new practice among male historians to gather for informal "conferences" that explicitly excluded women. The Berkshire group implicitly recognized that as women these historians had something in common. Although they insisted they were not a "pressure group," they were in fact an interest group and they exerted pressure in the name of women on the AHA.

From the first meeting, they discussed ways of improving the situation of women historians. They began with a plan to establish a program of exchange professorships so that women could have varied experiences outside the confines of their own institutions. This plan never was implemented, because of the impact of the Depression and because of other more pressing concerns. In the 1930s, in the face of informal discrimination—the preference for hiring men in women's colleges, for example—and of outright discriminatory laws against married women enacted by state and federal legislatures, the Berkshire Conference turned to "the professional outlook for women," examining the comparable hiring patterns, rank, and salary scales for women and men.[40] Emily Hickman, of the New Jersey College for Women, seems to have been the most outspoken and imaginative of the leaders. At one meeting she suggested that the American Association of University Women (AAUW) make "a statistical survey of the possibilities in academic life for women." She also thought that "biographies of eminent women" should be published "with a view to disproving rumors that none is suitable for a [college] presidency." And she turned the group's attention to the inclusion of women in positions of power in the AHA, sending in nomination after nomination, lobbying sympathetic men and urging them to support the nominees.[41]

The Berkshire Conference represented an organized effort to improve the situation of women historians, though it was confined to the East Coast. Acting with a sense of commitment to a feminist cause, women in other regions—sometimes clustered in women's colleges, sometimes isolated in coeducational institutions—also organized campaigns to place women in positions of power. An example is Mary Williams, a Latin American historian who had received the Ph.D. from Stanford in 1914, taught briefly at Wellesley and then at Goucher College, and who began agitating in 1933 (the year Louise Phelps Kellogg—a member of one of several informal women's networks—served on the Nominating Committee)[42] for the nomination of Nellie Neilson to the presidency of the Association.[43] The detailed story of these highly political efforts has yet to be written, but even a glance at them suggests a widespread and determined self-conscious effort by women to challenge the inequities they experienced because of their sex.[44] Unlike Lucy Salmon, these women advocated and undertook collective action to challenge structures of differentiation within their chosen profession.

Clearly, the general ferment of the 1930s contributed to the kinds of action they took. Not only were interest groups a visible part of social and political life during the New Deal; they were increasingly the focus of historians' attention. John Higham has characterized the "new history" that came into full prominence in the 1930s as "progressive history." It focused on conflicts between sections and economic groups; "rather than unity, [it] emphasized diversity."[45] The story of the American heritage told by progressive historians was one of social protest, of the organization of movements that struggled in the name of the less privileged for improvement and change. The idea that there existed a universal human subject did not disappear; indeed, the appeal for equality was made in the name of inalienable human rights. Neither was there change in the optimistic belief that the story of history was a story of progress toward (now social as well as) political democracy. The story was, however, increasingly complicated by the play of competing interest groups.

In this context, women identified themselves as an interest group. Their interest came not from some inherent need or sameness but from the experience of an externally imposed discrimination: shared negative treatment constituted them as a group. They argued that irrelevant biological differences had been invoked to deny them jobs, leadership positions, and power; intellectual capacity and professional ability, they insisted, had nothing to do with sex. Yet if the disabling effects of differentiation were to be fought, collective action by women, as women, was necessary. The point was to include women in whatever was considered human, to insist on the androgyny, as it were, of Universal Man.

Not only did women press their interest as members of the profession of history, they assembled archival sources and a few also wrote histories of women. The creation of new knowledge about women in the past had many goals, the chief of which was simply to establish the fact that women were, as Mary Beard's book title put it, "a force in history."[46] The stress was on women's positive contribution to the building of societies and cultures, a challenge to the presumed passivity or irrelevance of women and therefore to their invisibility in the historical record. Almost by definition, visibility would confer humanity, making self-evident the terms on which equality ought to be practiced.

Feminists of the 1920s and 1930s appealed to democratic principles and the belief in the literal universality of Man to justify their right to full participation in the profession. They assumed their interests were those of all historians; only prejudice prevented their fulfillment for women. On one level, there was nothing in the masculine representation of the historical subject to prevent women's identification with it; they thought of themselves as viable actors capable of effecting change. Yet equality proved more difficult to procure than to demand or organize to achieve, at least in part because Man was less susceptible to pluralization then it seemed. The claim to universality rested on an implied contrast with difference and particularity; as long as Man was universal, the mere existence of Woman demonstrated her specificity. This proved repeatedly to be the case in the AHA, despite articulate and forceful pressures brought to bear by feminists. Beatrice Hyslop pondered the frustrations of the situation in these terms:

> . . . but where a woman has the ability to be a prominent historian, why should there be discrimination just because she is a woman? A young man starting on a career wants an even chance to show his ability and to compete for rewards. Women historians ask for the same equality of opportunity. Too many times they are not even given a chance. . . . Is there something about history . . . that excludes competence on the basis of sex?[47]

Hyslop thought not, but I would suggest there was: differentiation on the basis of sex was implicit in the abstract, but no less gendered, concept of Man as the representative human subject. As long as historical actors and historians were represented as "he," it would be difficult for women to put into effect the equality they believed was their due.

[III]

The 1970s brought another kind of collective strategy by women historians. Committed to equalizing conditions for women and men, the new approach nonetheless emphasized difference in a way that some earlier feminists found discomforting, if not unacceptable. For attention to the interests of women as professionals, the organization of women's caucuses, the publication of separate journals, and the writing of a women's history, all ran the risk of validating, even if only inadvertently, the difference of women from men.

The new emphasis on difference took shape in a national context generated by government policies of affirmative action that established and legitimated movements of organized "interest" groups, of women, blacks, and others. For feminists, the creation by President John F. Kennedy in 1961 of national and state commissions on the status of women set in motion processes that resulted in, among other things, the founding of the National Organization of Women in 1966.[48] Within the AHA, the Coordinating Committee on Women in the Historical Profession (CCWHP) emerged in 1969 as the explicit voice of women's interests.[49] Its pressure led to the formation of the AHA committee that issued the Rose Report in 1970. That report opened a new era for women's participation in the AHA: after 1970 patterns of exclusion began to be reversed, women were appointed to key committees, they were elected to the Council, and they had a significant impact on Association policies, producing guidelines for departments of history, for example, on fairness in hiring and tenure.[50] The standing Committee on Women Historians (CWH), established in the wake of the Rose Report, was the motor for these changes (which were not necessarily permanent.) This committee had enormous practical and symbolic effects. It not only designated women a separate constituency, requiring an advocate of their own, but it gave them access to high-level policy deliberations.

The existence of the CWH at once acknowledged and sought to change the fact that gender differences were used to differentiate and thus to discriminate among historians; at the same time it furthered a separate collective identity for women historians. Women attained undeniable visibility as a definably different group and they won important concessions because of that visibility. Indeed, visibility made it possible to identify the negative operations of differentiation and thus to counter discrimination; it also enabled positive political action by women, as women historians. The difficulty came in establishing the terms of identity: did one simply reverse the valence, accepting differences already assigned to women but assessing them positively, did one substitute other unifying female traits, or did one define the common interest as a rejection of the terms of difference others had imposed? If the last, in what name could difference be refused? Humanity? Didn't that then return to issues of "Man," to women's always problematic relationship to that representation?

These questions (by no means yet answered) were posed even more acutely by another aspect of the feminist politics of the 1970s: the emergence of women's history as a major field of scholarly inquiry. The organizational visibility of women enabled their appearance as historical subjects in association with a general reconceptualization of history itself. Evident by the early 1960s, the new vision of history challenged earlier notions. It was preoccupied, according to Higham's account, "with the tendency of stable structures to break down," with "the disastrous erosion of all institutional authority."[51] It turned away from formal politics to various areas of human experience, including work, family, and sexuality. It questioned the single narrative line of history as progress toward democracy, as well as the accuracy of representing humankind in unitary terms. Historians wrote books about conflict and struggle, about changing modes of domination, social hierarchy, and resistance. In the process they introduced a plurality of historical actors whose special point of view, whose different story, had to be told because its contents and outcome were not the same as that of "typical" white men. Indeed, these formerly typical figures themselves became particularized as only one group among many. The Renaissance was not a "renaissance for women"; the discovery of America became, in part, a story of Indian removal; Manifest Destiny was exposed as an ideological justification for imperialist expansion; and slavery became not a "peculiar institution" but a chapter in the continuing story of American racism.[52] The different stories of women, blacks, the poor, and the colonized were not reducible to a single narrative line about the "American Man." But how could they be told?

For the most part histories of these different groups were necessarily written as separate narratives alongside or in opposition to what was dubbed "mainstream" history. Women's history became a subfield within the discipline, generating a prodigious new scholarship on the lives and experiences of women in the past. The new knowledge demonstrated what previous accounts implicitly denied: women were significant actors, and the history of their lives yielded insight not only into hitherto unstudied realms of human existence but also into well-studied processes of change such as industrialization and urbanization. At the same time, the new knowledge was often cast in terms that affirmed the separateness and difference of women in implicit contrast to the world of man or men already known to history: they had a separate "culture," distinct notions of the meaning of work or family, identifiable artistic or literary signatures, and "female" forms of political consciousness.[53] The documentation of this women's world could become an end in itself; simply establishing its existence was thought to be a sufficient challenge to the "mainstream." Historians assumed they knew what the category "women" was and spent little time investigating its production; rather they ascribed its negative aspects to "patriarchy" or male dominance, its positive aspects to women's resistance or "agency," without in either case examining how "women" acquired social and political meaning in particular contexts.[54] This kind of women's history provided the evidence for the existence of something that could be dubbed, indeed already was assumed to be, a separate female sphere. Having made women visible, historians had also established their difference. This at once could challenge *and* confirm the established narrative—challenge it because its typicality was no longer assured; confirm it because the different stories were so different as to be inconsequential, trivial, parallel but not central to the received story of American democracy.

Both effects are evident in current professional practice. On the one hand, there are historians like Carl Degler who recognize the need for a new concept of history. He writes:

> What is meant by history or the past will have to be changed before [women's history] becomes a part of it . . . since the conventional past was not only conceived (invented?) by men but includes almost by definition, only those activities in which men have been engaged, while ignoring almost entirely the historical activities of women. . . . The challenge is now to rethink our conception of the past we teach and write about so that women . . . are included.[55]

On the other hand, departments of history, for the most part, reject Degler's challenge and treat women's history as a separate field of study, hiring for positions in nineteenth- or twentieth-century social history those who have written about miners or railroad workers, but rejecting as "in the wrong field" those who have written about seamstresses or (female) textile operatives. The common explanation for this kind of action is that "we already have a women's historian." The subject of women for these historians is by definition a particularized subject that lies outside traditionally established fields. What is at stake is a refusal to recognize the particularity and the specificity of men—an inevitable consequence of the "fall" of Universal Man. In the face of this refusal, which evokes tradition, the legacy of civilization, and the return of narrative on its behalf, integrating women into history, just as including women as equals with men in the concept of humanity, is a daunting task.

The various strategies of women historians have all foundered on the issue of difference as a conceptual and structural phenomenon. How to recognize and refuse terms of discrimination, how to act collectively on behalf of women without confirming the "reality" of a separate female sphere—these have been persistent dilemmas, never fully resolved. Indeed, debates about how to resolve them are at the center of current theoretical discussions among feminists—historians and others. The questions posed by women's history are the same as those posed by women's collective action in the profession of history: Can the historical narrative—the great story of Western Civilization or American Democracy—sustain the pluralizing of its subject? Can we conceive of a notion of humanity that is not embodied—not, that is, constructed in gendered terms? Can we expand the concept of the human to include different embodiments of it? Is it possible to think about difference without reference to a standard or norm, without establishing a hierarchical ordering? Not easily or, at least, not yet. The ideal of democracy as the extension of rights (or access) to ever greater numbers of people is confounded by the history of the continuing inequality of different groups. Pluralism as a theory of democratic inclusion ignores the problem of power and the ways in which difference establishes and institutionalizes the various meanings of power. It has been impossible to demand equality without somehow recognizing difference; but too much insistence on difference (as Lucy Salmon pointed out) undercuts claims for equality. This conundrum is the result not of faulty strategies by those seeking equal treatment but of the inability of certain theories of liberalism to take difference—even as it defines equality—into account.[56]

The way out of the equality-difference dilemma seems to me to lie in another direction, one that critically analyzes the categories we most often take for granted: history, women, men, equality, difference, the terms of political theory itself. Instead of assuming we know the meaning of these terms, we need to examine them as they have been developed and used in specific historical contexts, as the products of culture, politics, and time. We cannot write women into history, for example, unless we are willing to entertain the notion that history as a unified story was a fiction about a universal subject whose universality was achieved through implicit processes of differentiation, marginalization, and exclusion. Man was never, in other words, a truly universal figure. It is the processes of exclusion achieved through differentiation that established man's universal plausibility that must, to begin with, constitute the focus for a different, more critical history. One aspect of those processes involved the definition of "women," the attribution of characteristics, traits, and roles in contrast to "men." The difference historians have documented in so much of women's history was produced by these processes, they did not arise from some essential quality inherent in the female sex. Thus "women's experience" or "women's culture" exists only as the expression of female particularity in contrast to male universality; each is a concept by which a certain vision of social life is implemented. Another aspect of these processes of differentiation involved the constant readjustment of the relationship between equality and difference. Equality has never been an absolute practice, rather it is the suspension for certain purposes in certain contexts of the exclusions enforced against certain differences; historically some differences have mattered more than others at different moments in time. Thus for purposes of access to the profession of history differences of sex were formally discounted; while for purposes of establishing leadership and allocating power within the AHA, differences of sex were taken into account. Gender seems to have been a crucial way of establishing hierarchy explained in terms of difference, though its definition and use have varied—as the history of women professional historians demonstrates.

The problem of difference complicates the story of democratization as a story of access, for it suggests that inequities persist even if physical barriers have been removed. It also calls attention to power relationships within persumably homogeneous organizations and indicates that these are related not only to sociological distinctions among practitioners but also to the very conceptions of knowledge produced and protected by a discipline or profession. This is not to say that access and concepts of difference are distinct issues, for there is clearly a relationship between them: lines of inclusion and exclusion are drawn in terms of difference, as are internal hierarchies, and the terms used are often similar if not the same. Still, it seems useful to distinguish different kinds of differentiation and not to conflate such questions as access and internal hierarchy, even when both involve drawing lines according to sex. These related processes have a history that requires precise recounting. Precision of focus and close analysis permit deeper appreciation of how varied and yet how persistent are the interconnections between gender and the politics of a discipline such as history.

Notes

Introduction

1. See especially Michel Foucault, *The Order of Things: An Archaeology of the Human Sciences* (New York: Vintage, 1973) See also his *Language, Counter-Memory, Practice* (Ithaca, N.Y.: Cornell University Press, 1977); *Discipline and Punish: The Birth of the Prison* (New York: Vintage, 1979); *Power/Knowledge: Selected Interviews and Other Writings, 1972–1977* (New York: Pantheon, 1980).

2. An interesting exchange among historians about the flexibility of cultural symbols is Roger Chartier, "Texts, Symbols and Frenchness," *Journal of Modern History* (1985) 57:682–95, and Robert Darnton, "The Symbolic Element in History," *Journal of Modern History* (1986) 58:218–34.

3. Teresa de Lauretis, ed. *Feminist Studies/Critical Studies* (Bloomington: Indiana University Press, 1986), "Introduction," p. 8. See also her *Technologies of Gender: Essays on Theory, Film and Fiction* (Bloomington: Indiana University Press, 1987).

4. Barbara Johnson, *The Critical Difference: Essays in the Contemporary Rhetoric of Reading* (Baltimore: Johns Hopkins University Press, 1980), p. 5.

5. *Ibid.*, pp. 4–5.

6. Jacques Derrida, *Of Grammatology,* translated by Gayatri Chakravorty Spivak (Baltimore: Johns Hopkins University Press, 1974).

7. On the processes by which history establishes its authority, see Michel de Certeau, "History: Science and Fiction," in *Heterologies: Discourse on the Other* (Minneapolis: University of Minnesota Press, 1986), pp. 199–221. See also Peter de Bolla, "Disfiguring History," *Diacritics* (1986) 16:49–58.

8. See, for example, De Lauretis, "Introduction," *Feminist Studies/Critical Studies;* Donna Haraway, "A Manifesto for Cyborgs: Science, Technology and Socialist Feminism in the 1980's," *Socialist Review* (1985) 15:65–107; Martha Minow, "Learning to Live with the Dilemma of Difference: Bilingual Education and Special Education," *Law and Contemporary Problems* (1984) 48:157–211; Barbara Johnson, "Apostrophe, Animation and Abortion," *Diacritics* (1986) 16:29–47; and Gayatri Chakravorty Spivak, *In Other Worlds: Essays in Cultural Politics* (New York: Methuen, 1987). See

also Michael Ryan, *Marxism and Deconstruction: A Critical Articulation* (Baltimore: Johns Hopkins University Press, 1982).

1. *Women's History*

1. Virginia Woolf, *A Room of One's Own* (1929; reprint ed., New York: Harcourt Brace Jovanovich, 1979), p. 68.

2. The American journals are *Signs, Feminist Studies, The Women's Studies Quarterly,* and *Women and History*. In France *Pénélope* published scholarly work in women's history until 1985. In Britain historical studies are published in the *Feminist Review,* and *History Workshop* is now a journal of socialist and feminist historians. *RFD/DRF* (*Resources for Feminist Research/Documentation sur la Recherche Féministe*) is the Canadian journal.

3. The largest of these is the Berkshire Conference on the History of Women, the seventh meeting of which was held in June 1987.

4. An overview is presented in Alice Amsden, ed., *The Economics of Women and Work* (London: Penguin Books, 1980). For specific interpretations of the relationship of economic development and women's work, see Patricia Branca, *Women in Europe Since 1750* (London: Croom Helm, 1978); Joan W. Scott and Louise A. Tilly, *Women, Work and Family* (New York: Holt, Rinehart and Winston, 1978; Methuen, 1987); Eric Richards, "Women in the British Economy since about 1700: An interpretation," *History* (1974) 59:337–57; Neil McKendrick, "Home Demand and Economic Growth: A New View of the Role of Women and Children in the Industrial Revolution," in Neil McKendrick, ed., *Historical Perspectives: Studies in English Thought and Society in Honour of J. H. Plumb* (London: Europa, 1974); Ann Oakley, *Women's Work: The Housewife Past and Present* (New York: Pantheon, 1974). On working women in America, see Gerda Lerner, "The Lady and the Mill Girl: Changes in the Status of Women in the Age of Jackson," in her *The Majority Finds Its Past* (New York: Oxford University Press, 1979); Barbara Mayer Wertheimer, *We Were There: The Story of Working Women in America* (New York: Pantheon, 1977); Alice Kessler-Harris, *Out to Work: A History of Wage-Earning Women in the United States* (New York: Oxford University Press, 1982); the essays in Milton Cantor and Bruce Laurie, eds., *Class, Sex and the Woman Worker* (Westport, Conn.: Greenwood Press, 1977); and Ruth Milkman, *Gender at Work* (Urbana: University of Illinois Press, 1987). On early textile factories in the United States, see Thomas Dublin, *Women at Work: The Transformation of Work and Community in Lowell, Massachusetts, 1826–1860* (New York: Columbia University Press, 1979). On domestic service, see David Katzman, *Seven Days a Week: Women and Domestic Service in Industrializing America* (New York: Oxford University Press, 1978); Theresa McBride, *The Domestic Revolution: The Modernization of Household Service in England and France, 1820–1920* (New York: Holmes and Meier, 1976); Leonore Davidoff, "Mastered for Life: Servant and Wife in Victorian and Edwardian England," *Journal of Social History* (1973–74) 7:406–28. On white-collar workers, see Lee Holcombe, *Victorian Ladies at Work: Middle-Class Working Women in England and Wales, 1850–1914* (Hamden, Conn.: Archon Books, 1973). On England, see Sally Alexander, "Women's Work in Nineteenth-Century London: A Study of the Years 1829–50," in Juliet Mitchell and Ann Oakley, eds., *The Rights and Wrongs of Women* (London: Pelican, 1976), pp. 59–111; Sally Alexander et al., "Labouring Women: A Reply to Eric Hobsbawm," *History Workshop* (1979) 8:174–82; Anna Davin, "Feminism and Labour History," in R. Samuel,

ed., *People's History and Socialist Theory* (London: Routledge and Kegan Paul, 1981), pp. 176–81; Barbara Taylor, " 'The Men Are as Bad as Their Masters . . . ': Socialism, Feminism and Sexual Antagonism in the London Tailoring Trade in the Early 1830s," *Feminist Studies* (1979) 5:7–40. For France, see Madeleine Guilbert, *Les fonctions des femmes dans l'industrie* (Paris: Mouton & Co., 1966); "Travaux de femmes dans la France du XIXe siècle," special issue of *Le Mouvement Social* (1978) 105; Madeleine Guilbert et al., eds., *Travail et condition féminine: Bibliographie Commentée* (Paris: Editions de la Courtille, 1977) is a thorough and comprehensive source for France.

5. Work on the demographic transition includes Robert V. Wells, "Family History and Demographic Transition," *Journal of Social History* (1956) 9:1–19; Daniel Scott Smith, "Parental Power and Marriage Patterns: An Analysis of Historical Trends in Hingham, Massachusetts," *Journal of Marriage and the Family* (1973) 35:419–28; James A. Banks, *Prosperity and Parenthood* (London: Routledge and Kegan Paul, 1954); James A. and Olive Banks, *Feminism and Family Planning in Victorian England* (New York: Schocken Books, 1972); Edward Shorter, "Female Emancipation, Birth Control and Fertility in European History," *American Historical Review* (1973) 78:605–40. On ideology, see Angus McLaren, "Contraception and the Working Classes: The Social Ideology of the English Birth Control Movement in Its Early Years," *Comparative Studies in Society and History* (1976) 18:236–51; Angus McLaren, "Sex and Socialism: The Opposition of the French Left to Birth Control in the Nineteenth Century," *Journal of the History of Ideas* (1976) 37:475–92; R. P. Neuman, "Working Class Birth Control in Wilhelmine Germany," *Comparative Studies in Society and History* (1978) 20:408–28. An analysis of the role of the state is in Anna Davin, "Imperialism and Motherhood," *History Workshop* (1978) 5:9–66. The relationship of feminism and reproduction in the political discourse of the period is analyzed in Atina Grossman, "Abortion and Economic Crisis: The 1931 Campaign Against #218 in Germany," *New German Critique* (1978) 14:119–37. On "domestic feminism," see Daniel Scott Smith, "Family Limitation, Sexual Control and Domestic Feminism in Victorian America," in M. Hartman and L. Banner, eds., *Clio's Consciousness Raised* (New York: Harper and Row, 1974), pp. 119–36. On women's sexual autonomy, see Linda Gordon, *Woman's Body, Woman's Right: A Social History of Birth Control in America* (New York: Penguin Books, 1977); Patricia Knight, "Women and Abortion in Victorian and Edwardian England," *History Workshop* (1977) 4:57–69; Angus McLaren, "Abortion in England, 1890–1914," *Victorian Studies* (1976–77) 20:379–400; Angus McLaren, "Abortion in France: Women and the Regulation of Family Size, 1800–1914," *French Historical Studies* (1977–78) 10:461–85. On reproduction, see Renate Bridenthal, "The Dialectics of Production and Reproduction in History," *Radical America* (1976) 10:3–11; Nancy Folbre, "Of Patriarchy Born: The Political Economy of Fertility Decisions," *Feminist Studies* (1983) 9:261–84.

6. Examples of histories of "women in public" are Jane Abray, "Feminism in the French Revolution," *American Historical Review* (1975) 80:43–62; the invaluable document collection by Patricia Hollis, *Women in Public* (London: Allen and Unwin, 1979); and the many studies of women's movements including Ellen Dubois, *Feminism and Suffrage: The Emergence of an Independent Women's Movement in America, 1848–69* (Ithaca, N.Y.: Cornell University Press, 1978); Andrew Rosen, *Rise Up Women! The Militant Campaign of the Women's Social and Political Union* (London: Routledge and Kegan Paul, 1974); Richard Evans, *The Feminist Movement in Germany, 1933–1934* (London: Sage Publications, 1976); Richard Stites, *The Women's Liberation Movement in Russia* (Princeton: Princeton University Press, 1978). On

working-class movements, unions, and socialism, see Mari Jo Buhle, *Women and American Socialism, 1870–1920* (Urbana: University of Illinois Press, 1981); Dorothy Thompson, "Women and Nineteenth-Century Radical Politics: A Lost Dimension," in Mitchell and Oakley, eds., *Rights and Wrongs of Women,* pp. 112–38; Jean H. Quataert, *Reluctant Feminists in German Social Democracy, 1885–1917* (Princeton: Princeton University Press, 1979); Marilyn Boxer and Jean H. Quataert, *Socialist Women* (New York: Elsevier North-Holland, Inc., 1978); Charles Sowerine, *Sisters or Citizens? Women and Socialism in France since 1876* (Cambridge: Cambridge University Press, 1982); Alice Kessler-Harris, "Where Are the Organized Women Workers?" *Feminist Studies* (1975) 3:92–110; Sheila Lewenhak, *Women and Trade Unions* (London: St. Martin's Press, 1977); Meredith Tax, *The Rising of the Women: Feminist Solidarity and Class Conflict, 1880–1912* (New York: Monthly Review Press, 1980). On women's culture in political movements, see Blanche Wiesen Cook, "Female Support Networks and Political Activism: Lillian Wald, Crystal Eastman, Emma Goldman," *Chrysalis* (1977) 3:43–61; Estelle Freedman, *Their Sisters' Keepers: Women's Prison Reform in America, 1830–1930* (Ann Arbor: University of Michigan Press, 1981); Mary Ryan, "A Woman's Awakening: Evangelical Religion and the Families of Utica, New York, 1800–1840," *American Quarterly* (1978) 30:602–33; Nancy Cott, *The Bonds of Womanhood: Women's Sphere in New England, 1780–1835* (New Haven: Yale University Press, 1977); Temma Kaplan, "Female Consciousness and Collective Action: The Case of Barcelona, 1910–1918," *Signs* (1981–82) 7:545–66; Ellen DuBois et al., "Symposium: Politics and Culture in Women's History," *Feminist Studies* (1980) 6:26–64.

7. The attempts at broad synthesis are disappointing. See, for example, Richard Evans, "Modernization Theory and Women's History," *Archiv fur Sozialgeschichte* (1980) 20:492–514, and Evans, "Women's History: The Limits of Reclamation," *Social History* (1980) 5:273–81. Far more successful are running commentaries on the schlarship, topically arranged. These include Elizabeth Fox-Genovese, "Placing Women's History in History," *New Left Review* (1982) 133:5–29; Barbara Sicherman, "Review Essay: American History," *Signs* (1975) 1:461–86; and Carolyn Longee, "Review Essay: Modern European History," *Signs* (1977) 2:628–50. A good example of a synthetic history based on broad reading of diverse sources is Jane Lewis, *Women in England, 1870–1950: Sexual Divisions and Social Change* (Sussex: Wheatsheaf Books, 1984).

8. Sheila Rowbotham, *Hidden from History* (New York: Pantheon, 1974); Renate Bridenthal and Claudia Koonz, *Becoming Visible: Women in European History* (Boston: Houghton Mifflin, 1977); Hartman and Banner, eds., *Clio's Consciousness Raised*; Berenice Carroll, ed., *Liberating Women's History* (Urbana: University of Illinois Press, 1976); Mitchell and Oakley, eds., *Rights and Wrongs of Women.* The two superb collections edited by Martha Vicinus, *Suffer and Be Still* (Bloomington: Indiana University Press, 1972) and *A Widening Sphere* (Bloomington: Indiana University Press, 1977), have titles more descriptive of their subject than of their mission, but the introductory essays deal with the same theme.

9. Extensive bibliographical treatment can be found in Barbara Sicherman, E. William Monter, Joan W. Scott, and Kathryn K. Sklar, *Recent United States Scholarship on the History of Women* (Washington, D.C.: American Historical Association, 1980). On North America, see Jill Kerr Conway, *The Female Experience in Eighteenth and Nineteenth Century America* (Princeton: Princeton University Press, 1985). For England, see Barbara Kanner, *The Women of England from Anglo-Saxon Times to the Present* (Hamden, Conn.: Archon Books, 1979), and her essays in Vicinus, ed., *Suffer and Be Still* and Vicinus, ed., *Widening Sphere.* For a review of scholarship in

France, see Karen M. Offen, "First Wave Feminism in France: New Work and Resources," *Women's Studies International Forum* (1982) 5:685–89.

10. Jill Liddington and Jill Norris, *One Hand Tied Behind Us: The Rise of the Women's Suffrage Movement* (London: Virago, 1978).

11. Steven Hause (with Anne R. Kenney), *Women's Suffrage and Social Politics in the French Third Republic* (Princeton: Princeton University Press, 1984). A sensitive account that locates the origins of one wing of the American feminist movement in a broad political and social context is Sara Evans, *Personal Politics: The Roots of Women's Liberation in the Civil Rights Movement and the New Left* (New York: Vintage, 1979).

12. Joan Kelly-Gadol, "Did Women Have a Renaissance?" in Bridenthal and Koonz, eds., *Becoming Visible,* pp. 137–64.

13. See my summary of this research in "The Mechanization of Women's Work," *Scientific American* (1982) 267:167–87. See also Lerner, "The Lady and the Mill Girl"; Susan J. Kleinberg, "Technology and Women's Work: The Lives of Working-Class Women in Pittsburgh, 1870–1900," *Labor History* (1976) 17:58–72; Ruth Schwartz Cowan, "The 'Industrial Revolution' in the Home: Household Technology and Social Change in the Twentieth Century," *Technology and Culture* (1976) 17:1–26; Joann Vanek, "Time Spent in Housework," *Scientific American* (1974) 231:116–20; Susan Strasser, *Never Done: A History of American Housework* (New York: Pantheon, 1982).

14. Joan Hoff Wilson, "The Illusion of Change: Women in the American Revolution," in Alfred Young, ed., *The American Revolution: Explorations in the History of American Radicalism* (DeKalb: Northern Illinois University Press, 1976), pp. 383–446; Albie Sachs and Joan Hoff Wilson, *Sexism and the Law: A Study of Male Beliefs and Judicial Bias* (Oxford: Martin Robertson, 1978); Darlene Gay Levy, Harriet Branson Applewhite, and Mary Durham Johnson, *Women in Revolutionary Paris, 1789–1795* (Urbana: University of Illinois Press, 1979). See also Lee Holcombe, "Victorian Wives and Property: Reform of the Married Women's Property Law, 1857–82," in Vicinus, ed., *Widening Sphere,* pp. 3–28; Elizabeth Fox-Genovese, "Property and Patriarchy in Classical Bourgeois Political Theory," *Radical History Review* (1977) 4:36–59; Susan Miller Okin, *Women in Western Political Thought* (Princeton: Princeton University Press, 1979); Linda Kerber, *Women of the Republic* (Chapel Hill: University of North Carolina Press, 1980); Mary Beth Norton, *Liberty's Daughters: The Revolutionary Experience of American Women 1750–1800* (Boston: Little, Brown, 1980).

15. Barbara Ehrenreich and Deirdre English, *For Her Own Good: 150 Years of the Experts' Advice to Women* (Garden City, N.Y.: Anchor Books, 1978); Barbara Welter, "The Cult of True Womanhood, 1820–60," *American Quarterly* (1966) 18:151–74; Peter T. Cominos, "Innocent Femina Sensualis in Unconscious Conflict," in Vicinus, ed., *Suffer and Be Still,* pp. 155–72; Blanche Glassman Hersh, *The Slavery of Sex: Feminist Abolitionists in America* (Urbana: University of Illinois Press, 1978); William Leach, *True Love and Perfect Union: The Feminist Critique of Sex and Society* (New York: Basic Books, 1980). A different sort of interpretation has emerged among a group of American scholars who argue that there was an improvement in women's social and family status with the adoption of the ideology of domesticity. See nn. 17, 18, 19 below.

16. Catherin M. Scholten, "On the Importance of the Obstetrick Art': Changing Customs of Childbirth in America, 1760–1825," *William and Mary Quarterly* (1977) 34:426–45; Mary Roth Walsh, *Doctors Wanted, No Women Need Apply: Sexual Barriers in the Medical Profession, 1835–1975* (New Haven: Yale University Press,

1977); James Mohr, *Abortion in America: The Origins and Evolution of National Policy* (New York: Oxford University Press, 1978); Frances E. Kobrin, "The American Midwife Controversy: A Crisis of Professionalization," *Bulletin of the History of Medicine* (1966) 40:350–63; Judy Barrett Litoff, *American Midwives, 1860 to the Present* (Westport, Conn.: Greenwood Press, 1978); Jane B. Donegan, *Women and Men Midwives: Medicine, Morality and Misogyny in Early America* (Westport, Conn.: Greenwood Press, 1978); Barbara Ehrenreich and Deirdre English, *Witches, Midwives and Nurses: A History of Women Healers* (Old Westbury, N.Y.: The Feminist Press, 1973); Judith Walzer Leavitt, *Brought to Bed: Childbearing in America, 1750–1950* (New York: Oxford University Press, 1986); Jacques Gelis, "La Formation des accoucheurs et des sage-femmes aux XVIIe et XVIIIe siècles," *Annales de démographie historique* (1977); "Médicins, médicine et société en France aux XVIIIe et XIXe siècles," special issue of *Annales ESC* (1977) 32; "La femme soignante," special issue of *Pénélope* (1981) 5. On the complicated history of wet-nursing in France, see George D. Sussman, *Selling Mother's Milk: The Wet-Nursing Business in France, 1715–1914* (Urbana: University of Illinois Press, 1982); Fanny Faÿ-Sallois, *Les nourrices à Paris au XIXeme siècle* (Paris: Payot, 1980). On the relationship between the professionalization of science and the position of women scientists, see Margaret Rossiter, *Women Scientists in America: Struggles and Strategies to 1914* (Baltimore: Johns Hopkins University Press, 1982). On the contributions of women scientists to debates about sexual equality, see Rosalind Rosenberg, *Beyond Separate Spheres: Intellectual Roots of Modern Feminism* (New Haven: Yale University Press, 1982).

17. Carroll Smith-Rosenberg, "The Female World of Love and Ritual: Relations between Women in Nineteenth-Century America," *Signs* (1975–76) 1:1–29.

18. Cott, *Bonds of Womanhood*; Nancy Cott, "Passionlessness: An Interpretation of Victorian Sexual Ideology, 1790–1850," *Signs* (1978–79) 4:219–36; Linda Gordon, "Voluntary Motherhood: The Beginnings of Feminist Birth Control Ideas in the United States," in Hartman and Banner, eds., *Clio's Consciousness Raised*, pp. 54–71; Linda K. Kerber, "Daughters of Columbia: Education Women for the Republic, 1787–1805," in S. Elkins and E. McKitrick, eds., *The Hofstadter Aegis: A Memorial* (New York: Knopf, 1974), pp. 36–59.

19. See, for example, Anne Firor Scott, *The Southern Lady: From Pedestal to Politics, 1830–1930* (Chicago: University of Chicago Press, 1970); Jacqueline Dowd Hall, *Revolt Against Chivalry: Jessie Daniel Ames and the Women's Campaign Against Lynching* (New York: Columbia University Press, 1979); Mary P. Ryan, "The Power of Women's Networks: A Case Study of Female Moral Reform in Antebellum America," *Feminist Studies* (1979) 5:66–85; Jill Conway, "Women Reformers and American Culture, 1870–1930," *Journal of Social History* (1971–72) 5:164–77; and Barbara Leslie Epstein, *The Politics of Domesticity: Women, Evangelism and Temperance in Nineteenth-Century America* (Middletown, Conn.: Wesleyan University Press, 1981).

20. Bonnie Smith, *Ladies of the Leisure Class: The Bourgeoises of Northern France in the Nineteenth Century* (Princeton: Princeton University Press, 1981).

21. Carl Degler, *At Odds: Women and the Family in America from the Revolution to the Present* (New York: Oxford University Press, 1980).

22. Ann D. Gordon, Mari Jo Buhle, and Nancy Schrom Dye, "The Problem of Women's History," in Carroll, ed., *Liberating Women's History*, p. 89.

23. For an interesting confrontation with this problem, see Claudia Koonz, *Mothers in the Fatherland: Women, the Family and Nazi Politics* (New York: St. Martin's Press, 1987).

24. In addition to the studies listed in n. 5 above, see Tamara K. Hareven, "Family Time and Industrial Time: Family and Work in a Planned Corporation Town, 1900–

1924," *Journal of Urban History* (1974–75) 1:365–89; Karen O. Mason et al., "Women's Work and the Life Course in Essex Country, Mass., 1880," in Tamara K. Hareven, ed., *Transitions: The Family and Life Course in Historical Perspective* (New York: Academic Press, 1978); Elizabeth H. Pleck, "A Mother's Wages: Income Earning among Married Italian and Black Women, 1896–1911," in Michael Gordon, ed., *The American Family in Social-Historical Perspective,* 2d ed. (New York: St. Martin's Press, 1978), pp. 490–510; Elizabeth H. Pleck, "Two Worlds in One: Work and Family," *Journal of Social History* (1976–77) 10:178–95; Carole Turbin, "And We Are Nothing but Women: Irish Working Women in Troy," in Carol R. Berkin and Mary Beth Norton, eds., *Women of America: A History* (Boston: Houghton Mifflin, 1979); "Immigrant Women and the City," special issue of *Journal of Urban History* (1977–78) 4; Dee Garrison, "The Tender Technicians: The Feminization of Public Librarianship, 1876–1905," in Hartman and Banner, eds., *Clio's Consciousness Raised,* pp. 158–78; Margery Davies, "Women's Place Is at the Typewriter: The Feminization of the Clerical Labor Force," *Radical America* (1974) 18:1–28; Claudia Goldin, "Female Labor Force Participation: The Origin of Black and White Differences, 1870 and 1880," *Journal of Economic History* (1977) 37:87–108; Linda Nochlin, "Why Have There Been No Great Women Artists?" in Thomas B. Hess and Elizabeth C. Baker, *Art and Sexual Politics* (New York: Collier Books, 1971).

25. See Martha Blaxall and Barbara Reagan, eds., *Women and the Workplace: The Implications of Occupational Segregation* (Chicago: University of Chicago Press, 1976); Valerie Kincaide Oppenheimer, *Female Labor Force Participation in the United States* (Berkeley: University of California Press, 1970); Scott and Tilly, *Women, Work and Family*: Jane Humphries, "Class Struggle and the Persistence of the Working Class Family," *Cambridge Journal of Economics* (1977) 1:241–58; Jane Humphries, "Working Class Family, Women's Liberation and Class Struggle: The Case of Nineteenth-Century British History," *Review of Radical Political Economics* (1977) 9:25–41; Louise A. Tilly, "Paths of Proletarianization: Organization of Production, Sexual Division of Labor and Women's Collective Action," *Signs* (1981–82) 7:400–17; Ellen Ross, "Fierce Questions and Taunts: Married Life in Working-Class London, 1870–1914," *Feminist Studies* (1982) 8:575–602; Jule Matthaei, *An Economic History of American Women* (New York: Schocken Books, 1982).

26. Joan Kelly-Gadol, "The Social Relations of the Sexes: Methodological Implications of Women's History," *Signs* (1975–76) 1:816. See also her "The Doubled Vision of Feminist History: A Postscript to the 'Woman and Power' Conference," *Feminist Studies* (1979) 5:216–27.

27. Natalie Zemon Davis, " 'Women's History' in Transition: The European Case," *Feminist Studies* (1976) 3:90.

28. Temma Kaplan, *Anarchists of Andalusia, 1868–1903* (Princeton: Princeton University Press, 1977).

29. Tim Mason, "Women in Nazi Germany," *History Workshop* (1976) 1:74–113 and (1976) 2:5–32.

30. Judith Walkowitz, *Prostitution and Victorian Society: Women, Class and the State* (Cambridge: Cambridge University Press, 1980).

31. Darlene Gay Levy and Harriet Applewhite, "Male Responses to the Political Activism of the Women of the People in Paris, 1789–93" (unpublished paper), and their discussion in Levy, Applewhite, and Johnson, eds., *Women in Revolutionary Paris, 1789–1795,* pp. 143–220. Lynn Hunt, *Politics, Cultures and Class in the French Revolution* (Berkeley: University of California Press, 1984), pp. 94–117. See also Maurice Agulhon, *Marianne au combat: L'imagerie et la symbolique républicaines de 1789 à 1880* (Paris: Flammarion, 1979).

32. There is a difference between describing a society's attribution of status to particular groups and reflecting that status without comment or ignoring it entirely. In the first case, the historian takes the construction of inequality as part of the story to be recounted; in the second, he or she accepts inequality as a "natural" or inevitable fact, and, in effect, removes its construction from historical consideration.

33. Teresa de Lauretis, *Feminist Studies/Critical Studies* (Bloomington: Indiana University Press, 1986), p. 14. See also Biddy Martin and Chandra Talpade Mohanty, "Feminist Politics: What's Home Got to Do With It?" *ibid.*, pp. 191–212.

34. Likewise if the status of blacks in white society is to be understood, race is an important analytic tool. In American society, ethnicity and class are yet other ways of marking difference. The common denominator for the study of particular groups (dominant and subordinated) is difference. The theoretical historical question is, How has difference been constructed?

35. Michel Foucault, *The History of Sexuality*, Vol. I: *An Introduction* (New York: Vintage, 1980), pp. 97–98.

2. *Gender: A Useful Category of Historical Analysis*

1. *Oxford English Dictionary* (Oxford: Oxford University Press, 1961) 4.

2. E. Littré, *Dictionnaire de la langue française* (Paris, 1876).

3. Raymond Williams, *Keywords* (New York: Oxford University Press, 1983), p. 285.

4. Natalie Zemon Davis, "Women's History in Transition: The European Case," *Feminist Studies* (1975–76) 3:90.

5. Ann D. Gordon, Mari Jo Buhle, and Nancy Shrom Dye, "The Problem of Women's History," in Berenice Carroll, ed., *Liberating Women's History* (Urbana: University of Illinois Press), p. 89.

6. The best and most subtle example is from Joan Kelly, "The Doubled Vision of Feminist Theory," in her *Women, History and Theory* (Chicago: University of Chicago Press, 1984), pp. 51–64, especially p. 61.

7. For an argument against the use of gender to emphasize the social aspect of sexual difference, see Moira Gatens, "A Critique of the Sex/Gender Distinction," in J. Allen and P. Patton, eds., *Beyond Marxism?* (Leichhardt, N.S.W.: Intervention Publications, 1985) pp. 143–60. I agree with her argument that the sex/gender distinction grants autonomous or transparent determination to the body, ignoring the fact that what we know about the body is culturally produced knowledge.

8. For a different characterization of feminist analysis, see Linda J. Nicholson, *Gender and History: The Limits of Social Theory in the Age of the Family* (New York: Columbia University Press, 1986).

9. Mary O'Brien, *The Politics of Reproduction* (London: Routledge and Kegan Paul, 1981), pp. 8–15, 46.

10. Shulamith Firestone, *The Dialectic of Sex* (New York: Bantam Books, 1970). The phrase "bitter trap" is O'Brien's, *Politics of Reproduction*, p. 8.

11. Catherine McKinnon, "Femininism, Marxism, Method, and the State: An Agenda for Theory," *Signs* (1982) 7:515, 541.

12. *Ibid.*, pp. 541, 543.

13. For an interesting discussion of the strengths and limits of the term "patriarchy," see the exchange among historians Sheila Rowbotham, Sally Alexander, and

Barbara Taylor in Raphael Samuel, ed., *People's History and Socialist Theory* (London: Routledge and Kegan Paul, 1981), pp. 363–73.

14. Friedrich Engels, *The Origins of the Family, Private Property, and the State* (1884; reprint ed., New York: International Publishers, 1972).

15. Heidi Hartmann, "Capitalism, Patriarchy, and Job Segregation by Sex," *Signs* (1976) 1:168. See also "The Unhappy Marriage of Marxism and Feminism: Towards a More Progressive Union," *Capital and Class* (1979) 8:1–33; "The Family as the Locus of Gender, Class, and Political Struggle: The Example of Housework," *Signs* (1981) 6:366–94.

16. Discussions of Marxist feminism include Zillah Eisenstein, *Capitalist Patriarchy and the Case for Socialist Feminism* (New York: Longman, 1981); A. Kuhn, "Structures of Patriarchy and Capital in the Family," in A. Kuhn and A. Wolpe, eds., *Feminism and Materialism: Women and Modes of Production* (London: Routledge and Kegan Paul, 1978); Rosalind Coward, *Patriarchal Precedents* (London: Routledge and Kegan Paul, 1983); Hilda Scott, *Does Socialism Liberate Women? Experiences from Eastern Europe* (Boston: Beacon Press, 1974); Jane Humphries, "Working Class Family, Women's Liberation and Class Struggle: The Case of Nineteenth-Century British History," *Review of Radical Political Economics* (1977) 9:25–41; Jane Humphries, "Class Struggle and the Persistence of the Working Class Family," *Cambridge Journal of Economics* (1971) 1:241–58; and see the debate on Humphries's work in *Review of Radical Political Economics* (1980) 12:76–94.

17. Kelly, "Doubled Vision of Feminist Theory," p. 61.

18. Ann Snitow, Christine Stansell, and Sharon Thompson, eds., *Powers of Desire: The Politics of Sexuality* (New York: Monthly Review Press, 1983).

19. Ellen Ross and Rayna Rapp, "Sex and Society: A Research Note from Social History and Anthropology," in *Powers of Desire,* p. 53.

20. "Introduction," *Powers of Desire,* p. 12; and Jessica Benjamin, "Master and Slave: The Fantasy of Erotic Domination," *Powers of Desire,* p. 297.

21. Johanna Brenner and Maria Ramas, "Rethinking Women's Oppression," *New Left Review* (1984) 144:33–71; Michèle Barrett, "Rethinking Women's Oppression: A Reply to Brenner and Ramas," *New Left Review* (1984) 146:123–28; Angela Weir and Elizabeth Wilson, "The British Women's Movement," *New Left Review* (1984) 148:74–103; Michèle Barrett, "A Response to Weir and Wilson," *New Left Review* (1985) 150:143–47; Jane Lewis, "The Debate on Sex and Class," *New Left Review* (1985) 149:108–20. See also Hugh Armstrong and Pat Armstrong, "Beyond Sexless Class and Classless Sex: Towards Feminist Marxism," *Studies in Political Economy* (1983) 10:7–44; Hugh Armstrong and Pat Armstrong, "Comments: More on Marxist Feminism," *Studies in Political Economy* (1984) 15:179–84; and Jane Jenson, "Gender and Reproduction: Or, Babies and the State," unpublished paper, June 1985, pp. 1–7.

22. For early theoretical formulations, see *Papers on Patriarchy: Conference, London 76* (London: n.p., 1976). I am grateful to Jane Caplan for telling me of the existence of this publication and for her willingness to share with me her copy and her ideas about it. For the psychoanalytic position, see Sally Alexander, "Women, Class and Sexual Difference," *History Workshop* (1984) 17:125–35. In seminars at Princeton University in early 1986, Juliet Mitchell seemed to be returning to an emphasis on the priority of materialist analyses of gender. For an attempt to get beyond the theoretical impasse of Marxist feminism, see Coward, *Patriarchal Precedents.* See also the brilliant American effort in this direction by anthropologist Gayle Rubin, "The Traffic in Women: Notes on the Political Economy of Sex," in Rayna R. Reiter, ed., *To-*

wards an Anthropology of Women (New York: Monthly Review Press, 1975), pp. 167–68.

23. Nancy Chodorow, *The Reproduction of Mothering: Psychoanalysis and the Sociology of Gender* (Berkeley: University of California Press, 1978), p. 169.

24. "My account suggests that these gender-related issues may be influenced during the period of the oedipus complex, but they are not its only focus or outcome. The negotiation of these issues occurs in the context of broader object-relational and ego processes. These broader processes have equal influence on psychic structure formation, and psychic life and relational modes in men and women. They account for differing modes of identification and orientation to heterosexual objects, for the more asymmetrical oedipal issues psychoanalysts describe. These outcomes, like more traditional oedipal outcomes, arise from the asymmetrical organization of parenting, with the mother's role as primary parent and the father's typically greater remoteness and his investment in socialization especially in areas concerned with gender-typing." Nancy Chodorow, *The Reproduction of Mothering*, p. 166. It is important to note that there are differences in interpretation and approach between Chodorow and British object-relations theorists who follow the work of D. W. Winicott and Melanie Klein. Chodorow's approach is best characterized as a more sociological or sociologized theory, but it is the dominant lens through which object-relations theory has been viewed by American feminists. On the history of British object-relations theory in social policy, see Denise Riley, *War in the Nursery* (London: Virago, 1984).

25. Juliet Mitchell and Jacqueline Rose, eds., *Jacques Lacan and the Ecole Freudienne* (New York: Norton, 1983); Alexander, "Women, Class and Sexual Difference."

26. Teresa de Lauretis, *Alice Doesn't: Feminism, Semiotics, Cinema* (Bloomington: Indiana University Press, 1984), p. 159.

27. Alexander, "Women, Class and Sexual Difference," p. 135.

28. E. M. Denise Riley, "Summary of Preamble to Interwar Feminist History Work," unpublished paper, presented to the Pembroke Center Seminar, May 1985, p. 11. The argument is fully elaborated in Riley's brilliant book, "*Am I That Name?": Feminism and the Category of "Women" in History* (London: Macmillan, 1988).

29. Carol Gilligan, *In a Different Voice: Psychological Theory and Women's Development* (Cambridge, Mass.: Harvard University Press, 1982).

30. Useful critiques of Gilligan's book are: J. Auerbach et al., "Commentary on Gilligan's In a Different Voice," *Feminist Studies* (1985) 11:149–62, and "Women and Morality," a special issue of *Social Research* (1983) 50. My comments on the tendency of historians to cite Gilligan come from reading unpublished manuscripts and grant proposals, and it seems unfair to cite those here. I have kept track of the references for over five years, and they are many and increasing.

31. *Feminist Studies* (1980) 6:26–64.

32. For a succinct and accessible discussion of Derrida, see Jonathan Culler, *On Deconstruction: Theory and Criticism after Structuralism* (Ithaca, N.Y.: Cornell University Press, 1982), especially pp. 156–79. See also Jacques Derrida, *Of Grammatology*, translated by Gayatri Chakravotry Spivak (Baltimore: Johns Hopkins University Press, 1974); Jacques Derrida, *Spurs* (Chicago: University of Chicago Press, 1979); and a transcription of Pembroke Center Seminar, 1983, in *Subjects/Objects* (Fall 1984).

33. Clifford Geertz, "Blurred Genres," *American Scholar* (1980) 49:165–79.

34. Michelle Zimbalist Rosaldo, "The Uses and Abuses of Anthropology: Reflections on Feminism and Cross-Cultural Understanding," *Signs* (1980) 5:400.

35. Michel Foucault, *The History of Sexuality*, Vol. I, *An Introduction* (New York:

Vintage, 1980); Michel Foucault, *Power/Knowledge: Selected Interviews and Other Writings, 1972–1977* (New York: Pantheon, 1980).

36. For this argument, see Rubin, "The Traffic in Women," p. 199.

37. *Ibid.*, p. 189.

38. Biddy Martin, "Feminism, Criticism and Foucault," *New German Critique* (1982) 27:3–30; Kathryn Kish Sklar, *Catharine Beecher: A Study in American Domesticity* (New Haven: Yale University Press, 1973); Mary A. Hill, *Charlotte Perkins Gilman: The Making of a Radical Feminist, 1860–1896* (Philadelphia: Temple University Press, 1980); Jacqueline Dowd Hall, *Revolt Against Chivalry: Jesse Daniel Ames and the Women's Campaign Against Lynching* (New York: Columbia University Press, 1974).

39. Lou Ratté, "Gender Ambivalence in the Indian Nationalist Movement," unpublished paper, Pembroke Center Seminar, Spring 1983; and Mrinalina Sinha, "Manliness: A Victorian Ideal and the British Imperial Elite in India," unpublished paper, Department of History, State University of New York, Stony Brook, 1984, and Sinha, "The Age of Consent Act: The Ideal of Masculinity and Colonial Ideology in Late 19th Century Bengal," *Proceedings*, Eighth International Symposium on Asian Studies, 1986, pp. 1199–1214.

40. Pierre Bourdieu, *Le Sens Pratique* (Paris: Les Editions de Minuit, 1980), pp. 246–47, 333–461, especially p. 366.

41. Maurice Godelier, "The Origins of Male Domination," *New Left Review* (1981) 127:17.

42. Gayatri Chakravorty Spivak, "Three Women's Texts and a Critique of Imperialism," *Critical Inquiry* (1985) 12:243–46. See also Kate Millett, *Sexual Politics* (New York: Avon, 1969). An examination of how feminine references work in major texts of Western philosophy is carried out by Luce Irigaray in *Speculum of the Other Woman*, translated by Gillian C. Gill (Ithaca, N.Y.: Cornell University Press, 1985).

43. Natalie Zemon Davis, "Women on Top," in her *Society and Culture in Early Modern France* (Stanford: Stanford University Press, 1975), pp. 124–51.

44. Caroline Walker Bynum, *Jesus as Mother: Studies in the Spirituality of the High Middle Ages* (Berkeley: University of California Press, 1982); Caroline Walker Bynum, "Fast, Feast, and Flesh: The Religious Significance of Food to Medieval Women," *Representations* (1985) 11:1–25; Caroline Walker Bynum, "Introduction," *Religion and Gender: Essays on the Complexity of Symbols* (Boston: Beacon Press, 1987).

45. See, for example, T. J. Clark, *The Painting of Modern Life* (New York: Knopf, 1985).

46. The difference between structuralist and post-structuralist theorists on this question rests on how open or closed they view the categories of difference. To the extent that post-structuralists do not fix a universal meaning for the categories or the relationship between them, their approach seems conducive to the kind of historical analysis I am advocating.

47. Rachel Weil, "The Crown Has Fallen to the Distaff: Gender and Politics in the Age of Catherine de Medici," *Critical Matrix* (Princeton Working Papers in Women's Studies) (1985), 1. See also Louis Montrose, "Shaping Fantasies: Figurations of Gender and Power in Elizabethan Culture," *Representations* (1983) 1:61–94; and Lynn Hunt, "Hercules and the Radical Image in the French Revolution," *Representations* (1983) 1:95–117.

48. Edmund Burke, *Reflections on the French Revolution* (1892; reprint ed., New York, 1909), pp. 208–9, 214. See Jean Bodin, *Six Books of the Commonwealth* (1606; reprint ed., New York: Barnes and Noble, 1967); Robert Filmer, *Patriarchia and Other*

Political Works (Oxford: B. Blackwell, 1949); and John Locke, *Two Treatises of Government* (1690; reprint ed., Cambridge: Cambridge University Press, 1970). See also Elizabeth Fox-Genovese, "Property and Patriarchy in Classical Bourgeois Political Theory," *Radical History Review* (1977) 4:36–59; and Mary Lyndon Shanley, "Marriage Contract and Social Contract in Seventeenth Century English Political Thought," *Western Political Quarterly* (1979) 3:79–91.

49. I am grateful to Bernard Lewis for the reference to Islam. Michel Foucault, *Historie de la Sexualité,* Vol. 2, *L'Usage des plaisirs* (Paris: Gallimard, 1984). On women in classical Athens, see Marilyn Arthur, "'Liberated Woman': The Classical Era," in Renate Bridenthal and Claudia Koonz, eds., *Becoming Visible: Women in European History* (Boston: Houghton Mifflin, 1977), pp. 75–78.

50. Cited in Roderick Phillips, "Women and Family Breakdown in Eighteenth Century France: Rouen 1780–1800," *Social History* (1976) 2:217.

51. On the French Revolution, see Darlene Gay Levy, Harriet Applewhite, and Mary Durham Johnson, eds., *Women in Revolutionary Paris, 1789–1795* (Urbana: University of Illinois Press, 1979), pp. 209–20; on Soviet legislation, see the documents in Rudolph Schlesinger, *Changing Attitudes in Soviet Russia: Documents and Readings,* Vol. I, *The Family in the USSR* (London: Routledge and Kegan Paul, 1949), pp. 62–71, 251–54; on Nazi policy, see Tim Mason, "Women in Nazi Germany, *History Workshop* (1976) 1:74–113, and Tim Mason, "Women in Germany, 1925–40: Family, Welfare and Work," *History Workshop* (1976) 2:5–32.

52. Elizabeth Wilson, *Women and the Welfare State* (London: Tavistock, 1977); Jane Jenson, "Gender and Reproduction"; Jane Lewis, *The Politics of Motherhood: Child and Maternal Welfare in England, 1900–1939* (London: Croom Helm, 1980); Mary Lynn McDougall, "Protecting Infants: The French Campaign for Maternity Leaves, 1890s–1913," *French Historical Studies* (1983) 13:79–105.

53. On English utopians, see Barbara Taylor, *Eve and the New Jerusalem* (New York: Pantheon, 1983).

54. Louis Devance, "Femme, famille, travail et morale sexuelle dans l'idéologie de 1848," in *Mythes et représentations de la femme au XIXe siècle* (Paris: Champion, 1977); Jacques Rancière and Pierre Vauday, "En allant à l'éxpo: L'ouvrier, sa femme et les machines," *Les Révoltes Logiques* (1975) 1:5–22.

55. Gayatri Chakravorty Spivak, "'Draupadi' by Mahasveta Devi," *Critical Inquiry* (1981) 8:381–401; Homi Bhabha, "Of Mimicry and Man: The Ambivalence of Colonial Discourse," *October* (1984) 28:125–33; Karin Hausen, "The German Nation's Obligations to the Heroes' Widows of World War I," in Margaret R. Higonnet et al., *Behind the Lines: Gender and the Two World Wars* (New Haven: Yale University Press, 1987), pp. 126–40. See also Ken Inglis, "The Representation of Gender on Australian War Memorials," *Daedalus* (1987) 116:35–59.

56. On the French Revolution, see Levy et al., *Women in Revolutionary Paris.* On the American Revolution, see Mary Beth Norton, *Liberty's Daughters: The Revolutionary Experience of American Women* (Boston: Little, Brown, 1980); Linda Kerber, *Women of the Republic* (Chapel Hill: University of North Carolina Press, 1980); Joan Hoff-Wilson, "The Illusion of Change: Women and the American Revolution," in Alfred Young, ed., *The American Revolution: Explorations in the History of American Radicalism* (DeKalb: Northern Illinois University Press, 1976), pp. 383–446. On the French Third Republic, see Steven Hause, *Women's Suffrage and Social Politics in the French Third Republic* (Princeton: Princeton University Press, 1984). An extremely interesting treatment of a recent case is Maxine Molyneux, "Mobilization without Emancipation? Women's Interests, the State and Revolution in Nicaragua," *Feminist Studies* (1985) 11:227–54.

57. On pronatalism, see Riley, *War in the Nursery,* and Jenson, "Gender and Reproduction." On the 1920s, see the essays in *Stratégies des Femmes* (Paris: Editions Tierce, 1984).

58. For various interpretations of the impact of new work on women, see Louise A. Tilly and Joan W. Scott, *Women, Work and Family* (New York: Holt, Rinehart and Winston, 1978; Methuen, 1987); Thomas Dublin, *Women at Work: The Transformation of Work and Community in Lowell, Massachusetts, 1826–1860* (New York: Columbia University Press, 1979); and Edward Shorter, *The Making of the Modern Family* (New York: Basic Books, 1975).

59. See, for example, Margaret Rossiter, *Women Scientists in America: Struggles and Strategies to 1914* (Baltimore: Johns Hopkins University Press, 1982).

60. Luce Irigaray, "Is the Subject of Science Sexed?" *Cultural Critique* (1985) 1:73–88.

61. Louis Crompton, *Byron and Greek Love: Homophobia in Nineteenth-Century England* (Berkeley: University of California Press, 1985). This question is touched on also in Jeffrey Weeks, *Sex, Politics and Society: The Regulation of Sexuality Since 1800* (London: Leyman, 1981).

3. *On Language, Gender, and Working-Class History*

1. See the editors' introduction to the special issue of the *Radical History Review* on "Language, Work and Ideology" (1986) 34:3: "As radicals, we are concerned about the languages of power and inequality: how words express and help to construct dominance and subordination." The conflation of "language" and "words" is exactly the problem that needs to be avoided and that I will address throughout this essay. See also Christine Stansell's critique of this essay in *International Labor and Working Class History* (1987) 31:24–29.

2. Here it is important to point out that being profemale—that is, in favor of women in the profession and even of women's history—is not inconsistent with being antifeminist—that is, opposing a philosophical analysis that tries to explain the subordination of women in terms of inequalities of power as they are constructed in and by systems of social relationships, including class. The outcry against feminism has often come from people who claim great sympathy for women; they just don't like to have to reinterpret the history they undertake in terms that take feminist analyses into account.

3. G. S. Jones, *Languages of Class: Studies in English Working Class History, 1832–1982* (Cambridge: Cambridge University Press, 1983).

4. William Sewell, Jr. has shown a similar logic at work among French laborers in the same period. See his *Work and Revolution in France: The Language of Labor from the Old Regime to 1848* (New York: Cambridge University Press, 1980).

5. The political theorist Carole Pateman argues that what was at stake in liberal theory and in concepts of fraternity was not only male property generally but men's (sexual) property in women's bodies. See *The Sexual Contract* (forthcoming, 1988).

6. Barbara Taylor, *Eve and the New Jerusalem: Socialism and Feminism in the Nineteenth Century* (New York: Pantheon, 1983).

7. On women in Chartism, see Dorothy Thompson, "Women and Nineteenth Century Radical Politics: A Lost Dimension," in Juliet Mitchell and Ann Oakley, eds., *The Rights and Wrongs of Women* (London: Pelican, 1976), pp. 112–38.

8. Sally Alexander, "Women, Class and Sexual Difference," *History Workshop* (1984) 17:125–49.

9. Eileen Yeo, "Some Practices and Problems of Chartist Democracy," in J. Epstein and D. Thompson, eds., *The Chartist Experience: Studies in Working-Class Radicalism and Culture, 1830–60* (London: Macmillan, 1982), pp. 345–80.

4. *Women in* The Making of the English Working Class

1. E. P. Thompson, *The Making of the English Working Class* (New York: Vintage, 1966), p. 12.
2. Fredric Jameson, *The Political Unconscious: Narrative as a Symbolic Act* (Ithaca, N.Y.: Cornell University Press, 1981), p. 19.
3. On this question, see Jacques Rancière, "The Myth of the Artisan: Critical Reflections on a Category of Social History," *International Labor and Working Class History* (1983) 24:1–16.
4. Thompson, *The Making,* p. 210.
5. Thompson, "Outside the Whale," *Out of Apathy* (London: New Left Books, 1960), p. 152.
6. Thompson, *The Making,* p. 9.
7. On the problem of experience in *The Making,* see William Sewell, Jr., "How Classes Are Made: Critical Reflection on E. P. Thompson's Theory of Working-Class Formation," in Harvey J. Kaye and Keith McClelland, eds., *E. P. Thompson: Critical Debates* (Oxford: Oxford University Press, 1987). See also Sande Cohen, *Historical Culture: On the Recoding of an Academic Discipline* (Berkeley: University of California Press, 1986), pp. 174–229.
8. "Interview with E. P. Thompson," in MARHO, *Visions of History* (New York: Pantheon, 1983), p. 7.
9. *Ibid.*
10. Thompson, "Outside the Whale," pp. 174–75.
11. Thompson, *The Making,* p. 11.
12. *Ibid.*, p. 9.
13. *Ibid.*, p. 11.
14. *Ibid.*
15. *Ibid.*, pp. 18–19.
16. *Ibid.*, p. 416.
17. *Ibid.*
18. *Ibid.*, p. 417.
19. *Ibid.*, p. 730.
20. Ivy Pinchbeck, *Women Workers and the Industrial Revolution* (London: Routledge and Kegan Paul, 1930).
21. Thompson, *The Making,* p. 415.
22. Thompson, "Outside the Whale," p. 173.
23. *Ibid.*
24. Thompson, *The Making,* p. 10.
25. *Ibid.*, p. 386.
26. *Ibid.*, p. 787.
27. *Ibid.*, p. 382.
28. E. J. Hobsbawm, "Methodism and the Threat of Revolution," *History Today* (1957) 7:124, and Hobsbawm, *Primitive Rebels: Studies in Archaic Forms of Social Movements in the Nineteenth and Twentieth Centuries* (New York: Norton, 1959), pp. 106–7; Barbara Taylor, *Eve and the New Jerusalem: Socialism and Feminism in*

the Nineteenth Century (New York: Pantheon, 1983); Deborah M. Valenze, *Prophetic Sons and Daughters* (Princeton: Princeton University Press, 1985).

29. Thompson, *The Making,* pp. 730–31.

30. For a psychoanalytic approach to this kind of analysis, see Neil Hertz, "Medusa's Head: Male Hysteria under Political Pressure," *Representations* (1983) 4:27–54.

31. Thompson, *The Making,* p. 706.

32. "Interview," p. 10.

33. Thompson, *The Making,* p. 832.

34. E. P. Thompson, *William Morris: Romantic to Revolutionary* (New York: Pantheon, 1977), p. 695.

35. *Ibid.,* p. 721.

36. *Ibid.,* pp. 793, 803.

37. Henry Abelove, "Review Essay: *The Poverty of Theory* by E. P. Thompson," *History and Theory* (1982) 21:132–42. For one vision of life in the British CP, see Raphael Samuel, "Staying Power: The Lost World of British Communism, Part II," *New Left Review* (1986) 156:63–113.

38. Abelove, "Review Essay," pp. 138–39.

39. Thompson, "Outside the Whale," p. 152.

40. Abelove, "Review Essay," p. 138.

41. This is a vast literature in which I include my own work, Tilly and Scott, *Women, Work and Family* (New York: Holt, Rinehart and Winston, 1978; Methuen, 1987). See also the notes for Chapter 1 of this book, especially n. 4).

42. Barbara Taylor, "Socialist Feminism: Utopian or Scientific?" in Raphael Samuel, ed. *People's History and Socialist Theory* (London: Routledge and Kegan Paul, 1981), p. 163. See also Taylor, *Eve and the New Jerusalem.*

43. Michel Foucault, *The Archaeology of Knowledge* (New York: Harper and Row, 1976); and his "Nietzsche, Genealogy, History," in *Language, Counter-Memory, Practice: Selected Essays and Interviews,* Donald F. Bouchard and Sherry Simon, eds. and trans. (Ithaca, N.Y.: Cornell University Press, 1977), pp. 139–64.

44. Sally Alexander, "Women, Class and Sexual Difference," *History Workshop* (1984) 17:125–49.

45. On "dual systems," analysis, see Jane Jenson, "Gender and Reproduction: Or, Babies and the State," unpublished paper, 1985, p. 21; Heidi Hartmann, "Capitalism, Patriarchy, and Job Segregation by Sex," *Signs* (1976) 1:137–70.

46. Jane Lewis, "The Debate on Sex and Class," *New Left Review* (1985) 149:120.

47. Denise Riley, "Does a Sex Have a History? 'Women' and Feminism," *New Formations* (1987) 1:35.

5. *Work Identities for Men and Women: The Politics of Work and Family in the Parisian Garment Trades in 1848*

1. See, for example, Bernard Moss, *The Origins of the French Labor Movement 1830–1914: The Socialism of Skilled Workers* (Berkeley: University of California Press, 1976); William H. Sewell, Jr., *Work and Revolution in France: The Language of Labor from the Old Regime to 1848* (New York: Cambridge University Press, 1980); Robert J. Bezucha, *The Lyon Uprising of 1834: Social and Political Conflict in a Nineteenth Century City* (Cambridge, Mass.: Harvard University Press, 1974); Joan W. Scott, *The Glassworkers of Carmaux: French Craftsmen and Political Action in*

a Nineteenth Century City (Cambridge, Mass.: Harvard University Press, 1974); Charles Tilly and Lynn Lees, "Le Peuple de juin 1848," *Annales ESC* (1974) 29:1061–91. French studies include Maurice Agulhon, *Une Ville ouvrière au temps du socialisme utopique: Toulon de 1815 à 1851* (Paris and The Hague: Mouton, 1970); Yves Lequin, *Les Ouvriers de la région lyonnaise (1848–1912)*, 2 vols. (Lyon: Presses Universitaires Lyon, 1977); Roland Trempé, *Les Mineurs de Carmaux 1848–1914*, 2 vols. (Paris: Les Èditions Ouvrières, 1971). A dissenting view of the origins of labor protest is Jacques Rancière, *La Nuit des prolétaires: Archives du rêve ouvrier* (Paris: Fayard, 1981).

2. On women's history, see "Travaux de femmes, dans la France du XIXe siècle," special issue of *Le Mouvement Social* (1978) 5. See also Louise Tilly, "Paths of Proletarianization: Organization of Production, Sexual Division of Labor, and Women's Collective Action," *Signs* (1981) 7:400–417; Michelle Perrot, *Les Ouvriers en Grève: France 1871–1890* (Paris and The Hague: Mouton, 1974), pp. 318–30. An invaluable source on the entire subject of working women in France is Madeleine Guilbert, *Les Fonctions des femmes dans l'industrie* (Paris and The Hague: Mouton, 1966).

3. Georges Duveau, *La Vie ouvrière en France sous le Second Empire* (Paris: Gallimard, 1946), p. 211.

4. Christopher Johnson, "Economic Change and Artisan Discontent: The Tailors' History, 1800–1848," in Roger Price, ed., *Revolution and Reaction: 1848 and the Second French Republic* (London: Croom Helm, 1975), pp. 87–114; Christopher Johnson, "Patterns of Proletarianization: Parisian Tailors and Lodève Workers," in John Merriman, ed., *Consciousness and Class Experience in Nineteenth-Century Europe* (New York: Holmes and Meier, 1979), pp. 65–84; Christopher Johnson, *Utopian Communism in France: Cabet and the Icarian Movement* (Ithaca, N.Y.: Cornell University Press, 1974), pp. 156–57, 183, 200–201; J. P. Aguet, *Les Grèves sous la Monarchie de Juillet, 1830–1847* (Geneva: Droz, 1954); Direction du Travail, *Les Associations professionnelles ouvrières* (Paris, n.d.) 2:601–67; Octave Festy, "Dix années de l'histoire corporative des ouvrier tailleurs d'habits (1830–1840)," *Revue d'Histoire des Doctrines Economiques et Sociales* (1912), pp. 166–99.

5. Remi Gossez, *Les Ouvriers de Paris: L'organisation, 1848–1851* (Paris: Société d'histoire de la Révolution de 1848, 1967), p. 172. Henriette Vanier, *La Mode et ses métiers: Frivolités et luttes des classes, 1830–1870* (Paris: Armand Colin, 1960), pp. 75–90, 107–24; Mäite Albistur and Daniel Armogathe, *Histoire du féminisme français*, Vol. II (Paris: Des Femmes, 1977), pp. 455–64; Claire Moses, "Saint-Simonian Men/Saint-Simonian Women: The Transformation of Feminist Thought in 1830s France," *Journal of Modern History* (1982) 2:240–67; Lydia Elhadad, "Femmes prénommées: Les prolétaires saint-simoniennes rédactrices de 'La Femme libre,' 1832–1834," *Les Révoltes Logiques* (1977) 4:63–88 and (1977) 5:29–60. Laure Adler, *A l'aube du féminisme: Les premières journalistes (1830–1850)* (Paris: Payot, 1979); Susan Hellerstein, "Journalism as a Political Tool: The St-Simonian Working-Class Feminist Movement," Honors thesis (Brown University, 1981); Sebastien Charléty, *Essai sur l'histoire de St-Simonisme* (Paris: 1896). The Saint-Simonian women's newspaper had a number of titles: *La Femme libre, La Femme d'avenir, La Femme nouvelle, Apostolat des femmes.* I have followed the usage of Claire Moses to minimize confusion (Moses, "Saint-Simonian Men/Women," p. 252, n. 27).

6. *Le Journal des Tailleurs* (Sept. 15, 1848), p. 175.

7. *Ibid.* (March 16, 1848), p. 48.

8. *Ibid.* (Aug. 16, 1848), p. 132.

9. Pierre Vidal, *Histoire de la corporation des tailleurs d'habits, pourpointeurs-chaussetiers de la ville de Paris* (Paris, 1923), p. 50.

10. For one account of the history of the trade, see "Délégations ouvrières à

l'éxposition universelle de Londres en 1862" (Paris, 1863), *Rapport des délégués tailleurs,* p. 6.

11. George Rudé, "La Population ouvrière parisienne de 1789 à 1791," *Annales Historiques de la Révolution Française* (1967) 39:15–33; Léon Cahen, "La Population parisienne au milieu du XVIIIe siècle," *La Revue de Paris* (1919) 16:148–70; J. Kaplow, *The Names of Kings: The Parisian Laboring Poor in the Eighteenth Century* (New York: Basic Books, 1972); François Furet, "Pour une définition des classes inférieures à l'époque moderne," *Annales ESC* (1963) 18:462, 466; Maurice Garden, *Lyon et les lyonnaise au XVIIIe siècle* (Paris: Les Belles Lettres, 1970); Olwen Hufton, "Women and the Family Economy in Eighteenth-Century France," *French Historical Studies* (1975) 9:1–22; Michael Sonenscher, "Work and Wages in Paris in the Eighteenth Century," in M. Berg, P. Hudson, and M. Sonenscher, eds., *Manufacture in Town and Country Before the Factory* (Cambridge: Cambridge University Press, 1983), pp. 147–172; and Michael Sonenscher, "Journeymen, the Courts and the French Trades, 1781–1791," *Past and Present* (1987) 114:77–109.

12. I have used the spelling of *appièceur* given in the chamber of commerce inquiry. Robert's dictionary gives it as *apièceur* and says that the use of the word as a noun first appeared in 1836.

13. Kaplow, *The Names of Kings,* p. 36; Cahen, "La Population parisienne," pp. 154–55.

14. On the history of *confection,* see Le Vicomte Georges Avenel, *Le Mécanisme de la vie moderne* (Paris, 1896), pp. 31–32; *A Propos du centenaire de la belle jardinière* (Paris, 1924); Pierre Parisot, founder of La Belle Jardinère, described his operations to the minister of agriculture and commerce, July 11, 1848, Archives Nationales (AN) F12 2337–38. On changes in the trade, see Johnson, "Economic Change and Artisan Discontent," pp. 95–96; Johnson, "Patterns of Proletarianization," p. 68; Michael Kirby, "Changing Structure in the Parisian Tailoring Trades, 1830–1867," Master's thesis (University of North Carolina, Chapel Hill, 1979), pp. 28, 36; Chambre de Commerce de Paris, *Statistique de l'industrie à Paris, 1860* (Paris, 1864), p. 313. Chambre de Commerce de Paris, *Statistique de l'industrie à Paris, 1847–1848,* 2 vols. (Paris, 1851), Vol. II, pp. 293, 294, 298.

15. Chambre de Commerce, *Statistique 1847–1848,* Vol. II, pp. 66, 285, 293–7; Chambre de Commerce, *Statistique 1860* (Paris, 1861) p. 310; *Rapport des délégués tailleurs* (1862), p. 19; Frédéric Le Play, *Les Ouvriers européens,* Vol. VI (Paris, 1878), ch. 8, "Tailleur d'habits de Paris (1856)," pp. 388–441. See also Albert Aftalion, *Le Développement de la fabrique à domicile dans les industries de l'habillement* (Paris: Librairie de la Société du Recueil J.-B. Siray et du Journal du Palais, 1906), p. 6.

16. *Le Journal de Tailleurs,* March 16, 1848.

17. Aguet, *Les Grèves,* pp. 75–90, 130–39, 169, 239, 240, 241; *Associations professionnelles ouvrières,* Vol. II, pp. 601–5; Johnson, "Economic Change and Artisan Discontent," pp. 103–9; Vanier, *La Mode et ses métiers,* pp. 63–70, AN, CC 585 (1833–34); R. Grignon, *Réflexions d'un ouvrier tailleur sur la misère des ouvriers en général* (Paris, 1833).

18. AN, C 930 C2394; Chambre de Commerce, *Statistique 1847–1848,* Vol. II, p. 74; AN, C 930 dos. 5 (April 23, 1848); Bibliothèque Historique de la Ville de Paris, Papiers E. Cabet, Folio 372; Tacheux, "Aux membres composant la commission des ouvriers tailleurs" (1848); Gillard, *Revue anécdotique des association ouvrières* (Paris, 1850), quoted in Jacques Rancière, *La Nuit des prolétaires,* p. 310. See also André Cochut, *Les Associations ouvrières: Histoire et théorie des tentatives de réorganisation industrielle opérée depuis la Révolution de 1848* (Paris, 1851), p. 43, and Vanier, *La Mode et ses métiers,* pp. 117–19.

19. *Le Journal des Tailleurs* (Sept. 15, 1848), p. 175.
20. *Ibid.* (April 1, 1848), p. 59.
21. Charles Dupin, *Discussion du projet de loi sur le travail des enfants, des adolescents, des filles et des femmes* (Paris, 1848), p. 27.
22. Lemann, confectionneur, *De l'industrie des vêtements confectionnés en France* (Paris, 1857), pp. 34–35.
23. *Rapport des délégués tailleurs* (1862), pp. 202–1. See also AN, C2257 cos. 4772, "Petition des tailleurs d'habits à l'Assemblée Nationale" (1848); and AN, C2394 dos. 683 (Paris, Oct. 3, 1849), letter from Gautier, *tailleur,* to the national representatives.
24. *Rapport des délégués tailleurs,* p. 21.
25. See, for example, the letter of the printer and Proudhonian Louis Vasbenter to Flora Tristan written in 1843, "La vie de la femme est la vie du ménage, la vie domestique, la vie intérieure." Alain Faure and Jacques Rancière, *La Parole ouvrière, 1830–1851* (Paris: Union générale d'éditions, 1976), p. 199. See also the comment in *L'Atelier,* cited in Vanier, *La Mode et ses métiers,* p. 78. On male workers' preference for the patriarchal models of Cabet and Proudhon over those of Fourier and Saint-Simon, see Louis Devance, "Femme, famille, et morale sexuelle dans l'idéologie de 1848," in *Mythes et représentations de la femme au XIXe siècle* (Paris: Champion, 1977), p. 99.
26. On histories of women garment workers, see J. Barbaret, *Monographies professionnelles,* Vol. V, "Les Couturières" (Paris, 1890), pp. 260–61. Gaston Worth, *La Couture et la confection des vêtements de femme* (Paris, 1895), p. 9. On the history of the corporation of *couturières,* see G. Levasnier, *Papiers de famille professionnelle, l'ancien communauté des couturières de Paris et le syndicat actuel de l'auguille 1675–1895* (Blois 1896). See also Chambre de Commerce, *Statistique 1847–1848,* Vol. II, pp. 249, 293; Commerce, *Statistique 1847–1848;* Vanier, *La Mode et ses métiers,* pp. 75–90; Aftalion, *La Fabrique à domicile,* passim; A. Parmentier, *Les Métiers et leur histoire* (Paris: A. Colin, 1908), "Tailleurs et couturières," pp. 45–51. On the more general question of the social construction of the concept of skill, see Charles More, *Skill and the English Working Class, 1870–1914* (London: Croom Helm, 1980); Veronica Beechey, "The Sexual Division of Labour and the Labour Process," in *The Degradation of Work* (London: Hutchinson, 1982); Anne Phillips and Barbara Taylor, "Sex and Skill: Notes Towards a Feminist Economics," *Feminist Review* (1980) 6:78–88.
27. On feminism in 1848, see Claire G. Moses, *French Feminism in the Nineteenth Century* (Albany: State University of New York Press, 1984), ch. 6. On the status of feminist discourse, see Richard Terdiman, *Discourse/Counter Discourse: The Theory and Practice of Symbolic Resistance in Nineteenth-Century France* (Ithaca, N.Y.: Cornell University Press, 1985), pp. 72–74.
28. Barbaret, *Monographies professionnelles,* Vol. V, p. 266; Chambre de Commerce, *Statistique 1847–1848,* Vol. II, p. 66; *La Voix des Femmes,* April 3, 1848; Alfred Picard, *Exposition Internationale de 1900 à Paris: Le bilan d'un siècle 1801–1900* (Paris: Imprimérie Nationale, 1906), Vol. IV, pp. 412–16.
29. *La Voix des Femmes,* April 15, 1848.
30. *Ibid.*
31. *Ibid.*
32. *Ibid.,* March 22, March 31, April 15, 1848.
33. *Ibid.,* April 21, 1848.
34. Vanier, *La Mode et ses métiers,* p. 114.
35. *Ibid.,* p. 112; *La Voix des Femmes,* April 18, 1848; Gossez, *Les Ouvriers de Paris,* pp. 170–71.

36. Vanier, *La Mode et ses métiers,* pp. 115–16; Octave Festy, *Procès verbaux du conseil d'encouragement pour les associations ouvrières, 11 juillet 1848—24 octobre 1849* (Paris, 1917), pp. 96, 106–7; Julie Daubié, *La Femme pauvre au XIXe siècle* (Paris, 1866), pp. 47–48.

37. *La Voix des Femmes,* April 26, 1848; May 30, 1848.

38. *Ibid.,* June 1–4, 1848.

39. *Ibid.,* April 10, 11, 1848. The St. Simonienne Suzanne Voilquin wrote, "Stress your title of mother, to claim from men your equality and the right to free passage on this earth. Motherhood! . . ." cited in Susan Grogan, "Charles Fourier, the St. Simoniennes and Flora Tristan on the Nature and Role of Women," unpublished D. Phil., Murdoch University (Australia) 1986, p. 227.

40. *La Voix des Femmes,* April 18, 1848.

41. *Ibid.,* April 29, 1848.

42. E. Cabet, *La Femme* (Paris, 1841), p. 19.

43. On the formative history of women in the Saint-Simonian movement, see Moses, "Saint-Simonian Men/Women," p. 25; Moses, *French Feminism,* pp. 41–60; Elhadad, "Femmes prénommées"; Adler, *A l'aube du féminisme*; and Suzanne Voilquin, *Souvenirs d'une fille du peuple* (Paris: Maspero, 1978). See also Kari Weil, "Male/Female and the New Morality of the Saint-Simoniennes," unpublished paper, Pembroke Center for Teaching and Research on Women, 1987.

44. Cited in Johnson, *Utopian Communism,* p. 90.

45. *Ibid.,* p. 85.

46. Faure and Rancière, *La Parole ouvrière,* pp. 384–95.

47. *La Voix des Femmes,* March 26, 1848.

48. On the varieties of usages, see, for example, Devance, "Femme, famille, travail"; Jacques Rancière and Patrice Vauday, "En allant à l'éxpo: L'ouvrier, sa femme et les machines," *Les Révoltes Logiques* (1975) 1:5–22; Michelle Perrot, "L'Éloge de la ménagère dans le discours des ouvriers français au XIXe siècle," *Mythes et représentations de la femme au XIXe siècle,* pp. 105–21; Christine Dufrancatel, "La Femme imaginaire des hommes: Politique, idéologie et imaginaire dans le mouvement ouvrier," in Dufrancatel et al., *L'Histoire sans qualités* (Paris: Editions Galilée, 1979), pp. 157–86; Christine Dufrancatel, "Les Amants de la liberté? Stratégies de femme, luttes républicaines, luttes ouvrières," *Les Révoltes Logiques* (1977), 5:76.

49. Louis Réné Villermé, *Tableau de l'état physique et moral des ouvriers employés dans les manufactures de coton, de laine et de soie,* 2 vols. (Paris, 1840); Honoré Antoine Frégier, *Des classes dangereuses dans la population des grandes villes et des moyens de les rendre meilleures,* 2 vols. (Paris, 1840). On the Academy itself, see Ernest Seillière, *Une académie à l'époque romantique* (Paris: E. Leroux, 1926). See also Hilde Rigaudis-Weiss, *Les Enquêtes ouvrières en France entre 1830 et 1848* (Paris: Les Presses Universitaires du France, 1936). Studies that discuss reformers' views of the working-class family are Louis Chevalier, *Classes laborieuses et classes dangereuses à Paris pendant la première moitié du XIXe siècle* (Paris: Plon, 1958), and Jacques Donzelot, *La Police des families* (Paris: Editions de Minuit, 1978).

6. *A Statistical Representation of Work:* La Statistique de l'industrie à Paris, 1847–1848

1. See, for example, Keith Michael Baker, *Condorcet: From Natural Philosophy to Social Mathematics* (Chicago: University of Chicago Press, 1975).

2. Louis Frégier, *Des classes dangereuses* (Paris, 1840), 1:59, cited in Michelle Perrot, *Enquête sur la condition ouvrière en France au XIXe siècle* (Paris: Hachette, 1972), p. 26. See also the classic discussion of these issues in Louis Chevalier, *Classes laborieuses et classes dangereuses à Paris pendant la première moitié du XIXe siècle* (Paris: Plon, 1958).

3. Alexandre J. B. Parent-Duchâtelet, *De la prostitution* (Paris, 1836), 1:22, cited in Perrot, *Enquête,* p. 31.

4. Cited in Gérard Leclerc, *L'observation de l'homme: Une histoire des enquêtes sociales* (Paris: Seuil, 1979), p. 184.

5. *L'Atelier* (October 1840) 2:13.

6. I could list many examples, but perhaps it is best to make this an exercise in self-criticism. In most of my work and notably in *The Glassworkers of Carmaux: French Craftsmen and Political Action in a Nineteenth Century City* (Cambridge, Mass.: Harvard University Press, 1974), *Women, Work and Family,* coauthored with Louise Tilly (New York: Holt, Rinehart and Winston, 1978; Methuen, 1987), and most recently, "Men and Women in the Parisian Garment Trades: Discussions of Family and Work in the 1830's and 40's," in *The Power of the Past: Essays for Eric Hobsbawm,* ed. P. Thane, G. Crossick, and R. Floud (Cambridge: Cambridge University Press, 1984), pp. 67–93, I have followed this procedure, harvesting "facts" from statistical sources whose categories, intentions, and politics I have rarely examined critically.

7. For the history of these statistical inquiries, see Bertrand Gille, *Les sources statistiques de l'histoire de France: Des Enquêtes du XVIIe siècle à 1890* (Geneva: Librairie Droz, 1964). See also Perrot, *Enquêtes,* and her preface to the new edition of Léon Bonneff and Maurice Bonneff, *La vie tragique des travailleurs* (Paris: Rivière, 1984); and T. Markovitch, "Statistiques industrielles et systèmes politiques," in *Pour une histoire de la statistique* (Paris: Institut National de la Statistique et des études économiques, 1977), pp. 318–21. For an original treatment, see Marie-Noëlle Bourguet, "Race et folklore: L'image officielle de la France en 1800," *Annales ESC* (1976) 31:802–23, and her impressive dissertation (University of Paris I), "Dechiffrer la France: La statistique départementale à l'époque napoleonienne." On the question of critically analyzing statistics, see Michel de Certeau, "History: Science and Fiction," chapter 15 of his *Heterologies: Discourse on the Other,* translated by Brian Massumi (Minneapolis: University of Minnesota Press, 1986), especially pp. 208–10.

8. Hilde Rigaudis-Weiss, *Les enquêtes ouvrières en France entre 1830 et 1848* (Paris: Les Presses Universitaires de France, 1936).

9. Chambre de Commerce de Paris, *Statistique de l'industrie à Paris, 1847–1848* (Paris, 1851). (The *Statistique* was published in one volume but had two separately numbered sections. I will hereafter cite the volume as CCF and refer to part 1 or 2.)

10. Chambre de Commerce de Paris, *Centenaire de la Chambre de Commerce de Paris, 1803–1903* (Paris, 1903), p. 48.

11. Adolphe Blanqui, cited in Perrot, *Enquêtes,* p. 16.

12. *Le Moniteur Industriel,* July 2, 1848.

13. AN, F12 2337, Notes remises par les industriels des 8e et 9e arrondissements après une conference avec le Général Cavaignac, July 1848.

14. AN, C926, "Procès verbaux des séances du Comité du commerce et de l'industrie."

15. See references in Perrot, *Enquêtes,* p. 16, and in Leclerc, *Observation,* pp. 202–3. See also F. de Luna, *The French Republic under Cavaignac, 1848* (Princeton: Princeton University Press, 1969).

16. *Le Moniteur Industriel,* July 2, 1848.

17. On this history, see Gille, *Sources,* pp. 151–211.

18. CCP, 1:11–15.

19. Louis R. Villermé, *Tableau de l'état physique et moral des ouvriers employés dans les manufactures de coton, de laine et de soie,* 2 vols. (Paris, 1840), 2:93 and 358, cited in Rigaudis-Weiss, *Enquêtes,* p. 111. For an interesting discussion of Villermé, see William Sewell, Jr. *Work and Revolution in France: The Language of Labor from the Old Regime to 1848* (New York: Cambridge University Press, 1980), pp. 223–32. See also William Coleman, *Death Is a Social Disease: Public Health and Political Economy in Early Industrial France* (Madison: University of Wisconsin Press, 1981); B.-P. Lécuyer, "Démographie, statistique et hygiène publique sous la monarchie censitaire," *Annales de démographie historique* (1977), pp. 215–45; B.-P. Lécuyer, "Médecins et observateurs sociaux: Les annales d'hygiène publique et de médecine légale, 1820–1850," in *Pour une histoire de la statistique,* pp. 445–76; and Jan Goldstein, "Foucault among the Sociologists: The 'Disciplines' and the History of the Professions," *History and Theory* (1984) 23:170–92.

20. For details on this, see Rigaudis-Weiss, *Enquêtes.* See also Jacques Rancière, *La nuit des prolétaires: Archives du rêve ouvrier* (Paris: Fayard, 1981); and Alain Faure and Jacques Rancière, *La Parole ouvrière, 1830–1851* (Paris: Union générale d'éditions, 1976).

21. *Recherches statistique de la ville de Paris,* 3 vols. (Paris, 1823–29).

22. *Statistique de la France: Industrie,* 4 vols. (Paris, 1847–52). On the history of this effort, see Gille, *Sources,* pp. 200–203.

23. *Le Journal du Peuple,* June 8, 1841, cited in Rigaudis-Weiss, *Enquêtes,* p. 170.

24. *Le Populaire,* November 1844, cited in Rigaudis-Weiss, *Enquêtes,* 173. See her extensive discussion of this, pp. 169–78.

25. Rigaudis-Weiss, *Enquêtes,* pp. 191–93; and Leclerc, *Observation,* pp. 197–204.

26. AN, C943, "Assemblée constituante, enquête sur le travail agriculture et industriel," law of May 25, 1848.

27. AN, C925, "Procès verbaux du Comité du travail," 3 vols., May 1848–March 1849, is a remarkably detailed source on the work of the committee charged with carrying out the *enquête* launched in May 1848.

28. CCP, 1:18–19, 21.

29. This kind of association between certain classifications of economic activity and conservative politics had long characterized the debates about France's economy. In 1841 the editors of the workers' newspaper *L'Atelier* bitterly rejected the conclusions of the Baron Charles Dupin this way:

"Further on, we see that there are today in France 1,416,000 heads of industry (*chefs d'industrie*). Included in this number, of course, are a crowd of men who, as heads of workshops in Lyon, have been reduced to a position like that of a worker, properly speaking. . . . But, let us admire the skill of the baron. He estimates four people for each family of landowners and the same number for the families of heads of industry. We thus find in France 24 million landowners and more than six million heads of industry. Conclusion: there remain in France 2 million of the helpless, lazy, undisciplined, and brawling, and these are the men who want to dictate laws to industry, raise the price of labor, and demand, without working for it, a part of the property of others. As you can see, reader, the bogeyman has come back!"

30. CCP, 1:11.

31. Chambre de commerce de Paris, *Centenaire de la Chambre de commerce,* p. 52, lists Horace Say as director of the inquiry and indicates he was assisted by Léon Say (see n. 33 below) and Natalis Rondot. Rondot was an economist who specialized in textiles, an editor of *Le Journal des Economistes,* and member of various societies of political economists. For information on him, see *Dictionnaire universel des con-*

temporains (Paris, 1861), p. 1512. For biographical information on Horace Say, see *Dictionnaire universel des contemporains*, p. 1573. See also Horace Say, *Rapport du Comité central d'instruction primaire* (Paris, 1845); Horace Say, *Études sur l'administration de la ville de Paris* (Paris, 1846); and P. Piazza, *Étude historique et critique sur l'organisation et le fonctionnement des tribunaux commerciaux en France* (Paris: Rousseau, 1918).

32. On Léon Say, see G. Michel, *Léon Say* (Paris, 1899), and G. Picot, *Léon Say: Notice historique sur sa vie* (Paris: Hachette, 1901).

33. Léon Say, *Discours prononcé à Mugron, à l'inauguration du monument élevé à la mémoire de Frédéric Bastiat* (Paris, 1878), pp. 10–11.

34. Jean-Baptiste Say, *Traité d'économie politique*, 6th ed., ed. Horace Say (Paris, 1841), p. 12. On the work of J.-B. Say, see E. Treilhac, *L'oeuvre économique de J-B Say* (Paris, 1927); Michelle Perrot, "Premières mesures des faits sociaux: Les débuts de la statistique criminelle en France, 1780–1830," in *Pour une histoire de la statistique*, p. 134; C. Menard, "Trois formes de résistance aux statistiques: Say, Cournot, Walras," in *Pour une histoire de la statistique*, pp. 417–20. See also Horace Say, ed., *Edition nouveau de J-B Say, Cours complet de l'économie politique* (Paris, 1890).

35. J.-B. Say, *Traité* , p. 586.

36. *Ibid.*, p. 371.

37. *Ibid.*, p. 592.

38. CCP, 2:206, 302, for examples.

39. CCP, 1:152.

40. CCP, 2:239.

41. CCP, 2:251.

42. CCP, 2:339.

43. CCP, 2:260.

44. CCP, 2:302.

45. CCP, 2:302.

46. J.-B. Say, *Traité*, p. 195, also pp. 190–94.

47. The best examples of these arguments are in R. Gossez, *Les ouvriers de Paris: L'organisation, 1848–51* (Paris: Société d'histoire de la Révolution de 1848, 1967).

48. J.-B. Say, *Traité*, pp. 86–89.

49. CCP, 1:54.

50. J.-B. Say, *Traité*, pp. 371–74.

51. CCP, 2:194, 246, 277.

52. CCP, 1:52, 54.

53. On this see Chevalier, *Classes laborieuses et classes dangereuses*, p. 394.

54. CCP, 1:70–71, 141, 154, 170.

55. CCP, 1:65.

56. CCP, 1:65.

57. CCP, 1:65.

58. CCP, 1:62–66.

59. CCP, 1:63.

60. CCP, 1:63; 2:206.

61. CCP, 1:64.

62. CCP, 1:106.

63. CCP, 1:64.

64. CCP, 2:277.

65. CCP, 2:83, 110.

66. CCP, 1:202.

67. The next step was to look more closely at the "matrimonial status" of workers,

which the minister of commerce sought to do in 1849. He asked for statistical information on the "état civil des ouvriers appartenant aux dix principaux établissements manufacturiers dans chaque département." Information was collected and sent to the statistical bureau during 1849–50 and is conserved in AN, F501. The records for the department of the Seine seem never to have been collected, at least they are not in the Archives.

68. CCP, 1:186.

69. CCP, 1:52.

70. CCP, 1:160.

71. CCP, 2:277.

72. CCP, 1:163. On the representation of political threats as sexual threats and on the use of female figures to accomplish that, see Neil Hertz, "Medusa's Head: Male Hysteria under Political Pressure," *Representations* (1983) 4:27–54. A suggestive and important discussion of the uses of female sexuality in political analysis is Therèse Moreau, *Le sang de l'histoire: Michelet, l'histoire et l'idée de la femme au XIXe siècle* (Paris: Flammarion, 1982).

73. J.-B. Say, *Traité,* p. 446. In this outlook, as in many others, Say shared the views of physiocrats such as Quesnay.

74. CCP, 2:252.

75. CCP, 2:266.

76. CCP, 2:260.

77. CCP, 1:201-4. The details presented in the section on *logements garnis* are extraordinarily thorough, more so than for any other section of the report. There are house-by-house descriptions of what the inspectors saw in each place and accounts of the lives of individual inhabitants. Coming at the very end of the report, this section leaves the reader with a distinctly negative impression of the disordered lives of the workers of Paris.

78. CCP, 2:272.

79. CCP, 1:11, 2:272.

80. On the importance of "seeing" for these scientific reports, see Perrot, *Enquêtes,* pp. 11, 21, 26, 28; and on the significance of categories as modes of "discipline," Foucault, *Discipline and Punish* (New York: Vintage, 1979), p. 189.

81. See chapter 7, n. 22.

82. The references to sexuality seem to be part of a more complicated process of class construction in which definitions of the middle class involve notions of sexual self-control and those definitions depend on negative examples, or social "others." In this case the social "other" is the working class; its "otherness" is indicated by its feminine representation.

83. On these developments, see Perrot, *Enquêtes,* pp. 18–20, and her "Note sur le positivisme ouvrier," *Romantisme* (1978) 21–22:201–4; also A. Savoye, "Les continuateurs de Le Play au tournant du siècle," *Revue française de sociologie* (1981), 22:315–44.

7. *"L'ouvrière! Mot impie, sordide . . .": Women Workers in the Discourse of French Political Economy, 1840–1860*

1. *The Second Empire: Art in France under Napoleon III* (Philadelphia: Philadelphia Museum of Art, 1978), p. 310.

2. *Ibid.,* pp. 309–10.

3. Claire G. Moses, *French Feminism in the Nineteenth Century* (Albany: State University of New York Press, 1984), pp. 151–72.

4. Denise Riley, "'The Free Mothers': Pronatalism and Working Women in Industry at the End of the Last War in Britain," *History Workshop* (1981) 11:110.

5. On the regulation of prostitution, see Alain Corbin, *Les filles de noce: Misère sexuelle et prostitution aux 19e et 20e siècles* (Paris: Aubier, 1978); and Jill Harsin, *Policing Prostitution in Nineteenth-Century Paris* (Princeton: Princeton University Press, 1985).

6. Chamber of Commerce of Paris, *Statistique de l'industrie à Paris, 1847–1848,* 2 vols. (Paris, 1851), 1:11. (Hereafter referred to as CCP.)

7. A. Parent-Duchâtelet, *De la prostitution dans la ville de Paris,* 2 vols. (Paris, 1836; 3d ed., 1857), vol. I, pp. 103–4, cited in Harsin, *Policing Prostitution,* p. 123.

8. Parent-Duchâtelet, *De la prostitution,* cited in Therèse Moreau, *Le Sang de l'Histoire: Michelet, l'histoire, et l'idée de la femme au XIXe siècle* (Paris: Flammarion, 1982), p. 77. Moreau points out that the editors of the third edition of Parent's work insisted that a taste for luxury was the sole cause of prostitution.

9. CCP, 2:277.

10. CCP, 2:252.

11. Charles Dunoyer, "De la concurrence," *Le Journal des Economistes,* ler serie (1842) 1:135. (*Le Journal des Economistes* will be hereafter cited as *JE.*)

12. Interestingly, there was almost no reference to servants in these discussions, although they were surely a problem in urban settings. Olwen Hufton, writing on discussions of urban prostitution in eighteenth-century Europe, notes a similar phenomenon: "the seduced servant has a very secondary role in such data as we possess." Olwen Hufton, "The Fallen Women and the Limits of Philanthropy in the Early Modern Metropolis: A Comparative Approach" (unpublished paper, presented at the Davis Center, Princeton University, April 1986), p. 38. The omission of servants from these discussions clearly merits further explanation.

13. Jean-Baptiste Say, *Traité de l'économie politique,* 6th ed., 2 vols. (Paris, 1841), p. 324. See also J. Garnier, "Etude sur la répartition de la richesse: Profits et salaires," *JE,* ler série (1847) 18:209; Vée (Maire du 5e arrondissement de Paris), "Du paupérisme dans la ville de Paris," *JE,* ler série (1845) 10:224–71; CCP, 1:52.

14. Say, *Traité,,* pp. 372–74.

15. *Ibid.,* p. 372.

16. *Ibid.*

17. *Ibid.,* pp. 593–94.

18. *Ibid.,* p. 595.

19. See Wally Seccombe, "Patriarchy Stabilized: The Construction of the Male Breadwinner Wage Norm in Nineteenth Century Britain," *Social History* (1986) 11:53–76, for a discussion of concepts of the wage in English working-class discourse. Seccombe's exclusive focus on "the proletariat" tends to underplay the importance of political economy's theories in setting in place the wage system. Similarly, Jeanne Boydston begins with Marx for a theoretical discussion of housework in relation to wages, when she might have looked first at the political economists to whom Marx directed his critique, but within whose framework he wrote. J. Boydston, "To Earn Her Daily Bread: Housework and Antebellum Working-Class Subsistence," *Radical History Review* (1983) 35:7–25.

20. *L'Atelier,* December 30, 1842, p. 31.

21. Eugène Buret, *De la misère des classes laborieuses en France et en Angleterre,* 2 vols. (Paris, 1840), vol. I, p. 287, cited in Moreau, *Le Sang,* p. 74.

22. "Prostitution is only a *specific* expression of the *general* prostitution of the *labourer,* and since it is a relationship in which not the prostitute alone, but also the one who prostitutes, fall—and the latter's abomination is still greater—the capitalist, etc., also comes under this head." K. Marx, *Economic and Philosophic Manuscripts of 1844* (Moscow: Foreign Languages Publishing House, 1959), note 1, pp. 99–100. See also Marx's various discussions of women's work and prostitution that cite and comment on the 1840s writings of French political economists, pp. 31–34. For one analysis of this notion, see Lisa Vogel, *Marxism and the Oppression of Women* (New Brunswick, N.J.: Rutgers University Press, 1983), p. 44.

23. Moreau, *Le Sang,* p. 240.

24. Giovanna Procacci, "Le Gouvernement de la Misère: La Question social entre les deux revolutions, 1789–1848" (unpublished thèse de 3e cycle, Université de Paris VIII, 1983). These are Procacci's characterizations of the representation of poverty by political economists. I share much of her analysis of the ways in which poverty was identified as an object of study, marginal to sound order and thus in need of regulation. But I think she misses an important aspect of her subject by neglecting the gendered representation of poverty that was developed. Poverty was depicted as feminine and that entailed important implications, both for the analysis of the state of the working classes *and* for the position and status of women. How that feminine representation worked is the focus of this essay.

25. Hufton reminds us that urban iconography frequently represents the city as a whore. "The Fallen Woman," p. 2.

26. Jules Michelet, *La Femme* (Paris: Flammarion, 1981), p. 91.

27. For one example, see Achille de Colmont, "De l'amélioration de la situation sociale des ouvriers," *JE,* ler série (1848) 20:195.

28. G. Procacci, "Social Economy and the Government of Poverty," *Ideology and Consciousness* (1979) 4:62. See also Louis Reybaud, "Introduction," *JE,* ler série (1842) 1:9.

29. Jacques Donzelot, *La Police des Familles* (Paris: Editions de Minuit, 1978).

30. Theodore Fix, "Situation des Classes Ouvrières," *JE,* ler série (1844) 10:39. See also Joseph Garnier, "Etude sur la repartition de la richesse," p. 210.

31. See A. Blaise, "Cour d'Economie Politique du Collège de France," *JE,* ler série (1842) 1:206, for an argument against the prevailing tendency to include moral science within political economy.

32. These views are cited in J-B Say, *Cours Complet d'Économie Politique,* 2 vols. (Paris, 1840), p. 180.

33. de Colmont, "De l'amélioration," p. 257.

34. Dunoyer, "De la concurrence," p. 32.

35. The issue of sexual boundaries seems to have become most heated in trades that, in fact, did not require great "muscular" strength, although the debates often accompanied some mechanization. Printing is one of the examples that needs more attention in this regard. See "Chronique Economique," *JE,* 2e série (1862) 34:324–25.

36. Say, *Cours Complet,* p. 548, and Julie-Victoire Daubié, "Quel Moyens des Subsistance out les femmes," *JE,* 2e série (1862) 34:361–62. (I have cited Daubié's articles and not her book in this essay because the book, when published in 1866, was a much expanded version of her initial essay. It seemed more useful to use the articles here both because of when they were written and because of where they were published.)

37. T. Fix uses this analogy in "Situation," pp. 9–10.

38. William Sewell, Jr., *Work and Revolution in France: The Language of Labor from the Old Regime to 1848* (New York: Cambridge University Press, 1980), pp. 223–32.

39. *Ibid.*, p. 227.

40. *Ibid.*, p. 229.

41. *Ibid.*, pp. 224–25. See also William Reddy, *The Rise of Market Culture: The Textile Trade and French Society, 1750–1900* (New York: Cambridge University Press, 1984), pp. 138–84.

42. Fix, "Situation," p. 31.

43. "Il est pire moralement dans les grandes manufactures, où les hommes et les femmes travaillent dans les mêmes heures, ce qui fait que les moeurs sont plus dissolues qu'ailleurs." "Enquête: de la condition des femmes," *L'Atelier*, December 30, 1842, pp. 31–32.

44. On this issue, see Isaac Joseph, Philippe Fritsch, and Alain Battegay, *Disciplines à Domicile: L'édification de la famille* (Paris: Recherches, 1977).

45. Terme et Monfalcon, *Histoire des enfants trouvés* (Paris, 1840), p. 196, cited in Rachel Fuchs, *Abandoned Children: Foundlings and Child Welfare in Nineteenth-Century France* (Albany: State University of New York Press, 1984), p. 39.

46. H. Baudrillart, "De l'enseignement de l'économie politique," *JE*, 2e série (1862) 38:180–81.

47. Jules Simon, *L'Ouvrière*, 2d ed. (Paris: Hachette, 1861), p. ii.

48. J. Daubié, "Travail manuel des femmes," *JE*, 2e série (1863) 39:97–98.

49. Simon, *L'Ouvrière*, p. i.

50. Daubié, "Travail manuel," *JE* 39:99.

51. Michelet, *La Femme*, p. 54.

52. Simon, *L'Ouvrière*, p. v.

53. *Ibid.*

54. *Ibid.*, p. 42.

55. *Ibid.*, p. 46.

56. *Ibid.*, p. 71.

57. *Ibid.*, p. 273.

58. *Ibid.*, p. 87–88.

59. *Ibid.*, p. 83.

60. *Ibid.*, p. 89–90.

61. See, for example, the writings of Alphonse Esquiros, *Les Vièrges Martyres* (Paris, 1846), p. 177: "Les soucis de la maternité sont en effect les seuls travaux naturels de la femme; les autres la déforment."

62. H. Dussard, "Compte rendu de *l'Ouvrière*," *JE*, 2e série (1861), 30:94.

63. Simon, *L'Ouvrière*, p. 277.

64. *Ibid.*, p. 168.

65. *Ibid.*, p. 46.

66. Daubié, "Quel moyens de subsistence," *JE* 34:365

67. Daubié, "Travail manuel," *JE* 39:94.

68. Daubié, "Quel moyens des subsistence," *JE* 34:378.

69. Daubié, "Travail manuel," *JE* 39:83.

70. *Ibid.*, p. 80.

71. *Ibid.*, p. 96.

72. *Ibid.*, p. 84.

73. Daubié, "Travail manuel," *JE*, 2e série (1863) 38:203.

74. *Ibid.*, p. 210.

75. It seems crucial for feminist critiques of conceptions of the wage to begin not

with Marx but with political economy. On this question, see Harold Benenson, "Victorian Sexual Ideology and Marx's Theory of the Working Class," *International Labor and Working Class History* (1984) 25:1–23. See also Rosalind Petchesky, "Dissolving the Hyphen: A Report on Marxist-Feminist Groups 1–5," in Zillah Eisenstein, ed., *Capitalist Patriarchy and the Case for Socialist Feminism* (New York: Longman, 1981), pp. 376–77.

8. *The Sears Case*

1. Legal attention has focused on the issue of pregnancy benefits. See, for example, Lucinda M. Finley, "Transcending Equality Theory: A Way Out of the Maternity and the Workplace Debate," *Columbia Law Review*, Vol. 86, No. 6 (October 1986), pp. 1118–83; Sylvia A. Law, "Rethinking Sex and the Constitution," in *University of Pennsylvania Law Review*, Vol. 132, No. 5 (June 1984), pp. 995–1040.

2. Historians, for example, have periodized feminist history in terms of equality and difference.

3. Ruth Milkman, "Women's History and the Sears Case," *Feminist Studies* (1986) 12:394–95. In my discussion of the Sears case I have drawn heavily on this careful and intelligent article, the best so far of the many that have been written on the subject.

4. Martha Minow, "Learning to Live with the Dilemma of Difference: Bilingual and Special Education," *Law and Contemporary Problems* (1984) 48:157–211; quote from p. 160; see also pp. 202–6.

5. There is a difference, it seems to me, between arguing that men and women have identical interests and arguing that one should presume such identity in all aspects of the hiring process. The second position is the only strategic way of not building into the hiring process prejudice or the wrong presumptions about differences of interest.

6. For the offers of proof, see *Signs* (1986) 11:757–79. The "Written Rebuttal Testimony of Rosalind Rosenberg" is part of the official transcript of the case, U.S. District Court for the Northern District of Illinois, Eastern Division, EEOC *vs* Sears, Roebuck & Co., Civil Action No. 79-C-4373. (I am grateful to Sanford Levinson for sharing the trial documents with me and for our many conversations about them.)

7. Appendix to the "Written Rebuttal Testimony of Dr. Rosalind Rosenberg," pp. 1–12.

8. Alice Kessler-Harris, *Women Have Always Worked* (New York: Feminist Press, 1982).

9. On the limits imposed by courtrooms and the pitfalls expert witnesses may encounter, see Nadine Taub, "Thinking About Testifying," *Perspectives* (American Historical Association Newsletter) (November 1986) 24:10–11.

10. On this point Taub asks a useful question: "Is there a danger in discrimination cases that historical or other expert testimony not grounded in the particular facts of the case will reinforce the idea that it is acceptable to make generalizations about particular groups?" (p. 11).

11. See the cross-examination of Dr. Alice Kessler-Harris, EEOC *vs* Sears, Roebuck & Co., pp. 16376–619.

12. The Rosenburg "Rebuttal" is particularly vehement on this question: "This assumption that all employers discriminate is prominent in her [Kessler-Harris's] work. . . . In a 1979 article, she wrote hopefully that women, 'harbor values, attitudes, and behavior patterns potentially subversive to capitalism'" (p. 11). "There are, of course,

documented instances of employers limiting the opportunities of women. But the fact that some employers have discriminated does not prove that all do" (p. 19). The Rosenberg "Rebuttal" raises another issue about the political and ideological limits of a courtroom or, perhaps it is better to say, about the way the courtroom reproduces dominant ideologies. The categorical notion that employers discriminate was unacceptable (but the categorical notion that women "prefer" certain jobs was not). Its unacceptability was underscored by linking it to subversion and Marxism, positions intolerable in American political discourse. Rosenberg's innuendos attempted to discredit Kessler-Harris on two counts: first, by suggesting she was making a ridiculous generalization and, second, by suggesting that only people outside acceptable politics could even entertain that generalization.

13. Milkman, "Women's History," p. 391.

14. Naomi Schor, "Reading Double: Sand's Difference," in Nancy K. Miller, ed., *The Poetics of Gender* (New York: Columbia University Press, 1986), p. 256.

15. Michael Walzer, *Spheres of Justice: A Defense of Pluralism and Equality* (New York: Basic Books, 1983), p. xii. See also Minow, "Learning to Live with the Dilemma of Difference," pp. 202–3.

16. Milkman, "Women's History," p. 384.

17. Nancy F. Cott, *The Grounding of Modern Feminism* (New Haven: Yale University Press, 1987) makes this point about feminism in the United States in the early twentieth century. For a similar approach to the British movement, see Susan Kingsley Kent, *Sex and the Suffrage in Britain, 1860–1914* (Princeton: Princeton University Press, 1987). See especially Denise Riley, "Does a Sex Have a History?: 'Women' and Feminism," *New Formations* (1987) 1:35–46.

18. For recent examples, see Linda Gordon, "What's New in Women's History," in Teresa de Lauretis, *Feminist Studies/Critical Studies* (Bloomington: Indiana University Press, 1986), pp. 26–27; Alice Kessler-Harris, "The Debate over Equality for Women in the Workplace: Recognizing Differences," in Laurie Larwood, Anne H. Stromberg, and Barbara Gutek, eds., *Women and Work I: An Annual Review* (Beverley Hills, Calif., 1985), pp. 141–61.

9. *American Women Historians, 1884–1984*

1. Cited in Arthur S. Link, "The American Historical Association, 1884–1984; Retrospect and Prospect," *American Historical Review* (1985) 90:5. The *American Historical Review* is cited hereafter as *AHR*.

2. Fewer than 100 scholars held the Ph.D. in history before 1900; among these were 8 women. Many more, however, held masters' degrees or were working on a Ph.D. degree. The other women recruited to the AHA in its early years were members of historical societies, archivists, librarians, and wives of male historians. See William Hessletine and Louis Kaplan, "Women Doctors of Philosophy in History," *Journal of Higher Education* (1943) 14:254–59.

3. Lawrence Veysey, "The Plural Organized Worlds of the Humanities," in A. Oleson and J. Voss, eds. *The Organization of Knowledge in Modern America, 1860–1920* (Baltimore: Johns Hopkins University Press, 1976), pp. 51–106, especially pp. 53–78. On the early history of the AHA, see J. Franklin Jameson, "The American Historical Association, 1884–1909," *AHR* (1909) 15:1–20, and "Early Days of the American Historical Association, 1884–1895," *AHR* (1934) 40:1–9. See also John Higham, "Herbert Baxter Adams and the Study of Local History," *AHR* (1984) 89:1225–39; and David D. Van Tassel, "From Learned Society to Professional Organization: The American Historical Association, 1884–1900," *AHR* (1984) 89:929–56.

4. Nellie Neilson, "A Generation of History at Mount Holyoke," *Mount Holyoke Alumnae Quarterly* (May 1939), cited in Penina M. Glazer and Miriam Slater, *Unequal Colleagues: The Entrance of Women into the Professions 1890–1940* (New Brunswick, N.J.: Rutgers University Press, 1987), p. 53.

5. Cited in John Higham, *History* (Englewood Cliffs, N.J.: Prentice Hall, 1965), p. 6.

6. *Ibid.*, p. 13.

7. Herbert Baxter Adams, *The Study of History in American Colleges and Universities* (Washington, D.C.: Bureau of Education, Circular 2, 1887), pp. 211–12.

8. *Ibid.*, pp. 213–17. See also Adams, *Methods of History Study* (Baltimore: Johns Hopkins University Press, 1883).

9. Adams, *The Study and Teaching of History* (Richmond, Va.: Whittet and Shepperson, 1898), p. 11.

10. *Ibid.*, p. 10.

11. Although the focus of much of this work was formal politics, it could extend to other kinds of institutions, even something as seemingly remote from politics as domestic service. Lucy Salmon, for example, who had written a master's thesis on the "History of the Appointing Power of the President," took up the question of domestic service in a book published in 1897, as part of her preoccupation with the history of democracy. Finding in the institution of service an aristocratic remnant that perpetuated dependence and subservience, she devised ingenious ways to study its history and current practice. She did not conceive of the project as a separate study of the family, the private sphere, or of women. Rather, her argument was that domestic service was an economic and political phenomenon and, as such, the proper province of scientific historical investigation. Lucy Maynard Salmon, *Domestic Service* (New York, 1897; reprint ed., New York: Ayer, 1972).

12. Adams, *The Study and Teaching of History,* p. 14.

13. AHA records, 1905, cited by Jacqueline Goggin, "Challenging the Historical Establishment: Women in the Historical Profession, 1890–1940" (unpublished paper, Berkshire Conference, June 1987), p. 30.

14. Cited in Van Tassel, "From Learned Society," p. 953.

15. *Ibid.*, p. 954. Salmon's perseverance resulted in an increase in female representation on AHA committees; at the end of her Council term in 1920, there were four women on various committees. See Goggin, "Challenging the Historical Establishment," p. 37.

16. Link, "The American Historical Association," p. 5.

17. Referring to the period 1926–39, one study concluded that "teaching history—or even holding positions in which graduate training in history is of some use—is predominantly a man's occupation. Part of the reason for this situation is the more limited job opportunities for women. No woman teaches history in a man's college, although men may teach in a woman's college. Coeducational institutions employ a far greater percentage of men than women." Hesseltine and Kaplan, "Women Doctors of Philosophy in History," pp. 255–56.

18. Link, "The American Historical Assocation," p. 5.

19. Howard K. Beale, "The Professional Historian: His Theory and His Practice," *Pacific Historical Review* (1953) 22:235.

20. In the early 1960s much of the discussion of women in the professions had assumed that an increase in numbers would end discrimination. Barnaby Keeney, then President of Brown University, wrote in 1962 that "all things being equal, 50% of the professors in the total of colleges and universities ought to be women." "Women Professors at Brown," *Pembroke Alumna* (1982) 27:8–9. See also Jessie Bernard, *Academic Women* (University Park, Pa.: Pennsylvania State University Press, 1964), p.

xii; and Lucille Addison Pollard, *Women on College and University Faculties: A Historical Survey and a Study of Their Present Academic Status* (New York: Ayer, 1977).

21. American Historical Association, *Report of the Committee on the Status of Women,* November 1970, p. i.

22. Jesse Dunsmore Clarkson, "Escape to the Present," *AHR* (April 1941) 46:544–48. See also *Annual Report of the American Historical Association for the Year 1940,* "Proceedings—1940," pp. 21 and 59. Merle Curti remembered receiving a letter of thanks for the recognition the program gave to women from the Secretary of the Berkshire Conference after the AHA meetings. "I felt ashamed we hadn't done more and that it had seemed appropriate to thank us for so little." Merle Curti, personal letter to J. Scott, March 25, 1987.

23. *Annual Report of the AHA,* "Proceedings—1939," p. 58. I am grateful to Noralee Frankel for helping me locate these materials.

24. "Historical News: The American Historical Association," *AHR* (1939–40) 45:745, cited in Goggin, "Challenging the Historical Establishment," p. 52. The members of the 1940 nominating committee were Howard K. Beale, Paul Buck, Curtis Nettles, and Judith Williams. Beale, its chairman, had long championed including blacks on the Council and other committees. That effort repeatedly failed (indicating the depths of racist sentiments in the AHA) but he supported the movement to name a representative of another "different" category—women.

25. Jessie Bernard, *Academic Women;* Patricia Albjerg Graham, "Expansion and Exclusion: A History of Women in Higher Education," *Signs* (1978) 3:759–73; Susan Carter, "Academic Women Revisited: An Empirical Study of Changing Patterns in Women's Employment as College and University Faculty, 1890–1963," *Journal of Social History* (1981) 14:615–97. For a study of the impact of the G.I. Bill (the Servicemen's Readjustment Act of 1944), which poured government money into universities for the enrollment of returning veterans, see Keith W. Olson, *The G.I. Bill, the Veterans, and the Colleges* (Lexington, Ky.: University of Kentucky Press, 1974).

26. Allan Nevins, speech at a history conference at Stanford University, reported in the New York *Times,* August 16, 1951, cited in Beale, "The Professional Historian," p. 246. An example of Cold War ideology and education can be found in *National Defense and Higher Education* (Washington, D.C.: The American Council on Education, 1951).

27. Beatrice Hyslop, Mt. Holyoke College, "Letters of the Class of 1919" (1969). For this and other information about Hyslop I am grateful to Ellen Bullington Furlough. See her "Beatrice Fry Hyslop: Historian of France" (unpublished Master's Thesis in History, University of South Carolina, 1978), p. 87.

28. Natalie Zemon Davis was president of the AHA for 1987.

29. It would also be interesting, if one had more time, to look at what might be called the uncritical strategies: those that insisted that individual excellence or tact could overcome the disabilities of sex. Thus the authors of a 1953 study of the Radcliffe Ph.D. ended their book by suggesting the best way for women to succeed: "The solution . . . is for women to do work of such high quality that no question of 'competition' arises. It would take a very prejudiced anti-feminist to refuse to employ, on the ground of sex, a women who has demonstrated ability and achievement clearly superior to that of the men available," *Graduate Education for Women: The Radcliffe PhD* (Cambridge, Mass.: Harvard University Press, 1956) p. 108. The book also contains reports from women Ph.D.'s on their strategies. One tells how she tries to "hide my mind" (p. 36); another does "not attempt to press forward as strenuously as a man would" (p. 39); another simply dismisses as trivial her exclusion from social

events "like clubs and stag dinners" (pp. 27–28). For many, any evidence of stridency or feminism constitutes dangerous behavior, to be avoided at all costs (pp. 26, 38). The point seems to be either to be so good that one's sex is excused or to be so discreet that it goes unnoticed. In either case, the evidence for consciousness of female difference is overwhelmingly clear.

30. Louise Fargo Brown, *Apostle of Democracy: The Life of Lucy Maynard Salmon* (New York: Harper and Row, 1943), p. 98. See the entry on Salmon by Violet Barbour in J. T. James, ed. *Notable American Women,* Vol. III (Cambridge, Mass.: Harvard University Press, 1971), pp. 223–25. See also Helen Lefkowitz Horowitz, *Alma Mater: Design and Experience in the Women's Colleges from Their Nineteenth-Century Beginnings to the 1930's* (Boston: Beacon Press, 1984), pp. 180, 186–87, 194.

31. Cited in Brown, *Apostle of Democracy,* pp. 101–2.

32. *Ibid.,* p. 132.

33. *Ibid.,* p. 136.

34. *Ibid.,* p. 256.

35. Cited by A. Underhill in his foreword to the posthumously published book by Lucy Maynard Salmon, *Historical Material* (New York: Oxford University Press, 1933), p. vii.

36. Higham, *History,* passim and pp. 124n., 206n.

37. Evidence of protest by women historians exists prior to the 1920s in individual expressions of anger and in concerted efforts to include women in the AHA leadership structure. It is not until the 1920s, however, that widespread evidence of collective action appears.

38. "U of M gets First Woman History Prof," *Detroit Free Press,* October 29, 1961, p. C-5; letter from Univeristy of Michigan History Department chair, John Bowditch, to Vice-President and Dean of Faculties, Marvin L. Niehuss, February 15, 1961. Information about Dr. Robinson and the provisions of her bequest was obtained from the University of Wisconsin (Madison) History Department. It took years for bequests such as these to generate enough income to pay the salaries the donors stipulated. Only in the 1960s and 1970s, when alumnae pressure and a new concern with increasing the numbers of women Ph.D.'s drew attention to the existence of these possibilities for women, were the chairs fully funded and permanently filled.

39. Schlesinger Library, Radcliffe College, Papers of the Berkshire Conference, MC267 (5). Letter of Louise R. Loomis, May 8, 1952. See also Kathryn Kish Sklar, "American Female Historians in Context, 1770–1930," *Feminist Studies* (1975) 3:171–84.

40. Papers of the Berkshire Conference, MC267 (2), March 16, 1931. The influence, however indirect, of labor movement concerns in this period is also evident here.

41. Papers of the Berkshire Conference, MC267 (3), Minutes, May 20–22, 1938.

42. Louise Phelps Kellogg was an archivist at the Wisconsin State Historical Society. She was the first woman president of the Mississippi Valley Historical Association (the forerunner of the current Organization of American Historians), elected in 1930.

43. It would be interesting to know exactly why Nellie Neilson was chosen as the women's nominee. She, of course, was an accomplished historian with an excellent reputation. That she was a medievalist also seems important in the light especially of the fact that Medieval History attracted or produced long lines of extraordinary women historians. I would speculate that there was a relationship between the skills (of esoteric languages and epigraphy) required of medievalists and women's entry into this field. Mastery of these difficult and erudite skills made a woman's competence unquestioned or at least hard to challenge. It secured a certain recognition that in other more accessible areas of history (where one had only to read English or a mod-

ern foreign language) might be harder to achieve. William Roy Smith wrote of Nellie Neilson that she "has an uncanny faculty for inspiring her students with a love for mediaeval history, but she also teaches them how to use manuscript material and enjoy the game." Cited in Goggin, "Challenging the Historical Establishment," p. 15, n. 24.

44. Jacqueline Goggin, of the J. Franklin Jameson papers at the Library of Congress, is at work on this history of women historians from 1884 to 1940.

45. Higham, *History,* p. 148.

46. Mary Beard, *Woman as a Force in History* (1946: reprint ed., New York: Octagon Books, 1985). For examples of women's history, see also Mary Sumner Benson, *Women in Eighteenth Century America: A Study of Opinion and Social Usage* (1938; reprint ed., New York: AMS Press, 1976); Elizabeth W. Dexter, *Colonial Women of Affairs: A Study of Women in Business and the Professions in America before 1776* (1931; reprint ed., Fairfield, N.J.: Augustus Kelley, 1972); and Julia Cherry Spruill, *Women's Life and Work in the Southern Colonies* (1938; reprint ed., New York: Norton, 1972). For extensive bibliographic treatment, see Jill K. Conway, *The Female Experience in Eighteenth and Nineteenth Century America: A Guide to the History of American Women* (Princeton: Princeton University Press, 1985).

47. Beatrice Hyslop, "Letter to the Editor," *AHR* (1956) 62:288–9, cited in Furlough, MA Thesis, p. 67.

48. The history of this period is told by Alice Rossi and Ann Calderwood, *Academic Women on the Move* (New York: Russell Sage, 1973). See especially the essays by Rossi, Jo Freeman, and Kay Klotzburger.

49. Hilda Smith, "CCWHP: The First Decade" (unpublished history of the Coordinating Committee on Women in the Historical Profession, 1979).

50. American Historical Association, *Report of the Committee on the Status of Women,* November 9, 1970. See also the annual reports of the Committee on Women Historians in the *Proceedings* of the AHA.

51. Higham, *History,* p. 225.

52. On women, see Joan Kelly-Gadol, "Did Women Have a Renaissance?" *Women, History and Theory: The Essays of Joan Kelly* (Chicago: University of Chicago Press, 1984); Gerda Lerner, *The Majority Finds Its Past* (New York: Oxford University Press, 1979); and Joan Hoff Wilson, "The Illusion of Change: Women and the American Revolution," in Alfred Young, ed., *The American Revolution: Explorations in the History of American Radicalism* (DeKalb: Northern Illinois University Press, 1976), pp. 383–446. On Native Americans, see Francis Jennings, *The Invasion of America: Indians, Colonialism and the Cant of Conquest* (New York: Norton, 1976); Michael Paul Rogin, *Fathers and Children: Andrew Jackson and the Subjugation of the American Indian* (New York: Knopf, 1975); Mary Young, *Redskins, Ruffleshirts and Rednecks: Indian Allotments in Alabama and Mississippi* (Norman, Ok.: University of Oklahoma Press, 1961). On racism, see George Fredrickson, *The Black Image in the White Mind: The Debate on Afro-American Character and Destiny, 1817–1914* (New York: Harper and Row, 1971); Winthrop Jordan, *White over Black: American Attitudes Toward the Negro, 1550–1819* (Chapel Hill: University of North Carolina Press, 1968); Edmund Morgan, *American Slavery, American Freedom: The Ordeal of Colonial Virginia* (New York: Norton, 1975). On Manifest Destiny, see Walter LaFeber, *The New Empire: An Interpretation of American Expansion, 1860–1890* (Ithaca, N.Y.: Cornell University Press, 1963); and William Appleman Williams, *The Roots of Modern American Empire* (New York: Random House, 1969).

53. A recent attempt to synthesize the new knowledge about women is Marilyn J. Boxer and Jean H. Quataert, *Connecting Spheres: Women in the Western World,*

1500 to the Present (New York: Oxford University Press, 1987). On "women's culture," see the symposium, "Politics and Culture in Women's History," *Feminist Studies* (1980) 6:26–64. On women's writing, see the special issue of *Critical Inquiry,* "Writing and Sexual Difference" (1981) 8; on political consciousness, see Temma Kaplan, "Female Consciousness and Collective Action: The Case of Barcelona, 1910–1918," *Signs* (1982) 7:545–66.

54. On the historical variability of the category "women," see Denise Riley, *"Am I That Name?": Feminism and the Category of "women" in History* (London: Macmillan, 1988).

55. Carl Degler, "What the Women's Movement Has Done to American History," *Soundings: An Interdisciplinary Journal* (1981) 64:419.

56. On the history of double arguments for equality and difference in American feminism, see Nancy F. Cott, *The Grounding of Modern Feminism* (New Haven: Yale University Press, 1987).

Index